ALL · IN · ONE

Microsoft Certified Azure Fundamentals

EXAM GUIDE

(Exam AZ-900)

ABOUT THE AUTHOR

Jack Hyman is the founder of HyerTek, a technology consulting and training services firm specializing in cloud computing, information security, learning management, and digital marketing solutions for the private sector and government agencies in North America. He is an enterprise technology expert with over 20 years of digital and cloud transformation experience, collaborative computing, usability engineering, blockchain, and systems integration. During his extensive IT career, Jack has led U.S. federal government agencies and global enterprises through multiyear technology transformation projects. Before founding HyerTek, Jack worked for Oracle and IBM. He has authored many books, provided peer-review guidance for scholarly journals, and developed training courseware. Since 2004, he has served as an adjunct faculty member at George Washington University, American University, and University of the Cumberlands. Hyman holds a PhD in Information Systems from Nova Southeastern University.

About the Technical Editor

Corro'll (KUH'rel) Driskell, Sr., is an accomplished information technology (IT) consultant and training facilitator with 25 years of service with expertise in architecting cloud computing, content management, collaboration, and messaging solutions for organizations.

Corro'll is an established Thought Leader with a broad knowledge in business processes, policy development, and IT specializing in systematically improving how organizations deploy, operate, and manage their cloud-based solutions.

A graduate of Georgia State University's Andrew Young School of Policy Studies with a degree in Urban Policy Studies with an emphasis on Local Government Management, in Atlanta, Georgia, Corro'll spends most of his free time with his wife Angie and son CJ, and enjoys reading about various technologies.

ALL · IN · ONE

Microsoft Certified Azure Fundamentals

EXAM GUIDE

(Exam AZ-900)

Jack A. Hyman

New York   Chicago   San Francisco
Athens   London   Madrid   Mexico City
Milan   New Delhi   Singapore   Sydney   Toronto

Microsoft Certified Azure Fundamentals All-in-One Exam Guide (Exam AZ-900)

1 2 3 4 5 6 7 8 9   LCR   25 24 23 22 21

Library of Congress Control Number: 2021941668

ISBN   978-1-264-26836-8
MHID   1-264-26836-X

Sponsoring Editor	**Technical Editor**	**Production Supervisor**
Lisa McClain	Corro'll Driskell	Thomas Somers
Editorial Supervisor	**Copy Editors**	**Composition**
Patty Mon	Richard Camp	KnowledgeWorks Global Ltd.
	Lisa McCoy	
Project Manager		**Illustration**
Neelu Sahu,	**Proofreader**	KnowledgeWorks Global Ltd.
KnowledgeWorks Global Ltd.	Tricia Lawrence	
		Art Director, Cover
Acquisitions Coordinator	**Indexer**	Jeff Weeks
Emily Walters	Claire Span	

To my children, Jeremy and Emily.
I hope you always love learning as much as I do.

CONTENTS AT A GLANCE

CONTENTS

ACKNOWLEDGMENTS

Writing a book is an extraordinary effort that requires not just the significant labors from an author but the help of many talented experts. It was a privilege to work with so many exceptional individuals during this project. Thank you to the McGraw Hill team, including sponsoring editor Lisa McClain, editorial coordinator Emily Walters, and editorial supervisor Patty Mon. Shepherding this book with your guidance made this project a success, as always.

To Carole Jelen, literary agent and vice president at Waterside Productions: Your ability to bring wonderful projects and share your industry guidance is beyond appreciated. I owe you countless thanks for all you do for me.

As an author, you are only as good as the technical experts you surround yourself with. The McGraw Hill team provided me a best-in-class technical editor, Corro'll Driskell. Thank you for providing sound advice during the writing of this book.

It is truly an honor and a great fortune to be among a group of highly respected professionals in the IT and education communities. For those colleagues in the Microsoft community who I've worked with during this project and over the years, thank you.

No project of this size is ever complete without a personal cheerleading squad. My family and friends have been my biggest champions. The most important three people within the group are my wife, Debbie, and my children, Jeremy and Emily. Thank you for allowing me to take on yet another major book project and see it through to the very end. This project would not be complete without you. I love the three of you to pieces.

INTRODUCTION

Microsoft Azure is a leading public cloud hosting platform used by commercial and public sector entities worldwide. The platform combines infrastructure, platform, and software as a service capabilities. Businesses, organizations, and individuals looking for sophisticated applications and operating solutions can deploy options in minutes using a graphical user interface experience through Azure Portal or many command-line tools such as Azure Power Shell, Azure Cloud Shell, or Azure CLI. The breadth of storage solutions in conjunction with the highly capable networking and security options make the cloud offering best-in-class. With a global footprint on six out of seven continents, Microsoft Azure offers any user type an option to transform their on-premises workloads to be cloud-ready.

As an Azure Cloud Fundamentals Certified professional, your goal is to learn the key capabilities across the Microsoft Azure platform from virtual machines, storage, database, and security to the uses of IoT, Machine Learning, and Advanced Analytics. The exam focuses on applying technologies offered across the entire Microsoft Azure platform, not just specific tools.

About the Exam

The Microsoft Azure Fundamentals Exam (AZ-900) exam has anywhere from 40 to 60 multiple-choice questions. You might be wondering why the discrepancy. The answer is: it depends on the questions you receive and the format of those questions. Some people get many more one-part multiple-choice questions, while others get several matching and drag-and-drop options. Be prepared for the lower end, based on the November 2020 exam outline update.

You have 90 minutes to complete the exam. Whether you are taking the exam in a testing center or using the online-proctored platform, the type of questions will be the same. Microsoft states that there are no requirements for hands-on Azure access. That is true. You are expected to know more about the conceptual capabilities of key platform features instead of "in the weeds" code. The key business areas that Microsoft expects learners to understand include:

- Identify the benefits and considerations of using cloud services
- Describe the differences between categories of cloud services
- Describe the differences between types of cloud computing
- Describe the core Azure architectural components
- Describe core solutions available in Azure

- Describe Azure management tools
- Describe Azure security features
- Describe Azure network security
- Describe core Azure identity services
- Describe Azure governance features
- Describe privacy and compliance resources
- Describe methods for planning and managing costs
- Describe Azure Service-Level Agreements (SLAs) and service lifecycles

As you can see, the topics are broad. A detailed review of those specific topics can be found throughout the chapters. More specifically, each of these line items is mapped against the exam areas listed in the objectives map (see Appendix A).

As stated earlier, you can take the exam at an official Microsoft testing site convenient to you. Alternatively, you may complete the exam using the online-proctored environment, using the Pearson Vue online platform. This vendor manages the exam process on behalf of Microsoft. Should you require testing accommodations, reach out to Pearson Vue well in advance as this is not something that can be handled the day of the exam.

Exam Experience

The recent changes on the AZ-900 come with some changes to the formatting of questions that may surprise exam takers. Whether you are taking the exam online or in a test center, you will be asked to answer questions in a multiple-choice format or use a combination of matching definitions, true and false series, yes and no series, scenario-based questions, and diagrams. Here's an example of the question layouts:

	True	False						Yes	No
Question 1	◯	◯		Definition 1	Answer A		Question 1	◯	◯
Question 2	◯	◯		Definition 2	Answer B		Question 2	◯	◯
Question 3	◯	◯		Definition 3	Answer C		Question 3	◯	◯
True/False				**Definition Based**			**Yes/No**		

Complete the following statement:

The *definition term* would be listed here. You would need to decide if it is correct or incorrect.

a. Statement A (Accurate)
b. Statement B (Inaccurate)
c. Statement C (Inaccurate)
d. Statement D (Inaccurate)

Select the appropriate term

The exam has around 75 to 100 questions in reality given many of the questions are stacked; however, with the mixture of formats, the actual number of questions is set at 40. Microsoft does, at times, supply trial questions. You will not know which are actual questions and which questions are for experimental purposes. Don't guess, because you won't be able to figure it out.

The actual exam itself is set at 60 minutes. You then have 30 minutes to supply feedback on questions, review your answers, and help Microsoft improve the exam. Bear in mind, then, that this is not an opportunity to go ahead and change your answers. This is a way for you to help evaluate the exam and review the questions. Providing feedback is optional. It has no bearing on your score whatsoever.

The most important advice is to pace yourself with each question. Some application-type questions require you to understand a few complex concepts, especially in storage, database, and virtual machines.

Exam-Taking Strategies

As said earlier, you are given 60 minutes to complete a mixture of 40 question types. You then have 30 more minutes to give feedback on the exam. Some questions present one question against one response, while others present three or four questions in a single exam question. Each question must be answered in 90 seconds or less. Throughout the exam, there are various icons you may click so that you can review any question you were uncertain of or did not answer.

A reliable test-taking strategy is to read the question first. Next, remove all the answers you know are incorrect. If you can reduce half of the choices, you should focus on answering that question before moving on. Assuming you are still uncertain of the response, it is strongly recommended that you pick the response that is the best fit. Once you select the answer, make sure you click the button to review the question later before submission. Whatever you do, do not spend too much time on a single question, because you only have so much time for the exam.

 EXAM TIP Microsoft is notorious for presenting questions where there are subtle word differences. They may present the same response and change only one or two words to trick you. Watch out! Remember to pick the most logical choice for the question.

As you go through each question, some questions may supply hints for previous questions you answered. Use the flag feature if you believe that you want to refer back to the question at the end of the exam for one final review.

At the very end of the exam, you are presented with your entire answer sheet. If you have time, you should check your responses again. Once you are certain all answers are the way you would like them to be, click Submit.

About the Book

The *Microsoft Certified Azure Fundamentals All-In-One Exam Guide* is designed to help you become better acclimated to Azure, not only for the exam, but also as an Azure cloud practitioner. The goal is that after the exam is over, you can use this text as a platform reference guide for key Azure capabilities.

Using this textbook can surely be a significant study aid for your exam preparation, but it will not be your only study aid. You will need to reference the Microsoft website documentation many times and practice many of the exercises in the text using the Azure platform.

The book has seven chapters. Each chapter focuses on a specific exam objective except for Chapters 2 and 3. I deliberately broke those two chapters out as I felt they deserved dedicated attention due to their importance on the exam. The content is in chronological order for all purposes, although some sections are repeated a few times. In those instances, you should pay attention as they are likely to appear on the exam at least one or two times.

At the end of each chapter, you are presented with a chapter summary and a series of questions and answers. Unlike most certification exam books, the way the questions are presented in this book and on the TotalTester exam mimic the structure and rigor of what you will find on the actual exam. The questions all employ a similar tone and style to help you become more familiar with what to expect on the exam. If you practice the exam questions several times and pass each series of questions with confidence, you should do just fine passing the AZ-900 exam.

Lastly, the book comes with two full-length sample exams using the TotalTester platform. Each of the companion exams supplies 40 sample questions, above and beyond the number of questions you will have on your actual AZ-900 exam. Again, the TotalTester mimics the format of the actual Microsoft environment from a user experience perspective to the best of its ability. The only difference is that you will not be able to drag and drop or select the matching options questions due to technical limitations although the images offer a like-kind experience. All answers are multiple choice, although the images convey matching or definition-like questions. It is a limitation of the platform.

Book Coverage

The book covers each exam objective by following the Microsoft exam outline using the November 2020 guidelines. Microsoft says there are six major coverage areas. This book breaks those six coverage areas out over seven chapters to simplify some rather complex concepts. Each chapter is constructed with a concise introduction and then provides an overview of the major themes followed by a more in-depth discussion of the topics that Microsoft feels you should be aware of for the respective units. Each chapter has numerous exam hints and technical tips to guide you on best practices and test-taking strategies.

Chapter 1: Cloud Computing Concepts In the first chapter, you are introduced to cloud computing concepts. Microsoft wants you to understand the transformation from on-premises to cloud computing. The topics covered include the technical, financial, and operational aspects of computing across various enterprises.

Chapter 2: Azure Concepts and Architecture Components Chapter 2 addresses the organization and architectural logistics of cloud computing. When an organization decides to stand up a cloud infrastructure, they must decide where to host the infrastructure and to what degree they would like the cloud infrastructure to be managed across one or more geographic regions. Also, the organization of the resources and infrastructure is of the essence. Throughout this chapter, you learn the difference between resource management, templates, and subscriptions in the Azure Cloud.

Chapter 3: Azure Resources While Chapter 2 and Chapter 3 are considered a single unit on the exam, it is broken out deliberately in this text. IaaS concepts are discussed at great length on the exam. The topics within this section are quite robust. Therefore, you will find that separating the architectural concepts from the technology discussion will help you as a learner. In this chapter, you learn about the key IaaS, PaaS, and networking functionality necessary to support an enterprise in Azure. That includes virtual machines, database solutions, storage, and a host of networking options to support your IaaS and PaaS infrastructure.

Chapter 4: Management Tools and Solutions Other cloud vendors have technical offerings that require cloud administrators to utilize command-line tools to handle management and solution offerings. That is not the case with Azure. In fact, Microsoft offers every solution first and foremost in their Azure Portal. A second choice is to use PowerShell, CLI, or Cloud Shell. Solution offerings under Azure are plentiful. For the exam, Microsoft wants you to focus on specific IoT, data warehousing, artificial intelligence, machine learning, data analytics, serverless computing, and DevOps solutions. While not all Azure solutions are covered in the chapter, those that you must know for the AZ-900 exam help organizations extend the digital transformation of on-premises cloud operations to either hybrid cloud or cloud-native solutions using Azure.

Chapter 5: Core Security and Network Security Chapter 5 focuses on how to protect your cloud instructions using application-based and network security with Azure cloud. Microsoft has developed a series of solutions that addresses many of the pain points that organizations face using security information event management (SIEM) and security orchestration automated response (SOAR). Also, there are many automated predictive guidance tools to help mitigate risk and offer strong policy compliance, security alerts, measure security using a scoring system, and provide resource hygiene covered as part of the unit, all of which Microsoft expects you to know for the exam. As for network security, you will need to familiarize yourself with key concepts involving DDoS, Network Security Groups, network defense in depth, and Azure Firewalls.

Chapter 6: Identity, Governance, Privacy, and Compliance   The past several chapters have focused on implementing technologies within Azure Cloud. Microsoft feels it is just as important for you to understand the nuances of how to support the cloud infrastructure by applying the proper regulations, laws, and compliance measures to those cloud resources. That's why a chunk of the exam is spent applying the policies that protect Azure Cloud globally. Not only does Microsoft go over the policies, but they also want you to know about their own identity management and policy-based solution. The first half of the chapter goes over the technologies that address the identity management and governance functionality that power the Azure cloud. The latter half of the chapter discusses where you can find those policies on Azure Cloud and its implementation. Topics covered include authentication and authorization, Azure Active Directory, conditional access, multi-factor authentication (MFA), and single sign-on (SSO), Azure governance features, resource tags, resource locks, Azure Policy, Azure Blueprint, Cloud Adoption Framework for Azure, Microsoft Privacy Statement, Online Services Terms (OST) and Data Protection Addendum (DPA), Trust Center, Azure compliance documentation, and the Azure Sovereign Regions.

Chapter 7: Cost Management and Service-Level Agreements   The last chapter of the book addresses service delivery costs from a reduction and expense perspective. You also learn how to calculate the cost of delivering Azure services using the Pricing calculator and Total Cost of Ownership calculator. When an organization signs up to use Microsoft Azure, specific service terms for those services are agreed to between Microsoft and the organization. The last sections of the book discusses those service-level agreements and delivery metrics for the product lifecycle phases, from Private Preview to General Availability.

Objective Map
The objective map included in Appendix A has been constructed to help you cross-reference the official exam topics from Microsoft with the relevant coverage in the book. Official exam objectives have been provided exactly as Microsoft has presented them in their exam outline.

Supplementary Online Exam Tool
Using this book alone is just one step in preparing for the Microsoft Azure Fundamentals Exam. McGraw Hill includes a digital practice exam preparation solution featuring the TotalTester exam software, which allows you to generate two complete practice exams. See Appendix B for more information.

Cloud Computing Concepts

In this chapter, you will learn to
- Define cloud computing
- Differentiate cloud deployment options and architecture models
- Explain the advantages and disadvantages for cloud adoption
- Understand the technical and financial benefits for cloud computing

Cloud computing is a rich part of the information technology fabric. Many who embark on their certification journey assume that cloud technologies originated during the mid-1990s. Surprisingly, cloud computing has gradually evolved over several decades through numerous technical movements. Suppose one looks back at network-oriented computing architectures such as grid computing, utility computing, and application service provisioning. All share some resemblance to cloud computing. Ultimately though, each computing transformation has one thread in common—computing resources connect using a global network, the Internet.

In 1969, a groundbreaking concept was introduced by an associate professor at the Massachusetts Institute of Technology (MIT) for the potential of interconnected computing networks. The computer science expert, Joseph Carl Robnett (J.C.R.) Licklider, suggested that connecting many digital systems to communicate with one another may create an interconnected communication platform. Referred to as the Intergalactic Computer Network, the computing network concept and prototype demonstrated that users worldwide could potentially interconnect and access programs or data, from any location, at any time. Licklider's vision and the work of other Department of Advanced Research Project Agency (DARPA) fellows went on to create the first government model version of the Internet, the Department of Defense–funded Advanced Research Projects Agency Network (ARPANET). This small network was the first network that allowed digital sources to share data among one or more computers that were not in the same geographic location.

This government-funded initiative engendered several additional projects, including one started by Vinton Cerf and Robert Kahn that developed the framework we commonly refer to today as the Internet's architecture—the procedures known as the Transmission Control Protocol/Internet Protocol, or TCP/IP. The *TCP/IP* allows any computer, whether it is a supercomputer, desktop PC, tablet, or mobile device, to share data on the Internet.

Another commonality among these pivotal projects is that these computer scientists envisioned a world where everyone could connect via a network, accessible by programs and data, regardless of a bound location. Infrastructure and software could even be different. If this sounds familiar, it should. Today, we refer to this as cloud computing. While cloud computing has increased in complexity over the past two decades, the underlying technology concepts remains consistent.

There are countless reasons to move from a traditional computing environment to the cloud. However, most focus on removing the unnecessary technical and financial burdens an enterprise faces long term. A cloud provider, such as Microsoft Azure, allows one to take advantage of many infrastructure methods instead of just the ones found in your organization to reduce the cost of expensive computing investments. And consistency across data and application systems make it easier to ensure that an organization is working smarter and saving money to invest in innovative projects—IT or otherwise.

Cloud computing offers a range of opportunities. Organizations that are not technologically mature can quickly grow with affordable pre-built offerings, including solutions enabling backup, recovery, security, privacy, and compliance control. There are plenty of options for the mature organization to host, build, and deploy cost-efficient custom data and application solutions in the cloud, rather than investing in infrastructure and on-premises resources cyclically.

There are many considerations to address to appreciate the full value proposition of cloud computing. While some cloud service providers offer a complete set of best-in-class industry solutions, others provide a lightweight public data infrastructure. Only you and your organization know your exact needs. To figure out those needs, you should begin by understanding cloud computing requirements.

This first chapter is conceptual, using Microsoft Azure and as a cloud computing developer in general. You learn about the benefits, both technical and financial, for using the cloud, many services available for those considering cloud computing, their deployment, and delivery model types, and many of the features offered by Microsoft Azure.

An Introduction to Cloud Computing

Enterprise computing involves the delivery of many computing services. Examples of these services might include servers, storage, databases, networking, software, analytics, artificial intelligence, Internet of Things, and workflow capabilities. You may find that your organization will deliver these capabilities inside a data center, over the Internet, or using a hybrid approach. When an organization takes a cloud-first strategy, they offer services with flexibility in mind using the Internet. Their goal is to provide their user base with innovative, flexible resources and capabilities that continually scale based on demand at a given point in time. Unlike data center computing, cloud computing enables an organization to pay only for those cloud resources the organization consumes. Resources are measured precisely so that your organization does not spend any more than it uses; this is not the case in the data center environment. The outcome is simple: cloud computing helps lower operating costs, run infrastructure more efficiently, and drive business efficiency as needs change over time.

From the Data Center to the Cloud

If you were to purchase a computer, you would select the features appropriate for a given use case. For example, a graphic designer may require a significant amount of memory and storage. In contrast, an individual who requires a personal computer to check e-mail and browse the Internet may require only a lightweight desktop or laptop. If that individual ever needed to increase their machine's capacity, there would be numerous limitations. Besides, to make the change would likely not be instantaneous as you must research your choices and then purchase the new technology. Cloud computing is quite different because of its built-in ability to quickly reconfigure users' resources based on their changing needs and can can scale up and down rapidly. Here is a question: Who is responsible for managing a personal computer's upkeep? The answer, of course, is the owner. The same reasoning is applicable for servers in the enterprise data center. Organizations may purchase a support agreement with the manufacturer or vendor for onsite support, but such an agreement comes with an additional cost and time delay, one seldom encountered with cloud computing. Why? The *cloud provider* handles all aspects of the operational maintenance for the users and his or her organization.

On the other hand, a *data center* is a centralized hub for an organization and its shared IT operations, including its equipment for storing, processing, and disseminating data and applications. An organization may have one or more data centers critical to housing an organization's data assets. That is why organizations require constant assurance of reliability, including in staffing the operations. With cloud computing, though, the liability is not solely on the organization; it is often shared with the cloud hosting provider delivering the services to the end customer.

Choosing a Cloud Service Provider

Selecting a cloud service provider, such as Microsoft Azure, requires that you and your organization consider your capabilities, processes, and practices. For example, an organization with one location and five staff members may need less compute capacity than an organization halfway around the world with several locations and 50 staff members. It all depends on the activities that the business engages in on a day-to-day basis. In Table 1-1, you will find a list of attributes to consider when selecting a cloud service provider.

The list in Table 1-1 provides a framework, not a definitive list, which an organization should use as criteria for selecting a cloud service provider. Throughout this list are ideas one should consider in selecting any cloud service provider, as these are are all forward-thinking practices to follow during the evaluation process.

Cloud service providers, such as Microsoft, work with many business partners globally to help businesses large and small grow based on their unique technical profile. Whether you are using this book to prepare for certification or general reference, recognize that developing a cloud computing platform is quite a dynamic journey.

Attribute	Process, Capability, or Practice
Technical	<ul><li>**Deployment, Management, and Upgrade Simplicity** Users require that a provider ensure all software and hardware deployed in the cloud are easy for an organization to deploy, manage, and upgrade.</li><li>**Standardized user interfaces (UI) and customer experiences (CX)** A cloud provider will offer standard APIs and support data transformation through streamlined interfaces so that organizations can quickly build connections for applications and data sources in a single environment.</li><li>**Hybrid Availability** While not every organization initially requires the use of both on-premises and cloud-based support, make sure the cloud service provider offers such capabilities. Planning long term is an essential attribute for designing and developing cloud infrastructure.</li><li>**Event Management** A provider should have a built-in system for recording events integrated within its monitoring and management system, often as part of its security information and event management system (SIEM) functionality.</li><li>**Change Management** A provider should document and formalize processes for all requests, logging activities, approvals, testing, and acceptance actions.</li></ul>
Business	<ul><li>**Financial Stability and Reliability** There are hundreds of cloud hosting providers in the market. However, are you aware that many of the providers manage their assets by leveraging the assets of five or six larger IT solution providers? Therefore, the provider must prove that they have a track record of financial stability, with sufficient capital to handle unexpected events to their infrastructure footprint.</li><li>**Organizational governance, planning, and risk management** Any provider you consider must have formal management structures in place and make them widely available to the public, preferably on their website. These policies should establish best practices for assessing third-party providers and vendors at any given point in time. Microsoft makes all their governance, planning, and risk management policies available at https://docs.microsoft.com/en-us/azure/.</li><li>**Relationship Built on Trust** Make sure you feel comfortable with the company you will enter into a business partnership with and agree with its underlying corporate principles. It is important to know who some of its customers are, identify its business partners, and learn more about its reputation. Also, would you want to go into business with someonewho lacks experience and integrity? Before establishing a long-term relationship, try to speak with customers like yourself to see if the provider is a good fit.</li><li>**Business Knowledge and Domain Expertise** Look for a cloud solution provider with a team of experts that understands the technology and the industry.</li><li>**Assurance through Compliance** Providers need to prove that they can validate their platforms, including complying with not only government regulatory requirements but your organizational needs as well. A good indicator that an organization is highly reliable is an investment in third-party audits certifications, such as CMMI, ISO/IEC, and IEEE.</li></ul>

Table 1-1 Considerations for Selecting a Cloud Solution Provider *(continued)*

Attribute	Process, Capability, or Practice
Security	• **Infrastructure Protection** Regardless of service or feature, security options should be available to protect all hardware and software offerings offered within a provider's platform. • **Policies and Procedures** Comprehensive security policies and procedures should be enforceable to control operational systems. • **Identity and Access Management** Providers should ensure any application service or hardware component offers the appropriate level of personal, group, or corporate-wide authorization or authentication at a granular level, even if role based. Both gaining access to any application or system should require user authentication to make changes to data. • **Data Backup and Retention** Making sure data is always recoverable in an emergency is essential. Policies and procedures must be enforceable to ensure organizational integrity so that an organization can recover from any unexpected data loss or unplanned outage. • **Physical Security** If your data center was protected and secured with physical controls such as biometrics, video surveillance cameras, digital padlocks, or motion detectors, would you not want the same assurances from your cloud service provider? Controls, both physical and environmental, should ensure that cloud infrastructure and data are secured even during a disruptive event. The provider should have numerous redundant backup networking and power protection strategies, and these measures must be available as part of any disaster recovery and business continuity plans.
Administrative	• **Service-Level Agreements** Providers need to offer a basic service level to accommodate a customer's operational needs that can be met at all times. • **Performance Reporting** Providers should offer analytics to benchmark their performance. By providing regular reports to a customer, a service provider shows they are being held accountable to the terms set in one or more service-level agreements. • **Resource Monitoring and Configuration Management** System monitoring should be sufficient to allow the customer to identify any issues that may occur, including when system modifications arise. • **Billing and Accounting** Financials should be automated so that you or anyone responsible for resource management can monitor the cost of utilizing a system at any given point in time. Since cloud computing follows a "pay for what you use" model, you should not experience any unexpected charges. When you receive an invoice, you should be familiar with all the charges, including support costs, tied to the account.

Table 1-1   Considerations for Selecting a Cloud Solution Provider

Reasons to Consider Cloud Computing

Cloud computing is not limited to replacing infrastructure in the enterprise data center. Quite the opposite. If you have ever used an online service to listen to music, watch a movie, store a picture, play a video game, send an e-mail, make a video call, store a picture, or chat on social media, you are familiar with cloud computing capabilities

Capability	Cloud Service Opportunity
Cloud Native Applications	Quickly build, deploy, and scale applications such as web, mobile, and API functionalities. Apps may include cloud-native technologies such as container and Kubernetes-based solutions, microservice architecture applications, API communication options, and the use of DevOps. Delivery is generally via Platform as a Service (PaaS).
Store, Back up, and Recover Data	Protecting data allows cost-efficiency at scale and speed. Transferring data over the Internet using cloud storage options to one or more data locations can ensure organizational integrity. Delivery of services such as storage, backup, and recovery is best achieved via Infrastructure as a Service (IaaS).
Test and Build Applications	Minimize application development costs and expenses by using appropriate cloud infrastructure to scale up or down (applying scalability or elasticity principles). These are often delivered using IaaS best practices.
Analyze Data	Ability to streamline data that is siloed inside an organization or across many locations in the cloud. The data is often accessible via a team, division, unit, or other grouping using a service to uncover insights allowing more informed decision-making. Data sources can vary in size and capacity.
Embed Intelligence	Create specific models that help define goals and objectives to gain targeted insights from intelligent data captured.
Deliver Software on Demand	Complete applications delivered entirely over the Internet versus the desktop, on-demand. The advantage is that anytime the developer or vendor deploys an upgrade, the customer can acquire this capability instantly over the Internet, no matter where they are. The concept of "any time, anywhere" connectivity holds for software delivery on demand, which follows the principle of software as a service (SaaS).
Stream Multimedia Content	Multimedia, such as audio, video, and images, should be consistent in quality. Allowing an audience to connect anywhere, anytime using a device via cloud provides global distribution options.

Table 1-2   Potential Uses of Cloud Computing

whether you know it or not. Table 1-2 explores some of the cloud computing capabilities and cloud service opportunities that one might consider using in the enterprise.

Cloud Computing Deployment Options

No two organizations have the same computing needs. The same is also true for the options and services available as part of each computing deployment. One of your first tasks is determining what kind of cloud deployment is optimal for your project as a developer. A *cloud deployment* describes how a person or an organization intends to access the resources and services needed as part of a solution. You need to consider the architecture needs and the services that you or your team may use as part of the solution. Microsoft Azure offers three types of cloud deployments: private, public, and hybrid cloud. As you continue preparing for the AZ-900 exam, it will become quite evident there are many ways to configure a solution using Microsoft Azure.

Private Cloud

Private cloud deployments best serve organizations looking for dedicated computing resource management from a cloud service provider. Sometimes, a private cloud environment remains at a company's onsite data center. Organizations often take an alternate route, however, paying a third-party service provider, such as Microsoft, to host their private cloud infrastructure. Under these circumstances, a private cloud is where the services and infrastructure are maintained using a private network.

A private cloud will either deliver computing services over the Internet or over a private internal network to select users, instead of everyone on the world wide web. Often referred to as an internal or corporate cloud alternative, private cloud computing gives enterprise businesses many benefits that public cloud computing affords, such as self-service, scalability, elasticity, high availability, disaster recovery, and high performance, with one significant added bonus: the ability to add customization and control to dedicated resources on one's computing infrastructure.

Organizations whose primary objective is to ensure systems meet security and regulatory requirements often prefer private cloud deployments. Such additional layers of security ensure sensitive data is not accessible to third-party providers. Other benefits that organizations focus on when they need to choose between private and public cloud offerings include flexibility, control, and scalability. There is one drawback, though, with implementing a private cloud deployment. The IT organization is fully responsible for all financial and management costs in managing the cloud infrastructure. Since private cloud hosting requires staffing, infrastructure management, and maintenance expenses, cost savings are limited compared to a public cloud alternative.

Private cloud deployments allow for the delivery of two service models, discussed in the next section: Infrastructure as a Service (IaaS) and Platform as a Service (PaaS). Infrastructure abilities are specific to compute, network, and storage services. In contrast, platform services enable an organization to deliver cloud-based applications of various sizes to the enterprise. Private clouds can be combined with public cloud infrastructure or cloud infrastructures available to the general public to create a hybrid cloud. By creating a hybrid cloud offering, an enterprise can take advantage of *cloud bursting*; that is, when a private cloud needs additional capacity during a peak period of IT demand, public cloud resources can be utilized to pick up the slack.

Public Cloud

By far, the public cloud deployment model is the most common. With the *public cloud*, an organization will share infrastructure accessible on a public network with one or more organizations. All the cloud service providers' resources, including storage, memory, processing capacity, and networking capacity, are shared. Examples of public cloud providers include Microsoft Azure, Amazon Web Services (AWS), Google Cloud Platform (GCP), Alibaba Cloud, IBM Cloud, Salesforce, and Oracle Cloud.

Unlike a private cloud option, where the organization must configure the provided cloud server space, a public option offers preset infrastructure configurations and maintenance. The most challenging decision for you and your organization is determining which service provider most closely fits your business needs. Once you decide, your organization can easily begin to configure on-premises resources by scaling quickly and efficiently using configurable tools to provision the environment. Since the cloud provider has already made the capital resource investment, the organization is often responsible for selecting the configuration appropriate for the business objective.

There are numerous benefits to adopting a public cloud deployment approach. The most obvious is that the cost barrier is far lower than an on-premises or private cloud deployment model. Since there is no need to purchase dedicated hardware and software or rely on dedicated personnel for cloud maintenance, the costs are much lower. Another reason why prices are significantly lower is that with a public deployment most maintenance costs become the cloud service provider's responsibility, not the organization's. By shifting the financial burden, you are freeing up capital to focus on other projects.

Spotlight on CapEx vs. OpEx

When you shift responsibility from the data center (on-premises) to the cloud, you will need to adjust your entire financial mindset. Long-term purchases such as servers, storage, network equipment, backup and archive devices, and even technical personnel managing the infrastructure are all considered capital expenditure (CapEx) costs. You can't take a tax deduction for these items immediately; you need to cost these out over time (usually over three to five years). On the other hand, the water, gas, electricity, and even that website you might host with Microsoft Azure using a pay-as-you-go plan, those are all operational expenditure (OpEx) costs. Why? These are paid based on consumption. Since there are no upfront cost that are known, you only pay for the products or services as they are used. The greatest benefit with an OpEx cost is that it's tax deductibility occurs in the same calendar year it occurs. Learn more about capital expenditures and operational expenditures at the end of this chapter.

In terms of the technical benefits, public cloud infrastructure requires an incredibly robust set of technical resources, including networks, servers, storage, and compute power, to operate for many businesses. Solution providers, therefore, offer near unlimited scalability and high reliability. A single organization is not likely capable of replicating such scale on-premises.

 EXAM TIP When dealing with the public cloud, you may often hear the terms single- or multi-tenancy discussed. Make sure you understand these for the exam. Private cloud environments are associated with a single available tenant cloud environment (single organizations). Resources are exclusive to a single organization. On the other hand, organizations that share resources align with a multi-tenant cloud environment (multiple organizations using the same cloud infrastructure).

Hybrid Cloud

Suppose you are looking to deliver a cloud platform that supports private and public options. In that case, a hybrid environment is ideal for your organizational needs. An example of a hybrid environment might be a Microsoft 365 instance running in the public cloud but with a private cloud instance storing several data sets for one or more of the Microsoft 365 applications.

Many companies often start with a hybrid cloud implementation because they need to migrate their legacy data and applications to the cloud slowly. It usually takes a bit of time to make the transition. However, since business objectives should not delay using specific application resources or features, the transition to the cloud often begins using a phased approach. While this is the case for some organizations, this is not true all the time. There are instances where organizations have two environments running at the same time. Until the cloud environment is fully operational, both infrastructures are working concurrently. Eventually, the on-premises environment is shut down using a big bang approach.

Network connectivity is an essential part of any hybrid deployment model. For the cloud environments to communicate with one another, there must be a trusted relationship. Providers such as Microsoft must have different networking connectivity types, including virtual private connections and virtual private networks, to support cloud communication. Hybrid cloud connectivity is addressed in Chapter 3.

Cloud Service Models

At this point, you have already learned that there are three deployment options: private, public, and hybrid computing. When an organization decides to shift from the data center, the goal is to consider moving from an *on-premises business model* to a *shared responsibility model.* For those organizations whose computing resources are *on-premises*, that means the business purchases the physical resources, including all hardware and software, to meet the needs of the business's IT needs. Usually, the assets are physically consumable, which means they are procured for more than one year. Therefore, the purchase is considered a capital expenditure, a long-term procurement. Later in the chapter, we will discuss this financial model.

On-premises acquisitions are generally kept for three to five years until they are sunsetting resources or internally phased out of those capabilities. Although most computing assets are paid for after three to five years, that does not mean they are no longer used. The end of life for many IT assets can be several years later. Implementing on-premises technology is not ideal for those looking to evolve their IT environment with best-in-class solutions, because maintaining legacy technology means stifling innovation. Additionally, many organizations often take months, if not years, to fully configure new environments with hardware acquired through an on-premises requisition.

The cloud computing model is not reliant on any form of long-term purchase commitment. If you were to think of significant purchases such as purchasing a car or a home versus renting a house or leasing a car in comparison to cloud technologies, the analogy is quite similar. Instead of having to make a one-time lump sum investment on hardware, software, and personnel, you and your team will only procure the physical assets needed at a given point in time. By no longer focusing your technology budget on long-term investments, you can now scale your business for day-to-day needs. Operational expenses, including storage capacity, project requirements, labor, staffing utilization, and potential future customer projections, are trackable using time-based metrics.

When you purchase at scale, there are often many benefits tied to pricing. The same holds with cloud consumption costs. When cloud resources experience significant usage, discounts are usually applicable. Since a cloud-hosting provider pools resources together for many organizations, the provider is responsible for making an upfront investment, not the organization. Because the cloud provider pays for most resources in advance, the organization can realize cost savings based on an increase in cloud utilization to reduce the provider's investment. Another way the provider may reduce the overall expense to the organization is by offering commitment discounts. In summary, most cloud providers follow the basic savings principle known as *economies of scale.*

Computing Based on Consumption

Suppose you were to go ahead and buy a series of expensive servers for your organization and have your IT staff manage those servers. In that case, that expense is likely a one-time cost, also known as a capital expense. Once you buy the equipment, it is yours for good until you either sell it or dispose of it. All the costs associated with the upkeep are your responsibility. Does that sound like a cost-savings model over time?

Cloud computing costs, on the other hand, are based soley on consumption, meaning cloud providers charge the customer only for precisely what they use and nothing more. What does this mean? If you do not consume a computing resource, you do not pay for the resource.

Keep in mind, however, that cloud consumption invoicing applies to many levels within the cloud infrastructure. There is not just a single feature or function that you pay for. Cloud infrastructures scale to use resources as needed. For example, an application may only require the use of one virtual machine. Over time, capacity demand may require more disk storage at one point and then additional CPU and memory utilization later on. Adding these features onto the virtual machine each time will require a system adjustment and incur a separate charge increase. The additional capacity increases costs, just as a decrease in storage and CPU utilization would reduce the monthly invoice.

Another feature that providers such as Microsoft offer is paying for only the time an application or code is running. For example, suppose you have an application running a batch job only two hours per day. The remainder of the time, the application is idle. In that case, your organization will only pay for those two hours of operational use. At the end of the month, the invoice will only reflect, at most, 62 hours of usage for the batch operation, assuming a 31-day calendar month.

Cloud Computing as a Shared Responsibility

There are significant differences among cloud services deployment and delivery approaches as well as the architectureal components. An organization can deploy one or more cloud computing service models as part of a private, public, or hybrid deployment.

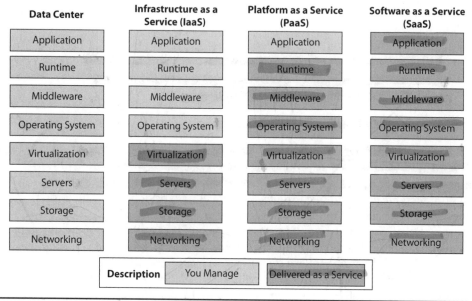

Figure 1-1   Cloud computing architecture model

However, each of the services comes with a different level of responsibility for managing the services. In Figure 1-1, one can better understand who is responsible for handling each cloud computing model's duties.

Suppose an organization was to maintain a traditional data center. In that case, the responsibility is entirely on the organization to handle all service ownership. For Infrastructure as a Service (IaaS), application, runtime, middleware, and operating system responsibilities reside with the organization. All other activities are delivered as a service. Since the only responsibility for an organization is to develop the application, all other services are delivered as a service with Platform as a Service (PaaS). Finally, for software as a service (SaaS), all features are services-based given the vendor has complete control. There is no specific combination to determine the advantages and disadvantages of one architecture over the next. Organizations need to figure out what is best for their growth trajectory.

Software as a Service (SaaS)

Instead of installing software applications onto an individual personal computer, software can be delivered over the Internet on-demand, often on a subscription basis. This cloud delivery model is referred to as *software as a Service* (SaaS). With SaaS, a cloud service provider, or in some instances the software vendor acting as the cloud service provider for that specific need, will host and manage the software application. The cost of utilizing the software consists of the infrastructure (hardware) and any maintenance, including software upgrades and security patches. A user will log in to the application over an Internet connection, using their device of choice with a Web browser, based on the application's systems requirements. Additional characteristics and benefits to using SaaS include:

- Access to the latest versions of sophisticated software applications
- Paying for only those applications and IT resources that you use
- Better support for a mobile and agile workforce
- Access application data anytime, anywhere

Most applications delivered as SaaS require some form of subscription. A subscription is the delivery of a service or product, such as a software application or infrastructure component, on a reoccurring payment plan, monthly, quarterly, or yearly. Occasionally, SaaS products are delivered to customers perpetually, a type of license where you pay one time for a service and get to use the product for an indefinite period.

Examples of SaaS-based applications you might be familiar with include e-mail, calendaring, spreadsheet, and business productivity tools such as those found in Microsoft 365. Perhaps if you have ever used a web conference or telepresence platforms such as Microsoft Teams or Skype, that too is a SaaS platform. Each of these applications provides a complete software solution purchased on a pay-as-you-go basis from a cloud service provider such as Microsoft. Instead of making a one-time purchase, you rent the application for the number of users necessary to connect to the Internet for a given period. Vendors such as Microsoft offer licensing terms as short as a month. Many offer long-term agreements that can extend beyond one year.

Unlike those responsible for managing computing resources in an enterprise environment, an organization choosing to compute using SaaS solutions frees itself from worrying about managing the hardware and software, based on the terms of its service agreement. In return, the provider ensures its technology is always available, including all data and security controls in place, without any upfront investment.

Use Case: SaaS

Whether you are a startup or a mature organization, one of the first decisions that you will likely consider making as part of your IT toolkit is what business productivity suite best meets your needs. Also, suppose your organization requires marketing management, enterprise resource planning, and collaboration functionality. In that case, these tools are often procured simultaneously. All these solutions are available by numerous enterprise IT vendors, including Microsoft.

For example, suppose you were to procure the full line of capabilities described (business productivity, CRM, ERP, and collaboration). In that case, your organization is likely to procure solutions including Microsoft 365, Microsoft Dynamics Sales Professional, Microsoft Dynamics Financials and Operations, Microsoft SharePoint 365, and Microsoft Power Automate for a specified number of users. If other vendors are preferred, your organization can easily select another SaaS solution to fit the technical need should systems integration between the systems be necessary. The organization would procure the number of licenses necessary at a given point in time. If the organization's footprint experiences a reduction in the workforce, the IT team can reduce their license count; if an increase in the license is necessary, the license count may also increase proportionally.

Infrastructure as a Service (IaaS)

Infrastructure is associated with the hardware that your applications consume. IaaS refers to the virtualized infrastructure offered by cloud providers such as Microsoft. An IaaS resource such as a virtual machine allows compute operations to be handled over the Web through the cloud provider rather than in an on-premises data center. A virtual machine requires only a few resources, such as a basic operating system that can be installed for you. Figure 1-2 provides an example of the initial setup of a virtual machine in Microsoft Azure.

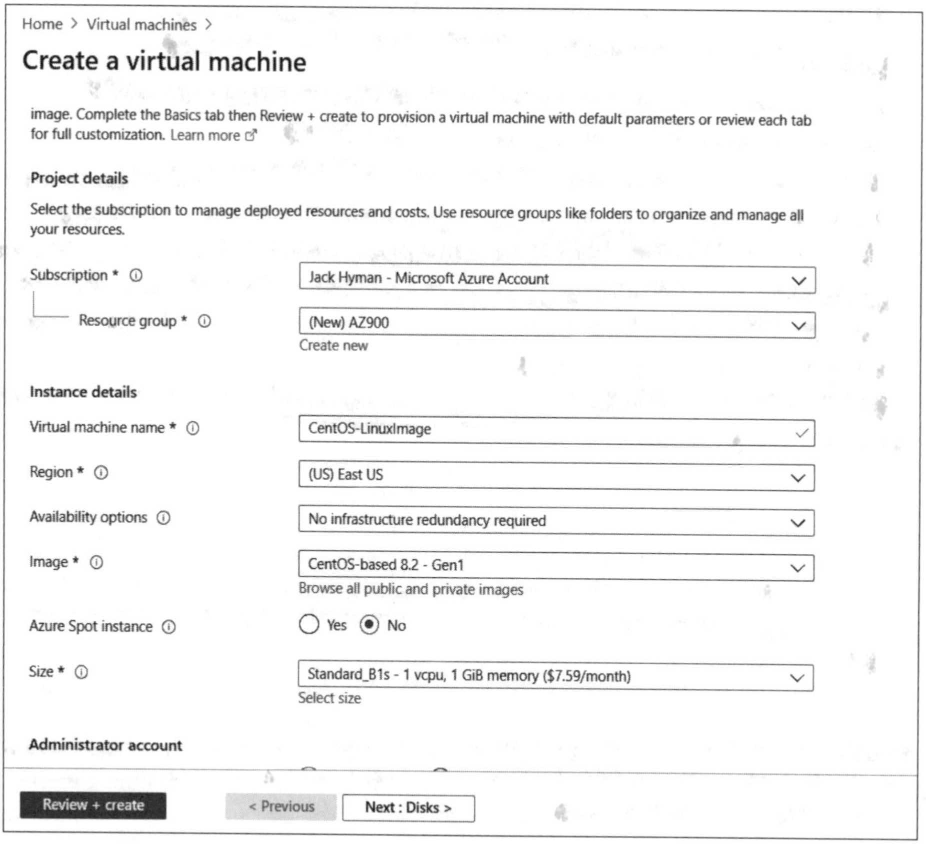

Figure 1-2 Creating a virtual machine instance in Microsoft Azure

The cloud provider may offer you, the client, the hardware; however, the responsibility is entirely yours to install all the necessary services and applications to make the environment operational.

In an IaaS environment, the organization manages the system configuration, including the operating system and that of most other services. One advantage of IaaS is that you have complete autonomy over your cloud resources. However, keep in mind that such independence can be a disadvantage because it holds the organization responsible for any operating system and security patch updates. If there are any system performance issues, the IT operations team is often responsible for troubleshooting the environment. The bounds of where the cloud service provider's responsibility ends and where your responsibility begins are at the provisioning of the virtual machine instance.

Your organization benefits from the underlying hardware being managed by a cloud service provider. The service provider is also held accountable for managing all hosting and maintenance ownership, including scalability, elasticity, fault tolerance, and disaster recovery. The provider takes on this responsibility; your organization holds limited liability. There are numerous business and technical advantages:

- Although, elimination of one-time business costs is never fully recognized when procured on-premises, ongoing costs are far less utilizing IaaS.
- Ability to better manage business continuity and disaster recovery.
- Greater flexibility in advanced technology is available to innovate rapidly.
- Businesses can respond quickly to shifting conditions.
- By moving to an operational business model, IaaS frees up developers to focus on core business needs and innovative projects, rather than infrastructure tasks.
- Since the cloud service provider is responsible for infrastructure support, there are assurances for increased stability and supportability based on mandatory SLAs.
- Security options in an IaaS offering are often better than what is available in a traditional data center setting.
- Delivery of any service offering is quicker, at scale, and can be done globally with greater ease.

The opportunities to scale quickly in the cloud are limitless for an organization, regardless of size. Often, the catalog of features available to support infrastructure growth by a cloud service provider can help you build a robust platform while also controlling your costs. Another reason organization may choose to utilize an IaaS model over another cloud model or an on-premises option is that cloud resources can be used temporarily. An organization can create resources quickly, use them as needed, gain all the processing power required, and dispose of those resources when the resources are no longer necessary.

In summary, IaaS is a preferred option when your organization requires someone to have control over the infrastructure to manage applications, system configurations, and how that operating system runs. While the cloud provider may set up the hardware footprint and potentially the initial operating system, they have limited responsibility for customizing the environment beyond the baseline. Additionally, for those businesses who only want to pay for their uptime system utilization whereby they control when to turn on and off the environment, this is another compelling reason to consider IaaS.

Use Case: IaaS

The cost of purchasing servers on-premises may appear relatively inexpensive as hardware costs have dropped dramatically in the past several years. That does not mean that an organization with a rapidly growing developer workforce should continue to procure new hardware every two to three months. Instead of having to purchase new servers to deploy a lightweight virtual machine environment such as those that maintain the Microsoft Azure B-series burstable profile, you can offer employees the option to deploy new virtual machine instances using pre-built Azure templates already built by Microsoft.

As is the case with a Microsoft B-series burstable profile, an employee will be able to create a virtual machine template that consists of features that offer a configured operating system with a lightweight operating system, memory, and CPU resources, a web server, a lightweight database, and development test environment. Should the developer require burstable performance requirements, these capabilities are configured in place. The VM is appropriate for those that are price and resource conscious. As the technical demand grows, so does the footprint of the virtual machine instance.

Platform as a Service (PaaS)

Platform as a service (PaaS) is a development and deployment environment in the cloud. Instead of supporting enterprise applications on an on-premises server, you can deliver every service from a cloud-based environment without having to worry about maintenance and support on a pay-as-you-go basis.

Like Infrastructure as a Service (IaaS) arrangements, all your servers, storage, and network costs are paid for as part of your expenses. The difference between IaaS and PaaS, though, is that depending on the cloud service provider, with PaaS your costs include middleware, development tools, and software capabilities such as business intelligence (BI), database management, and security options. PaaS helps reduce the costs for organizations that want to build complete web applications throughout the entire lifecycle, including building, testing, deploying, managing, and updating. There are many advantages to adopting a PaaS strategy:

- Reduces the cost of development and coding using pre-built assets and features
- Adds development capabilities without requiring technical personnel
- Ability to build multiple platform solutions using a single code base quickly and affordably

- Affordable development tools that may not have been otherwise available to those in a traditional technical deployment model
- Distributed geographic support for development teams that can work and collaborate on projects at scale

Examples that reflect PaaS solutions include development frameworks, analytics, and business intelligence solutions, and data-centric application solutions. Development frameworks often provider custom capabilities to the developer. If you have ever created a macro for an Excel workbook, you likely understand the model to develop built-in software components associated with cloud platforms. Cloud features including scalability, high availability, and multi-tenancy capabilities are included with these toolsets, often reducing the required coding a developer is responsible for completing. Additionally, analytics and business intelligence solutions are associated with PaaS platforms. Finally, application integration services to create enhancements such as workflows, directory services, and security fall into the category of PaaS.

In Figure 1-1, the example architecture shows that the difference between IaaS and PaaS is the resource requirements. Whereas with PaaS the only resource not delivered as a service is the application, the IaaS architecture requires the setup of an application, runtime, and the operating system. All those components must be in place before the development of the application even begins. In a PaaS environment, you and your organization are limited to deploying the standalone web application. All the resources mentioned are configurable as a service by the cloud provider. In Figure 1-3, you have a Web application in the Azure Web Service. The example is a standalone Python Web application with a dedicated URL. Upon developing and deploying code in the PaaS environment, the application is visible at the URL listed on the right-hand side of Figure 1-3.

Like other cloud providers, Microsoft Azure offers the ability to publish an entire application using code or through a Docker image. A developer can create an application using numerous application frameworks, including ASP.NET, Java, Python, PHP, or Node.js. Each framework usually contains multiple versions, from the latest version

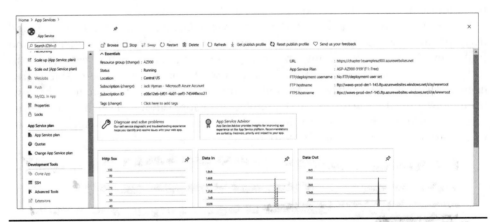

Figure 1-3   PaaS example of Azure Web application, Python standalone Web app

through at least one or two previous versions to ensure backward compatibility with your application. Having more than one version is also often necessary to ensure component compatibility.

Docker images allow a developer to use Docker to package their application and the application components into a single image file. The image file can be used in another environment, assuming Docker is installable. With Azure App Services, Docker is automatically installable on any services-run virtual machine delivered by Azure. Therefore, management and maintenance are handled by Microsoft.

Use Case: PaaS

Many vendors promote their data platforms as an infrastructure service. Not Microsoft. You will find that if your organization is looking to build an application, query a data source, or seek data for analytics evaluation, the cloud computing model best suited is PaaS. Products that fall under this category include Azure Database, Azure Database for MySQL, Azure Database for PostgreSQL, HDInsight, and Databricks.

 EXAM TIP   It is not uncommon on a Microsoft Fundamentals exam to find a mixture of definitions and use case–based questions. An individual preparing for certification should be comfortable with the definitions and example use cases provided in Azure platform documentation.

Serverless Computing

While not an "as a service" architecture directly, serverless computing is considered a fourth architecture type by Microsoft. Serverless computing often overlaps with many of the capabilities offered under PaaS. *Serverless computing* allows developers to build lightweight applications to eliminate the management of infrastructure required to run code. Serverless architectures are highly scalable and event driven. Two ways in Azure that serverless works includes the use of functions and triggers. A *function* is a single event that executes without providing or managing infrastructure explicitly. A *trigger* is an explicit action that is invoked once the Azure Function is told to run. Unless activity is occurring, a function remains idle. While lightweight, a serverless application is still built on a core set of resources provided by a service provider. The difference between a virtual machine and a serverless application is simple: backend features are automatically provisioned, scaled, and managed to run on your behalf. Code runs with a serverless application. That is not the case with a virtual machine. Serverless computing helps increase productivity while optimizing resources since the developer can focus on development almost exclusively. A more robust discussion of serverless computing, Azure functions, and logic apps can be found in Chapter 4.

Technical Benefits of Cloud Computing

To understand cloud computing benefits, one must first understand what is meant by the data center or physical environment versus the cloud environment. Employing a cloud-first strategy is associated with numerous innovative synergies not possible to those making one-time information technology acquisitions. Those that consider a data center approach must face ongoing ad hoc maintenance and uncertainty of the environment's stability over time—costs beyond the technology itself. Costs must consider the facility, electricity, gas, water, heating, cooling, physical security, personnel cost, and compliance expenses as part of a general equation. With cloud computing, what you are paying for is an all-inclusive price.

High Availability

When an organization is responsible for its infrastructure, there is a predetermined set of standards set for operational norms in uptime, system availability, and maintenance windows. You may find that an organization will indicate systems are available 95 percent of the time, 24/7/365 (meaning 24 hours a day, seven days a week, 365 days a year). The organization may have a weekly maintenance window, say, between 1:00 and 4:00 A.M. EST on Sunday, which is agreed upon between IT and other functions of the business. The procedural terms are called *service-level agreements* (SLAs). An SLA is a contract between a service provider, such as Microsoft, and an organization to document what services the provider is obligated to provide an organization. Cloud service providers, unlike on-premises providers, commit to a more stringent level of service quality. One of those qualities is to ensure that operational performance, usually uptime, exceeds a higher-than-average standard. The standard, known as *high availability*, implies that systems depending on the service provider can operate continuously without failure. The infrastructure for the service provider is well-tested and is supported by multiple system redundancy levels in case of some form of outage (power, network, application failure, or natural disaster). Most systems offered by cloud service providers guarantee operational performance levels exceeding 99.9 percent over a relevant period.

Scalability

What do you think about when you think of a rubber band: the ability to become big or small instantly, right? For those who are delivering cloud services, organizations that offer cloud servers at scale provide IT resources such as power, storage, network capacity, bandwidth, and memory, among capabilities on demand anytime, anywhere. *Scalability* measures a system's ability to increase or decrease performance and cost in response to changes to operational changes with applications or systems. Figure 1-4 demonstrates how one can scale up (increase memory and storage) from a development environment to a production environment for a standalone Python Web app.

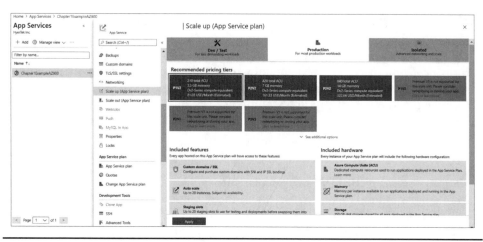

Figure 1-4 Scaling up from a development to production environment in Azure

Depending on how an enterprise grows, its cloud footprint depends on two considerations: resource management (vertical scaling) and workload support (horizontal support).

- **Cloud Vertical Scaling** Associated with adding more centralized processing unit (CPU), memory, and input/output (I/O) resources to an existing server or replacing outdated servers with more robust infrastructure. There are two options to scale vertically in Microsoft Azure. Your first option is to modify the instance size. A second option is to purchase a new appliance and replace the legacy instance. Since Azure offers numerous option sizes, scaling alternatives is an appropriate option most times.

- **Cloud Horizontal Scaling** When an organization says it needs to scale horizontally, adding additional servers to meet capacity. Another interpretation might be splitting up a workload (the different projects and jobs) between servers to limit the requested job limit. For those using Microsoft Azure, horizontal scaling means adding additional virtual machine instances instead of moving to a larger size server.

Use Case #1: Azure Database Example

Assume your organization runs a single-instance Azure MySQL Database for its online ecommerce store (based on WordPress and WooCommerce). The store has a total of 100 transactions. As the business grows, especially as you approach major holiday events, there tends to be a spike in resource demand. The database application, like the website traffic, will often see an increase in transactional activity. For the IT manager controlling the system, it is essential to know the business's growth rate, focusing on the database, so that the organization can purchase the appropriate amount of provisioned infrastructure. Metrics to be concerned with

(continued)

include compute, network, and storage capacity. The manager needs to be sure that the database and the network can grow with the traffic to ensure maximum performance and capacity. To scale performance with user demand, the IT manager should make sure that the system can scale appropriately without worrying about meeting the SLA pay-as-you-grow solution conditions.

Use Case #2: Virtual Desktop Example

Many organizations have transformed their physical office presence into a 100 percent virtual footprint. The first step in that transformation is identifying the necessary IT resources needed to create an efficient IT operation. That includes its hardware and software infrastructure. Instead of requiring employees to use desktop or laptop computers to complete everyday tasks, most organizations opt for a lightweight computer. So how do these organizations deliver the necessary IT software and services to operate their corporate systems through a virtualized desktop environment? The Microsoft Azure Windows Virtual Desktop experience enables a secure remote desktop experience from anywhere.

A virtual desktop experience allows the worker to access all the traditional workplace functionality using a Web browser. The opportunity costs are tremendous because there is a reuse of the same licenses based on the number of users who access the environment. In this use case, an organization may only need ten licenses, assuming they have ten employees on staff. However, if they downsize half their organization, they will not incur the cost of those five additional licenses. What happens, though, if there was a capacity surge? To support the maximum number of users and meet the SLA between the organization and Microsoft Azure, the IT manager simply provisions additional licenses and adds the necessary infrastructure capacity in the Azure portal.

 EXAM TIP It is not uncommon to find use cases such as the one presented throughout this chapter on the AZ-900 exam analyzing a best practice, circumstance, or condition. When trying to solve the question, look for the most logical answer, not necessarily the best answer that fits just one specific use case.

Elasticity

Elasticity is the ability to quickly expand or decrease the compute processing capacity to meet demand. Processing capacity includes memory and storage resources. Elasticity often requires modification during peak usage periods. As part of a cloud developer's planning process, it is essential to conduct capacity planning and engineering evaluations of the organization's current needs and understand its future opportunities.

Managed by system monitoring tools, system resources can match operational needs because elasticity scales in a computing environment to ensure resource allocation avoids operational disruptions. Cloud elasticity helps organizations only pay for the resources they require. Remember, you only pay for what you use, which means an organization will not pay for excess capacity or idle resource utilization. The organization also avoids paying for resources, equipment, labor, and maintenance unless necessary. One final benefit to consider is that elasticity provides efficiency and autonomy. Given that elasticity allows for automatic scaling while traditional IT requires human administration, there is no need to worry about continuous availability of services or operational slowness, system degradation, interruptions, or outages.

Agility

Quickly deploying and configuring cloud resources is one of the reasons why many organizations shift to the cloud. As requirements change, organizations cannot afford to wait to go through a drawn-out process of procurement, design, implementation, development, and testing. This constant cycle is simply too expensive, especially when application requirements are often so changeable. *Agility* refers to the rapid development, testing, and launching of a technical capability, whether it is a software application or infrastructure component, that drives business. In the cloud computing context, agility is not limited to provisioning and maintenance exclusively; it also focuses on security, monitoring, and analysis.

Disaster Recovery

Organizations hope they never have to deal with a disaster; however, it is always an essential part of IT planning. *Disaster recovery* requires you to understand how to restore application functionality when there is an outage of any sort or a catastrophic loss, including natural disasters. An organization needs to determine its tolerance for reduced functionality as part of its disaster recovery process, as business decisions are tied to application operations. While one application may be business critical because every user corporate-wide requires access to the system, another solution may only be used by a handful of employees, which means reduced functionality is acceptable for a period. As part of your business continuity planning, which means to create plans to keep the business operational during a period of disaster, an IT organization should better evaluate its organization's needs against network service, application failure, power demands, reliance on third-party systems, and system infrastructure such as virtualized infrastructure. In doing so, the organization will be better prepared to configure its systems if it decides to build a private cloud. Alternatively, if the organization decides to shift from the data center to the public cloud, it will be advantageous to foster a working relationship with the cloud solution provider to implement a standard that can monitor the health of cloud resources and take notice when resources are unhealthy, ensuring the cloud is *fault tolerant*.

Financial Benefits of Cloud Computing

When discussing cloud computing, there are often three fiscal outcomes every organization looks to address when making a significant decision: revenue, cost, and profit. *Revenue* is understood to be how much money a business can make as a result of the sale of goods and services. *Costs* are understood to be how much money is spent to bring the product or service to market, including all the backend requirements, including the technology infrastructure. The third facet is *profitability*. When looking to address transformation, there is always the potential to increase revenue and decrease costs. The result is a profit outcome.

With cloud computing, service providers offer organizations services without any significant upfront costs and equipment setup time. Why is this important to consider? If an organization invests a large portion of its revenue toward computing expenses, they are spending money on physical infrastructure upfront and then reducing that expense from their profits. This investment approach is called *capital expenditure (CapEx)*, which reduces the value of the investment over time. On the other hand, when the organization decides to buy products and services on an as-needed basis, they can only deduct those expenses during that same fiscal year. The financial approach to buy on an as-needed basis is called *operational expenditure (OpEx)*. There are a few differences here. First, the outlay of expenses is marginal relative to capital expenditure. Second, scaling based on supply and demand usage is allowed here while being able to put the funds that would have been used otherwise to other important priorities. Examples of CapEx include servers, storage, network, backup and archive, organization continuity and disaster recovery, data center, and technical staffing, whereas OpEx examples include leasing software, scaling charges based on usage/demand for hardware/capacity (storage, memory, CPU, etc.), and billing at the user/organization level (for a specific application, resources, and features).

The challenge with CapEx is simple: if demand and growth are unpredictable, resulting in unknowns to revenue, costs, and profit, the impact can be catastrophic to the financial stability of an organization, especially if an organization is actively growing. If an organization can precisely predict expenses from the start to finish of a project period (and the costs are fixed), including the budget, an organization may find comfort with using a CapEx model. Under all other circumstances, companies needing to regularly try new products and services, frequently upgrade and update services, and pay as little as possible to invest in other innovations should consider looking at an OpEx-based delivery model. If your organization has any unknowns or your demands fluctuate, cloud services using an OpEx model is the best approach to delivering agility in business.

Chapter Review

In Chapter 1, the focus is on general cloud computing concepts. You begin to familiarize yourself with why organizations become interested in moving to the cloud from a data center, whether the move is motivated by business, technical, or financial reasons. You learn the difference between cloud delivery models and cloud architecture. A cloud deployment model represents the delivery of services. In contrast, cloud architecture is the different services that make up the cloud service. There are three deployment models:

private, public, and hybrid. Similarly, there are three architecture options: Infrastructure as a Service (IaaS), software as a Service (SaaS), and Platform as a Service (PaaS).

Private cloud deployments are best suited for organizations needing dedicated resources for their organizations exclusively. These organizations look to have more control within their infrastructure, affording the business dedicated self-service, scalability, elasticity, high availability, disaster recovery, and high performance. A more affordable option where an organization can share infrastructure resources is that of a public cloud deployment. Unlike a private cloud offering where the organization holds almost all responsibility in maintaining the hosted infrastructure, the public infrastructure is managed almost exclusively by the cloud service provider. Some organizations look for the best of both worlds, both public and private cloud deployments. In that case, an organization will opt for a hybrid deployment. When migrating from a traditional data center environment, referred to as on-premises, most organizations tend to start with a hybrid approach because there are costs to moving legacy systems over to the cloud.

As for cloud architectures, there are three one should remember: IaaS, SaaS, and PaaS. With IaaS, compute infrastructure resources are managed by a cloud provider operations center over the Web versus in the organization's data center, which may include the operating system. Features managed also have storage, security, networking, and security capacity. Organizations looking to avoid making software procurements based on a fixed number of seats and instead purchase on-demand will prefer purchasing under an SaaS delivery model. Unlike the good old days where you buy a piece of software and installed it on the computer countless times, a user logs into the online platform to access the software using a Web browser. An organization only pays for the licenses they need. The organization can scale up or down at any time. The final architecture model, PaaS, delivers the development and deployment environment to create new applications in the cloud. Instead of supporting enterprise applications on servers in a hosted environment, the organization can centralize delivery using the cloud to mitigate common maintenance management concerns. Interestingly, some of the applications delivered using a PaaS deployment can be serverless. These are lightweight, function- or event trigger–based applications that only run when called. Otherwise, the application remains idle.

There are many reasons organizations pause before leaping to cloud computing, most of which have to do with company culture and time commitment. However, the technical and financial benefits are plentiful, often outweighing the disadvantages. Technical benefits include high availability, agility, scalability, elasticity, and disaster recovery at scale. Organizations that shift to the cloud establish a service-level agreement (SLA), a contract, to ensure that any service provides a certain standard. Unlike on-premises measures, cloud service providers such as Microsoft must offer high availability or continuous operation without fail for its customers. Also, since a service provider is responsible for many organizations' technical needs, they need to ensure that their systems can increase capacity at a moment's notice. That means the system must be scalable (increase and decrease performance) and elastic (quickly expand or decrease processing capacity) for memory and storage during peak periods. The last but most critical service an organization must have in place is disaster recovery solutions. In the unlikely event a system experiences an unplanned disruption, the organization should make sure that it has an appropriate contingency plan based on the criticality of the application in place.

By far, the biggest motivator for an organization to make the switch to the cloud is money. A significant distinction between traditional on-premises computing and cloud computing is the costs to deploy and maintain IT operations. An organization needs to decide whether they should pay an upfront expense for on-premises expenses, reducing their ability to invest revenue in other high-priority projects. The other perspective is, should the organization migrate to the cloud, allowing the organization to pay only as resources are consumed based on changing needs. Besides, the more resources procured, the more affordable those resources become, following economies of scale. Many organizations often need to weigh the decision between capital expenditure (CapEx) spending (initial spending with long-term asset procurement) versus operational expenditure (OpEx) spending (spending based on consumption and demand). Given that most organizations recognize the benefits outweigh the disadvantages regardless of delivery approach and architecture, cloud computing has quickly accelerated in the IT marketplace in recent years. This trend will undoubtedly continue, with innovative vendors such as Microsoft leading the way.

Questions

1. Which of the following statements is not true about Infrastructure as a Service (IaaS)? (Select one.)

   A. An IaaS security posture is often more robust than those in an on-premises data center due to regulatory and compliance mandates the provider's customers must adhere to.

   B. The cloud service provider is responsible for all facets of infrastructure and application support given there are assurances in place for increased stability and supportability using a mandatory service-level agreement (SLA).

   C. Elimination of one-time business costs that are never fully recognized when procured on-premises.

   D. Delivery of any service offering is quicker, at scale, and can be done globally with greater ease.

2. Which of the following statements regarding a private cloud delivery model are inaccurate? (Select two.)

   A. A private cloud only delivers services over the public Internet.

   B. A reason to consider private cloud options over a public cloud is when your organization requires customization to meet business needs, looks to gain control over resources that may be shared in a public setting, and is aware that the environment has the potential for a significant increase in activity.

   C. A reason to consider a private cloud option over a public cloud is when your organization requires strict enforcement of technical standards to streamline business needs, looks to lock down controls to ensure users are unable to modify settings, and recognizes that system scalability is limited.

   D. Private cloud supports only two service architectures, Infrastructure as a Service (IaaS) and Platform as a Service (PaaS).

3. An organization has decided to host its website on Microsoft Azure using WordPress. The CFO would like to know what the best delivery model is for all customers. The CFO wants to be assured the website is publicly accessible. What would you recommend?

  A. Public cloud

  B. Private cloud

  C. Hybrid cloud

  D. Serverless cloud

4. Your company has decided it is time to move its data and resources off an old Microsoft Access database. It would like to use the Microsoft Azure SQL migration wizard to move the records. The database administrator indicates that that Microsoft Azure SQL is a Software as a Service (SaaS) delivery offering. Is that statement accurate?

  A. Yes

  B. No

5. Your organization, a health care practice, is required by law to maintain patient records for seven years. Recently, the organization invested in an electronic health records (EHR) system. The business has been in practice for 18 years and still maintains 5,000+ previous patient files from the past. By law, all these records must be digitized. What type of cloud solution deployment model should the EHR company suggest the health practice implement?

  A. Private cloud

  B. Public cloud

  C. Hybrid cloud

  D. Serverless cloud

6. You are the member of a large accounting firm that works with large corporations. By law, the corporations are required to file quarterly tax reports. Traffic is extremely light to the applications except during specific filing periods, usually one week per quarter. Which of the Azure Cloud Service benefits best reflects the usage behavior that should be addressed?

  A. Scalability

  B. Agility

  C. High availability

  D. Elasticity

7. Your organization has recently instituted a 100 percent telework policy in order to reduce expenses. As part of the planning, the IT operations team is looking for ways to utilize as many enterprise vendors' pre-built software solutions so that there is no need to install custom applications and maintain a dedicated helpdesk. Which cloud architecture should you include in your suggestion to leadership?

   A. Software as a Service (SaaS)

   B. Platform as a Service (PaaS)

   C. Infrastructure as a Service (IaaS)

   D. Desktop as a Service (DaaS)

8. Select the appropriate architecture to match the applications from the following drop-down menus.

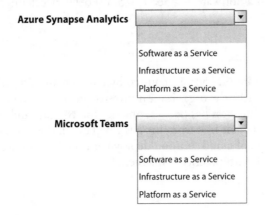

   A. Infrastructure as a Service, Platform as a Service

   B. Infrastructure as a Service, Software as a Service

   C. Platform as a Service, Software as a Service

   D. Software as a Service, Platform as a Service

9. Is the following statement true or false with regards to a hybrid cloud offering?

   A company can extend its internal network capacity using the public cloud when using cloud bursting.

   A. True

   B. False

10. What is the difference between fault tolerance and disaster recovery?

   A. A cloud service that scales horizontally is defined as fault tolerance, whereas disaster recovery is when a cloud service supports recovery after an outage or catastrophic event occurs.

   B. A cloud service that is available after an event occurs is defined as fault tolerance, whereas disaster recovery is when a cloud service supports recovery after an outage or catastrophic event occurs.

   C. A cloud service that offers rapid development, testing, and launching of a technical capability is referred to as fault tolerance, whereas disaster recovery is when a cloud service becomes available after an event occurs.

   D. A cloud service that is available after an event occurs is defined as disaster recovery, whereas fault tolerance is when a cloud service supports recovery after an outage or catastrophic event occurs.

11. Indicate if the following statements are true (Yes) or false (No) based on the questions regarding capital expenditure (CapEx) and operational expenditure (OpEx).

	Yes	No
An organization that procures more storage in the Azure Portal should consider the expense a Capital Expenditure.	○	⊗
An organization that procures 20 Microsoft Surface Laptops with a 36-month subscription should consider this a Capital Expenditure.	⊗	○
An organization that maintains part of its data center until its transition to the cloud is complete will charge expenses such as electricity and facility costs to the Capital Expenditure budget.	○	⊗

   A. Yes, No, No

   ✗ **B.** No, Yes, No

   C. No, Yes, Yes

   D. No, No, Yes

12. Which of the following as a service types are best aligned with serverless computing?

   A. Infrastructure

   ✗ **B.** Software

   C. Platform

   D. Database

13. When an administrator shuts off a virtual machine instance, which of the following statements regarding operational costs is accurate?

   A. Even though you are shutting off the virtual machine, you are still charged to keep the instance, including the storage operational.

   B. While you may not pay for operating the virtual machine, you will still be charged for the storage in use until deleted.

   C. Once a virtual machine is turned off, you do not pay for any additional fees.

   D. If the virtual machine is inactive, you are charged a subscription fee for inactivity use per virtual instance of $5.00 per day per VM.

14. In order to assure that an organization has a commitment from its cloud service provider for guaranteed uptime, service reliability, and continuous operations, a service-level agreement is signed to ensure what?

    A. Principle of economic scale

    B. High availability

    C. Disaster recovery

    D. Agility

15. What is meant by multi-tenancy in describing a public cloud deployment model?

    A. Many organizations share the same set of resources within a cloud infrastructure across one or more geo-distributed locations.

    B. A single organization has exclusive access to resources within a cloud infrastructure across one or more geo-distributed locations.

    C. A single organization shares the same set of resources within a cloud infrastructure across one or more geo-distributed locations.

    D. Many organizations are restricted to a specific set of cloud infrastructure resources in a bound geographic region.

Answers

1. B. While a cloud service provider is responsible for maintaining the infrastructure (hardware and installation of the operating system for an organization), they are not responsible for application level support. An SLA is put in place to ensure increased stability and reliability within the infrastructure, but not for applications unless they are specific to the operating system or maintaining the infrastructure itself.

2. B, D. Private cloud is an appropriate deployment option when an organization requires customization to meet business needs, looks to gain control over resources that may be shared in a public setting, and is aware that the environment has the potential for a significant increase in activity. In addition, only IaaS and PaaS are supported for private cloud.

3. A. Public cloud is intended for user consumption over the Internet. Private cloud is intended for internal consumption exclusively. Hybrid cloud allows for a mixture of internal and external resource utilization. Since there is no mention of requiring resource from within the organization, hybrid is not necessary. Serverless cloud is not necessarily a deployment model as much as it is an approach to deliver applications that are event-driven based on a function or trigger.

4. B. Microsoft Azure SQL is a Platform as a Service, not a Software as a Service, delivery offering given it is a data service that supports one or more applications.

5. **C.** A hybrid cloud is the optimal solution given the health care practice must maintain a public-facing EHR that patients access. However, the practice also maintains internal clinical records and system storage that is being updated as part of the digital modernization project to preserve the paper copies of all 5,000+ patients specific to the practices private cloud instance.

Connecting the public and private cloud instances together offer the best implementation alternative. Selecting a private cloud exclusively does not allow patients to access their data, a requirement by law for those offering EHR systems. By selecting public cloud, the health data is being exposed to unnecessary parties, violating policies such as protection of PII and HIPAA. Serverless computing is not applicable in this case.

6. **D.** Elasticity is the most appropriate choice since it allows for one to increase or decrease compute capacity quickly and at scale. While other options may seem reasonable, D is the best choice. Scalability measures a system's ability to increase or decrease performance and cost in response to operational changes with an application or system. Agility refers to the rapid development, testing, and launching of a technical capability, whether it is a software application or infrastructure component that drives a business. High availability ensures that systems depending on if a service provider can operate continuously without failing.

7. **A.** The organization is looking to reduce as many internal functions as possible, and they are aiming to use enterprise vendor commercial off-the-shelf (COTS) solutions. SaaS aligns best with that model. An organization may have some custom applications; however, in this use case, the goal is to shift away from custom and move toward pre-built offerings. The organization may need to procure some IaaS services; however, for this use case, this is not the main objective. Desktop as a Service is not a deployment model.

8. **C.** In the illustration, Azure Synapse Analytics maps to Platform as a Service in the first drop-down menu. Microsoft Teams maps to Software as a Service in the second drop-down menu. All other option combinations are inaccurate.

9. **A.** When a private cloud (internal network) needs additional capacity during a peak period of IT demand, it will require the use of public cloud resources. Therefore, the use of a special configuration known as *cloud bursting* is a great option for scaling a private cloud when necessitated.

10. **B.** Fault tolerance is defined as a cloud service that is available after a disrupting event occurs. Disaster recovery describes a cloud service that supports recovery after an outage or catastrophic event occurs.

11. **D.** No. The first condition describes procuring more cloud storage. Since cloud services are considered operational expenses, not capital expenses.

No. The second condition describes a subscription service. While the organization is procuring 20 devices, they will not own the devices outright, they are only leasing them for a monthly fee. At the end of the 36-month period, the devices must be returned. This too describes an operational expense.

Yes. The final condition describes expenses associated with maintaining data center operations. By default, any expense to maintain on-premises operations is tied to capital expenses.

12. **C.** Platform as a Service is associated with the development and design of applications. Serverless computing, like PaaS, focuses on the creation of lightweight applications that are event-based functions, set off by a trigger. Serverless applications are fully supported by the cloud service provider except for the application development functionality. IaaS is incorrect as infrastructure alone is not enough to support a serverless environment. It is the underpinning of the serverless capabilities though. SaaS is software delivered by another vendor, a third party; it is not applicable to serverless computing. Database as a service is not a formal architectural option to consider.

13. **B** is the best choice. You will still need to pay for storage regardless of a VM being active or inactive when managing an IaaS Instance.

14. **B.** High availability is the best selection, because it ensures that systems depending on a service provider can operate continuously without failing.

15. **A.** Multi-tenancy is when many organizations share the same set of resources within a cloud infrastructure across one or more geo-distributed locations.

Azure Concepts and Architecture Components

In this chapter, you will learn to

- Select Azure Support, Billing, and Subscription options
- Evaluate Azure architectural components
- Identify Azure design and deployment principles for core services

Microsoft Azure is a set of cloud services that can help an organization meet business challenges. The cloud services platform allows a user to build, manage, and deploy applications on one of the world's largest global networks.

You might be wondering what services and feature sets are available when you decide to utilize Microsoft Azure. With Microsoft Azure, you are getting a platform of services that allows an organization to use the cloud as a development and deployment environment. Some may use the cloud infrastructure as an alternative data center option, while others may create custom applications.

Azure allows organizations to grow as quickly as they want or to take their time. Microsoft is firmly committed to all application options, including open source. Besides, virtually all programming languages and frameworks are supported. It is up to the user to decide how to leverage features available in the platform.

In Chapter 1, you became familiar with hybrid computing as a capability of Azure. When an organization has resources that must remain on-premises but need the infrastructure to scale, Azure offers the best of all these options at an affordable price. You can select what tools to utilize and how to meet your organizational workload needs. In order to succeed, you must become familiar with how to organize and distribute the Azure resources, whether it is in your local geography or across many data centers. By the time you complete this chapter, you'll understand key Azure business principles and architectural concepts. The framework defined in Chapter 2 can help you successfully implement a robust infrastructure and well-built applications.

Azure Portal

The Azure Portal is your single location to view and manage all your cloud applications. Whether you have web apps, databases, virtual machines, virtual networks, storage appliances, or virtual desktop instances, you can access all cloud functionality as an administrator from the Azure Portal. The Azure Portal, presented in Figure 2-1, is a graphical user interface–based portal. However, you can utilize the integrated command-line utility provided by selecting the Azure Cloud Shell (Figure 2-2) or connect to the Azure Portal using the Windows PowerShell application to complete cloud-based support actions.

 EXAM TIP Make sure you know the difference between Azure Portal (http://portal.azure.com), Azure Cloud Shell, and Windows Power Shell.

One of the reasons your team may want to utilize the Azure Portal over a command-line utility is the ease of use and personalization. The Azure Portal creates a unified graphical hub that significantly simplifies building, deploying, and managing all cloud resources.

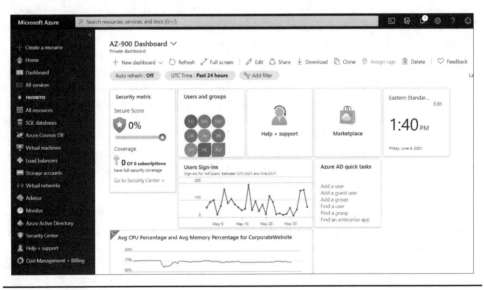

Figure 2-1   Azure Portal

Figure 2-2
Azure Cloud
Shell icon

In Figure 2-3, you can see critical services available from the Azure Portal Dashboard. You can focus on activities that matter the most to you and your organizational requirements by creating dashboards, pins, and tiles that are meaningful. The portal is the single location to handle all administrative functions, including subscriptions and provisioning requirements should you have those system responsibilities.

Many administrators prefer using Azure Portal over a command-line utility because visualizing fine-grain access controls, especially role-based access controls (RBAC), can become cumbersome. Role-based access limits user access based on their role in an organization. The Azure Portal's visual user experience presents you with an explicit user experience to manage access rights to account services and handle individual and group-level permissions.

Figure 2-3   Example Azure Services available on Azure Portal

Billing

Cloud computing measurement focuses on the consumption and utilization of resources. Organizations must keep track of the resources currently in use so that there are no unexpected billing charges. Within the Azure Portal, those with the appropriate permissions can gain visibility into current and projected costs. The portal allows the user to calculate existing charges automatically. A user can even forecast likely expenses based on current utilization, even if your enterprise runs hundreds of independent resources across various app types. Better yet, if you enable monitoring and diagnostics or servicing metrics, your organization can be alerted to any significant issues well in advance so that one can address billing errors before it is too late. In Chapter 7, we will go into greater depth about the pricing calculator and billing statement process. To access the Cost Management and Billing data, select the Cost Management and Billing plane seen in Figure 2-4 with the label 1.

Figure 2-4
Cost Management
and Billing as
well as Help
and Support
navigation plane

Support

Microsoft is one of the largest enterprise IT services providers, offering many channels to get support. When it comes to cloud services, any type of support you require is accessible directly from the Azure Portal exclusively at http://portal.azure.com. Whether you are looking to address alert notifications, view events and audit logs, or place a service request with a Microsoft support technician, a request must initiate in the Microsoft Azure Portal. To get started, Microsoft offers numerous how-to communities, knowledge bases, and troubleshooting solutions. If the self-help tools cannot resolve all your technical issues, you can access multiple feedback channels to Azure product development teams directly. To access the Help and Support features go to the Portal and select the Help and Support plane, as indicated in Figure 2-4 with label 2.

There are various support plans available in Microsoft Azure, from free to business-critical. Depending on the business criticality and workload demand, your pricing tier will vary. Table 2-1 reflects the options available to an organization and the features associated with each level. The key differentiators are the access to phone and e-mail support for Severity A and B requirements and the architectural guidance for businesses requiring enterprise-class implementation support. To select a support plan, a user will go to the Help and Support plan. Then the user will choose the Support Plan link on the left side, as seen in Figure 2-5.

EXAM TIP   Make sure to know the difference between the support plans. It is not uncommon for Microsoft to have several use cases on the exam asking which support plan is the most appropriate under a set of conditions.

Figure 2-5
Support Plan
Page link

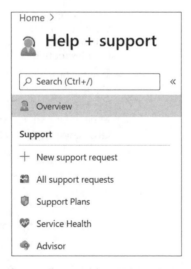

Support Type	Basic	Developer	Standard	Professional Direct
Scope of Service	Billing and subscription support; online self-help	Trial and non-production environments	Production workload environments	Business-critical operations
Customer Service and Communities	24×7 access to customer service, documentation, whitepapers, and support forums	24×7 access to customer service, documentation, whitepapers, and support forums	24×7 access to customer service, documentation, whitepapers, and support forums	24×7 access to customer service, documentation, whitepapers, and support forums
Best Practices	Access to Azure Advisor recommendations via Portal	Access to Azure Advisor recommendations via Portal	Access to Azure Advisor recommendations via Portal	Access to Azure Advisor recommendations via Portal
Health Status and Notifications	Access to personalized Service Health Dashboard and Health APIs	Access to personalized Service Health Dashboard and Health APIs	Access to personalized Service Health Dashboard and Health APIs	Access to personalized Service Health Dashboard and Health APIs
Technical Support		Business hours access to Support Engineers via e-mail	24×7 access to Support Engineers via e-mail and phone	24×7 access to Support Engineers via e-mail and phone
Who Can Open Cases		Unlimited contacts/ unlimited cases	Unlimited contacts/ unlimited cases	Unlimited contacts/ unlimited cases
Third-Party Software Support		Interoperability and configuration guidance and troubleshooting	Interoperability and configuration guidance and troubleshooting	Interoperability and configuration guidance and troubleshooting
Case Severity/ Response Time		Minimal business impact (Severity C) during working hours <8 business hours	Minimal business impact (Severity C) during working hours <8 business hours Moderate business impact (Severity B) <4 hours Critical business impact (Severity A) <1 hour	Minimal business impact (Severity C) during working hours <4 business hours Moderate business impact (Severity B) <2 hours Critical business impact (Severity A) <1 hour

Table 2-1   Azure Support Plans *(continued)*

Support Type	Basic	Developer	Standard	Professional Direct
Architecture Support		General guidance	General guidance	Architectural guidance based on best practice delivered by ProDirect Delivery Manager
Operations Support				Onboarding services, service reviews, Azure Advisor consultations
Training				Azure Engineering–led web seminars
Proactive Guidance				ProDirect Delivery Manager
Price Per Month	Free	$29.00	$100.00	$1,000.00

Table 2-1   Azure Support Plans

Azure Marketplace

There might be times when you or someone in your organization would like to leverage a pre-built solution already tested in Microsoft Azure by a trusted Microsoft partner, independent software vendor, or company offering IT services and solutions. The end product is optimized to run on Azure. How do you know it is optimized? Microsoft makes sure of it before it is posted live in its Azure Marketplace. As seen in Figure 2-6, the Azure Marketplace allows a customer to find solutions under numerous categories. Provisioned solutions are either "try before you buy" or free based on your requirements. You will find hundreds of offerings in the Marketplace from leading IT vendors and solution providers to help accelerate your deployment activity while also knowing that the configurations are specific for the Microsoft Azure Cloud.

 TIP   While some solution templates might indicate they are free to use, Microsoft still requires that you pay for the underlying storage cost. You will always pay a storage cost for a solution, even when the product is not in use.

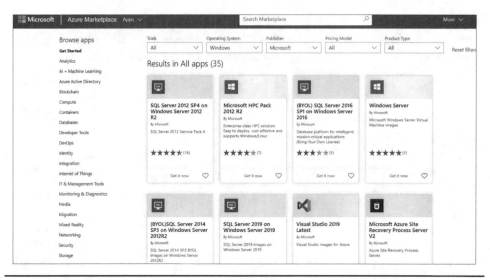

Figure 2-6   Azure Marketplace

The Azure Architecture Framework

When an organization decides to deploy a new Azure instance, a specific architecture is automatically generated based on provisioning. An organization must associate their instance with a Management Group, a subscription, one or more resource groups, and resources. Each of these four groups is tied by one or more geographic boundaries. The basic definitions are in Table 2-2. An architectural rendering of the Azure Architectural framework is seen in Figure 2-7.

Term	Definition
Management Group	A way to group accounts that can help you manage access, policy, and compliance for one or more subscriptions. Any subscription in a management group automatically inherits the conditions applied to the management group.
Subscription	A method of grouping together user accounts and the resources created or accessible for those accounts. Each subscription in Azure has designated limits or quotas tied to resources that can be created and used. Organizations use a subscription to identify their cost and the resources created at the user, team, and project level.
Resource Group	Brings together resources in a single group. Acts as a container for like-kind Azure resources such as web apps, databases, and storage accounts that are deployable and managed.
Resource	Instances of services that you create such as virtual machines, databases, or storages.

Table 2-2   Architecture Framework Concepts

Figure 2-7
Azure hierarchy
of organization
architecture

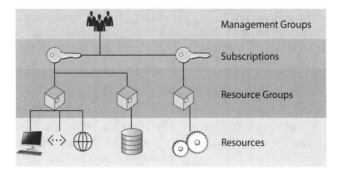

Management Groups

Subscriptions

Resource Groups

Resources

Azure Subscriptions

An Azure subscription serves as a single billing unit for Azure resources. Unless you have a subscription tied to your resources, there is no way for you or anyone in your organization to utilize any Microsoft Azure features or functionality. Once a subscription is associated with an account, it becomes the account invoiced for all billing activity. Each provisioned resource establishes an association with the subscription billing record.

In an organization, it is not uncommon for there to be several subscriptions. In fact, if a group of users has a specific purpose for their resources that requires differentiation from a billing perspective, a separate subscription is created. That means a different set of billing reports and invoices are also run, tied to the subscription. Should an organization decide to have several accounts, the individual responsible for handling the subscriptions becomes a global administrator across all accounts unless another party is designated control to manage an account otherwise.

Types of Subscriptions

There are several ways an organization or even an individual can acquire a subscription. Subscription acquisition is different from the payment arrangement between the customer and Microsoft. Each acquisition channel supports all payment arrangements on behalf of Microsoft.

- **Enterprise Agreement** Customers can acquire subscriptions in bulk given an upfront monetary and time commitment to agree to consumer resources and services throughout one or more calendar years.
- **Resellers** A third party who acts on behalf of Microsoft to help customers design and implement cloud infrastructure at scale and speed. A reseller provides the technical pre-sales support to fit a customer's needs appropriately.
- **Partners** Microsoft has pre-vetted Azure expert consultants who can help design and implement an Azure solution. Partners often sell Azure Cloud as a secondary channel through a reseller or broker the deal on behalf of your company with Microsoft.

- **Personal Account** The most common individual account for a Microsoft Azure user. Microsoft initially provides a user free credits to get started using Microsoft Azure. Once those credits expire, a customer must pay for their monthly consumption by check or credit card.

When you sign up for a Microsoft Azure account, asks the user a few questions so that you can select the appropriate subscription. There are four options. For consumers, they can choose from the Free Plan, Pay-As-You-Go, or Student Plan. If you are a business, there is an Enterprise option. Table 2-3 compares the account alternatives. Most consumers start with the Free Plan and eventually migrate to the Pay-As-You-Go. If you are a business, most times, you are going through a Microsoft Reseller or Solution Partner for setup and configuration.

Plan	Features
Free	A free account requires a user to submit an e-mail account and a form of payment (i.e., credit card). Microsoft provides the account with a $200.00 credit for the first 30 days of account operation. For the remainder of the first 12 months, all free accounts receive an entitlement to these free service features: up to 750 hours per month of B1S VM Linux- and Windows-based virtual machines, access to 64GB ×2 SDD managed disk space, 5GB of hot block blob storage space, 5GB file storage, 250 GB of SQL Server Database allocation, 400 RU/s Azure Cosmos DB, 15GB of outbound data transfer, and 5,000 transactions of AI/ML-based computer vision activity. If an account exceeds the usage limits, the administrator is charged the difference under the Pay-As-You-Go-Rate schedule prices. At the end of the 12 months, the free version is terminated and automatically becomes a Pay-As-You-Go account.
Pay-As-You-Go	Pay-as-you-go is a consumption-billable account where the user is billed for the resources utilized. At the end of each billing cycle, you or your organization will receive an invoice for one or more subscriptions based on the resources consumed during a given period. When an organization makes a long-term commitment to Microsoft Azure, there are often discounts applied to a Pay-As-You-Go pricing plan.
Enterprise	The Enterprise agreement is appropriate for businesses that plan on procuring a significant amount of cloud capacity. With the considerable volume and guaranteed commitments comes steeper discounts. If an organization bundles other Microsoft products with an Azure purchase, such as additional SaaS licenses and Software Assurance, there is often significant cost savings provided. These accounts usually have named account representatives assigned by Microsoft or may be associated with a Microsoft reseller.
Student	A student account provides anyone with a .edu address access to the full Azure platform for 12 months without using a credit card. The student will receive a $100.00 credit toward their account. Should the student require additional cloud resources, the account converts to the Pay-as-You-Go tier.

Table 2-3 Azure Subscription Plans

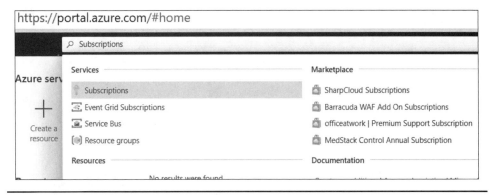

Figure 2-8   Subscription menu

If you are getting started with Azure, you will be prompted on the portal.azure.com homepage to initiate a subscription. Otherwise, if you need to add a new subscription to an existing account, complete the following steps:

1. Go to the Search dialogue at the top of the portal UI.

2. Type in the few letters for the subscription until it appears in the list.

3. Select Subscriptions (Figure 2-8).

4. On the following page, you would click Add to create your additional subscriptions (Figure 2-9).

5. Notice in Figure 2-9 that there are two existing subscriptions on the center of the page: one for Jack Hyman - Microsoft Azure Account and another for Visual Studio Enterprise Account.

 EXAM TIP   When you create a new subscription, you should create a descriptive name for the subscription. There is a subscription ID assigned to each subscription. On the exam, make sure you know the difference between the descriptive name and subscription ID.

Showing 2 of 2 subscriptions ☐ Show only subscriptions selected in the global subscriptions filter ⓘ

Subscription name ↑↓	Subscription ID ↑↓	My role ↑↓	Current cost	Status ↑↓
Jack Hyman - Microsoft Azure Account	e08e12eb-bf01-4a01-aef3-74544faccc21	Account admin	$23.56	✔ Active
Visual Studio Enterprise Subscription – M	28c96b3d-b7a6-4694-82df-932c45c7cbd1	Account admin	0.00	✔ Active

Figure 2-9   List of existing subscriptions page

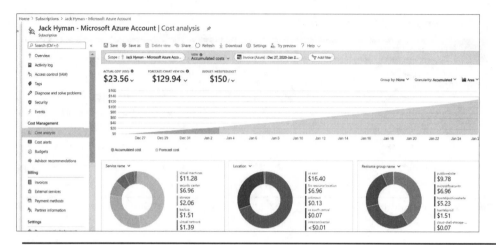

Figure 2-10   Example of Cost Analysis from a subscription

Another feature that you should be aware of when it comes to subscriptions is knowing how to drill down to Cost Management and Billing. Each subscription name is clickable. The subscription brings up its own set of navigation planes for Overview, Cost Management, Billing, and Settings. When you are looking to review existing subscription spend, analyze projected spend, set up a cost or budget alert, identify any recommendations, or review billing information, clicking on the named subscription link is appropriate. Example output from the subscription instance Jack Hyman - Microsoft Azure Account includes a current budget spend and forecasted spend, as seen in Figure 2-10.

Billing and Account Control Boundaries

Billing Boundaries enable a subscription to determine how an Azure account bills an organization when using Azure. Some subscriptions may have a single requirement, while others may have several different prerequisites. Azure can generate separate billing reports and invoices for each subscription or a master invoice for an entire organization so that it is easy to manage, monitor, and organize cost.

Billing controls often require access management policies to be applied at the subscription level so that only those users who need resources gain the appropriate control. Azure applies access management policies at the subscription level, and it is possible to create separate subscriptions to reflect different organization structures using access control boundaries. A hypothetical example is you have three departments in your company. Each department runs its own set of externally facing web applications for customers. Because each department must pay for the traffic out of its own budget, there must be an easy way to manage and control the resources based on a specific provisioning model. Having a distinct Azure subscription policy for each department is plausible because operational costs are bound to a department.

Organizing Subscriptions and Billing

There will likely come a time when your organization requires multiple subscriptions. The reason may include setting up various accounts to differentiate specific operating environments, better identify organizational structures, or help manage resource allocation as part of the billing process. In any of these scenarios, Microsoft Azures allows you to organize your invoices into sections. Each invoice section has a separate line item on an invoice that shows all charges incurred for that month. Some organizations may require their bill is split into departments, teams, projects, or systems.

Under any of these conditions, an administrator can configure multiples invoices within the same billing account. The only thing required is to create an additional billing profile. Every billing profile correlates to an individual monthly invoice and payment method. Figure 2-11 illustrates a prototypical multisubscription configuration. If your organization sets up an Enterprise License Agreement with Microsoft, the billing experience will vary slightly.

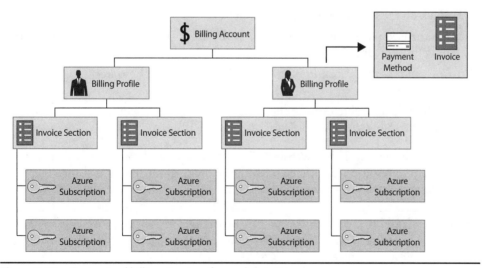

Figure 2-11   Customized billing structure for a subscription

Resources and Azure Resource Groups

A resource refers to an entity available and managed inside Azure. Any service such as a virtual machine, database, virtual network, or storage account constitutes an Azure resource. A resource does not stand alone in an Azure environment. In Azure, resources are pooled together in a resource group. Think of a resource group as a logical construct where all the items that work together to manage an entity's lifecycle and security can work together as a singular resource. For example, a group of resources that share a similar lifecycle, such as those tied together with a custom web application, may be created, modified, or deleted in a group.

 EXAM TIP   Resources in a Resource Group can only be associated with a single Azure subscription.

Resource groups store metadata about each resource contained inside the resource group. When you select your resource group's location, you are also specifying where the metadata is stored. As you are considering compliance, you must be sure that your data is in the proper region.

Locating Resources and Resource Groups in Azure

Drilling down to find a resource group and the associated resources in a resource group is easy from the Azure Portal homepage. To reach the homepage, type **http://portal .azure.com**. Once logged into the site, go to the search bar and type **Resource Group**, as seen in Figure 2-12.

1. Click on the menu option Resource Groups.
2. On the next page, you will see a page load with all the Resource Groups applicable for a filtered condition.
3. You can modify the condition to review all locations, all Resource Groups, all tags, and so on.
4. In this instance, all resource groups located in the Eastern United States that include the name PublicWebsite are displayed (Figure 2-13).

Clicking on the link PublicWebsite will open another web page. On this page, you will find all the resources associated with the resource group PublicWebsite. There are seven unique resources related to this Resource Group, as seen in Figure 2-14.

 EXAM TIP   For the exam, you are not required to know the process needed to create, modify, or delete a resource. You should only know how to locate a Resource and a Resource Group.

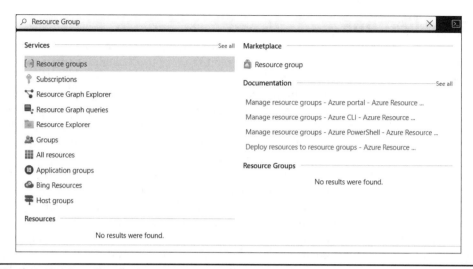

Figure 2-12   Searching for Resource Group in the Azure Search Bar

Figure 2-13   Expanded view of Resource Groups with filtered view

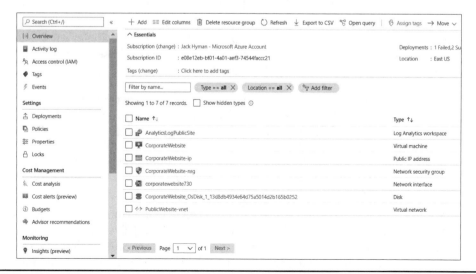

Figure 2-14   Resources listed in a Resource Group

Azure Regions

If you ask a person who knows absolutely nothing about cloud computing, technical ambiguity is common. Azure conceptually is a collection of technological constructs, but you know there are also physical components that make up each solution. We refer to this as infrastructure. What makes computing infrastructure different in the cloud is where the infrastructure resides. The infrastructure does not live in your data closet, or perhaps one or two specific locations defined by your organizations. Instead, a third-party vendor such as Microsoft is responsible for handling operations across a set of boundaries, defined using perimeters connected through a regional low-latency network.

An Azure *region* is a controlled data center deployment using a latency-defined perimeter that provides geographic-based management for data. The goal is to create a dedicated, structured network of regional data centers. Organizations offer flexibility for users to deploy applications and services where needed to support resiliency across a single region or many. A *geography* is a discrete part of the world, containing one or more Azure regions. Geographies are focused markets that maintain data residency often based on country-specific or regulatory-based measures. Customer-specific data centers usually require that data and applications be kept in proximity due to regulatory compliance, availability, and capacity requirements. Vendors such as Microsoft build geographies that are fault tolerant to ensure that complete regional failures never occur through dedicated networks built on high-capacity networks.

Regions Type

Not every region may have all service offerings and capabilities or the same degree of capacity. Azure's approach to managing services is by classifying a region as recommended or alternate.

- **Recommended Regions**   These offer the greatest number of service capabilities. Recommended regions support a range of Availability Zones.
- **Alternate Regions**   These offer an extension to the primary Azure data footprint boundary. An alternate region can help optimize data center latency should a secondary region be required for disaster recovery. The purpose of an alternate region is not to support Availability Zones.

Services are grouped into three categories throughout all Azure regions: foundational, mainstream, and specialized services. Service deployment varies from region to region, based on customer demand, service requirements, and region type.

- **Foundational**   Services are available across all recommended and alternate regions. The services are deemed generally available or will be available within 12 months of new foundational services availability.
- **Mainstream**   Services are available in a recommended region within 12 months and considered generally available. All these services are delivered in a demand-driven capacity only in alternate regions only. Services are often deployed into subsets of larger alternate regions but not active unless requested by the customer.

- **Specialized** Services offering in this category are industry-specific or custom-configured hardware solutions. All solutions are demand-driven across regions, given these are often deployable into larger recommended regions.

Selecting Azure Geographies

There are numerous geographic regions that Azure supports where both recommended and alternate capabilities are supported. Each geography often contains two or more regions, typically hundreds of miles apart. Azure data center footprint is available across all six continents except Antarctica. Each continent has a minimum of two available regions. In North America, data centers include East US, East US 2, South Center US, Central US, West US, West US 2 West US 3 Mexico Central, Canada Central, and Canada East.

For public sector clients, there is a specialized Azure data center solution available. For example, only US federal, state, local, and tribal governments and their partners have access to the US Gov and select US DoD dedicated instances. These regional data centers have specific controls that are screened explicitly for US citizens. Azure Government offers specific certification credentialing to meet US Federal and Defense Department compliance standards, including FedRamp and NIST 800-171. Similarly, mainland China services (China North/North 2 and China East/East 2) are is specialized due to political dynamics. Microsoft hosting and services are in partnership with 21Vianet.

 EXAM TIP Make sure you know there will always be a minimum of two data centers inside a region. Also, you should become familiar with the specialized data centers in the Microsoft Azure ecosystem.

Azure Regional Pairs

Microsoft Azure is available in over 60 regions around the world. Each Azure region hosts multiple datacenters with service offerings that enable global organizations to conduct business with Microsoft. Given each region has its footprint with distinct services available, customers must decide which region to select. However, it is not apparent that inside each region, there are multiple data centers paired together. What does a pair mean exactly? Specific Azure regions support one another for reliability and disaster recovery.

Azure regional pairs are a symbiotic relationship between two Azure regions, often within the same geographic region for disaster recovery purposes. If one of the regions experience a disaster due to an outage, the secondary region will manage all necessary services. For example, if the data center in East US fails, West US will be the default. Figure 2-15 illustrates the relationship between the East US and West US in a regional pair.

Azure regional pairs are not just a technical concept; the infrastructure is connected to support distribution and system redundancy. The geographical disparity also plays a significant part with Azure regions as it does with region pair. Part of why regions are placed where they are is not as much about disaster recovery; it has more to do with geopolitical concerns and internet connectivity within large communities.

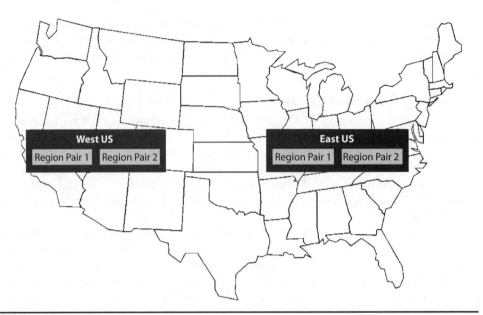

Figure 2-15   Regional pairs

As a rule of thumb, every Azure region is paired greater than 300 miles away from one another. The distance ensures that should there be a disaster, a single region's impact is minimized. Even if a natural disaster such as an earthquake, hurricane, tornado, or fire is widespread, the likelihood is that a significant distance of 300 miles will yield marginal impact to more than one datacenter. Because each region within an Azure region is interconnected to one another yet far enough to withstand isolation from any form of a regional disaster, Microsoft suggests that replicating data or interacting services across regions, Azure regional pairs should be used.

Data Residency and Regional Pairs

Where data is stored is often detrimental to an organization, especially if there are regulatory and compliance concerns. For example, companies that conduct business in the European Union must adhere to the General Data Protection Regulation (GDPR) regulations. The geopolitical and compliance implications can have significant consequences to any business based on where the data resides and how a company transacts. An enterprise should consider where their data is located to ensure that particular geography's bounds comply with the end user's privacy and security needs. One of the reasons why both regions in an Azure region pair are in the same geographic region is to assure there are no data residency conflicts.

Another concern that many organizations often worry about is system updates. Microsoft maintains one of the most extensive software and infrastructure footprints globally. When a system is updated, the change can impact many users. All Azure updates are automated and systematic. The sequence of events is as follows: Microsoft makes an update to systems in a single regional pair, validates the pair for errors, and then moves on to the next region once there are assurances that the systems are known to have no bugs and failures caused by the updates. Using Azure region pairs for replication and redundancy ensures that their applications and services are reliable regardless of the system state.

In the unlikely event of a widespread Azure outage, each Azure region pair has a single region that has one prioritized instance over another for recovery. System deployments also occur across multiple Azure regions within pairs. Deployments are guaranteed to have at least one Azure Region operate so that a recovery can occur with a high priority. Luckily though, some platform services offer automatic redundancy. Such services include geo-redundant storage pairing by default. For example, when you create an Azure Storage account and configure it for geo-replication, you are assigning the storage replication location to be the replication for all other provisioned configurations within the regional pair.

Availability Zones and Management Groups

Regions are physically separated by hundreds of miles to ensure that Azure datacenters are protected. Microsoft wants to assure Azure users that their data is not exposed to loss and unnecessary application outages. Whether it is by outages, caused by natural disasters, or otherwise, there is a need to ensure that systems remain available at all times. That is why Microsoft established dedicated physical locations within a given region that consist of an isolated zone made up of datacenters equipped with power, cooling, water supplies, and networking capacity to ensure fault tolerance and operational continuity. The infrastructure supports high availability, which includes any mission-critical applications and services. Datacenter failures redundancy and logical isolation of services are tolerant with the use of Availability Zones. Table 2-4 is a snapshot of available fundamental, mainstream, and specialized services supported in Availability Zones.

Foundational	Mainstream	Specialized
Account Storage	API Management	Azure API for FHIR
Application Gateway	App Configuration	Azure Analysis Services
Azure Backup	App Service	Azure Blockchain Service
Azure Cosmos DB	Automation	Azure Blueprints
Azure Data Lake Storage Gen2	Azure Active Directory Domain Services	Azure Database for MariaDB
Azure ExpressRoute	Azure Bastion	Azure Dedicated HSM
Azure SQL Database	Azure Cache for Redis	Azure Dev Spaces
Cloud Services	Azure Cognitive Search	Azure Digital Twins
Disk Storage	Azure Data Explorer	Azure Lab Services
Event Hubs	Azure Data Share	Azure NetApp Files
Key Vault	Azure Database for MySQL	Azure Quantum
Load balancer	Azure Database for PostgreSQL	Azure Spring Cloud Service
Service Bus	Azure Database Migration Service	Azure Time Series Insights

Table 2-4 List of Available Services Supported in an Availability Zone *(continued)*

Foundational	Mainstream	Specialized
Service Fabric	Azure Databricks	Data Box Heavy
Virtual Machine Scale Sets	Azure DDoS Protection	Data Catalog
Virtual Machines	Azure DevTest Labs	Data Lake Analytics
Virtual Network	Azure Firewall	Azure Machine Learning Studio (classic)
VPN Gateway	Azure Firewall Manager	Microsoft Genomics
	Azure Functions	Remote Rendering
	Azure HPC Cache	Spatial Anchors
	Azure IoT Hub	StorSimple
	Azure Kubernetes Service (AKS)	Video Indexer
	Azure Machine Learning	Virtual Machines (Various)
	Azure Private Link	Visual Studio App Center
	Azure Red Hat OpenShift	
	Azure SignalR Service	
	Azure Site Recovery	
	Azure Stack Hub	
	Azure Stream Analytics	
	Azure Synapse Analytics	
	Batch	
	Cognitive Services	
	Container Instances	
	Container Registry	
	Data Factory	
	Event Grid	
	HDInsight	
	Logic Apps	
	Media Services	
	Network Watcher	
	Notification Hubs	
	Power BI Embedded	
	Premium Blob Storage	
	Premium Files Storage	
	Storage: Archive Storage	
	Ultra-Disk Storage	
	Virtual Machines (Various)	
	Virtual WLAN	

Table 2-4   List of Available Services Supported in an Availability Zone

Figure 2-16
Availability Zones

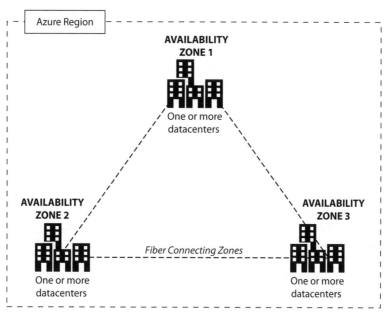

 TIP Availability Zones are not available across Azure regions. Additionally, depending on the services and application, support in a region may be limited.

When you deploy services to two or more Availability Zones, you are maximizing resource availability for a resource. More zone deployments yield a higher service-level agreement percentage. In the case of two zones, Microsoft will guarantee an SLA of 99.9 percent uptime for a virtual machine instance, assuming two or more machines have deployable resources in two or more zones. Figure 2-16 illustrates the benefits of running a system through multiple Availability Zones.

 EXAM TIP There is a big difference between an Availability Zone and an Availability Set. Availability Sets allow you to create two or more virtual machines in an Azure data center; however, the virtual machines are on different server racks. Microsoft provides a 99.95 percent SLA for availability sets. Availability Zones allow the deployment of two or more Azure services, not virtual machines, into two separate data centers in a given region. Microsoft commits to 99.99 percent SLA with Availability Zones.

Management Groups

When an organization has many subscriptions, managing access, policy, and compliance can be overwhelming. To efficiently group access, policies, and compliance responsibilities for subscriptions, Azure management groups provides a level of scope above a subscription to manager like-kind capabilities. With Azure, you place subscriptions into containers, called management groups. Each container contains a specific set of governance conditions, which you then associate with the management groups. Subscriptions in a management group inherit all conditions applied to a management group.

There are many benefits to using management groups in Microsoft Azure when managing subscriptions. No matter the scale of your deployment, management groups offer an organization enterprise-grade management enabling greater scalability regardless of the type of subscription you are using at a given point in time. A management group's subscription must establish a trust relationship with an Azure Active Directory tenant under all conditions.

When you create a hierarchy that applies a management group policy, it will set a limit to a location. For example, a policy based in the East US Region associated with a group called "Development" inherits all the rights applicable to the Enterprise Agreement (EA). Those rights are inheritable to all Virtual Machine instances under the subscriptions. You cannot modify any security policy created by the resource or the subscription owner, allowing for improved governance regardless of circumstance.

Azure management groups provide flexibility so that users can gain access to multiple subscriptions. Suppose you move multiple subscriptions under a management group. In that case, it allows for creating an Azure role assignment, which follows the principles of role-based access management. In this instance, role-based access management inherits access to all the subscriptions in a single management group instead of assigning access across different subscriptions individually. Figure 2-17 illustrates the flexibility of a management group inheriting various types of subscriptions.

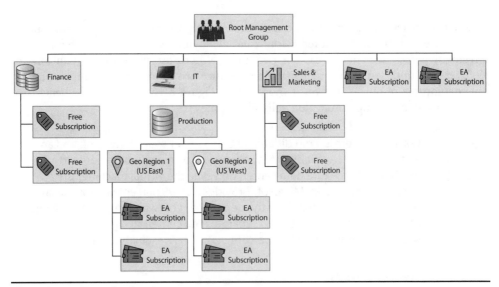

Figure 2-17   Example of an Azure management group

Management Group Limitations

Management groups have some hard limitations. Consider the following:

- There is a limit of 10,000 management groups in a single directory
- A management group tree can support up to six levels of depth, which does not include the subscription's root level.
- A management group and its subscription can only support a single parent.
- A management group can have many children.

Subscriptions and management groups must reside within a single hierarchy in a single directory.

Azure Resource Manager (ARM)

ARM is a deployment and management service, allowing Azure cloud administrators to create, update, and delete resources in a provisioned account. Suppose you have administrative access to management features such as access controls, locks, and tags to secure and organize resources after deployment. In that case, the Azure Resource Manager's use is a viable option for repeatable activities once an initial deployment occurs.

Resources must be already in place for Azure Resource Manager to function. Once the resources are in place, a user will send a request from any Azure tool, API, or SDK. The Azure Resource Manager receives the request. Upon receipt of the offer, the data is authenticated and then authorized. The Azure Resource Manager directs the request to the appropriate service, which triggers an action. Since all rights are handled using the same API, consistent results are noticeable across all tools. Figure 2-18 demonstrates a high-level diagram explaining how the Azure Resource Manager takes a request in Microsoft Azure.

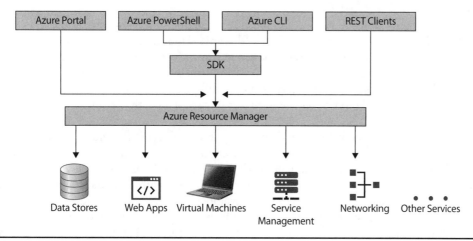

Figure 2-18   Azure Resource Manager

From a reliability perspective, resources alone do not offer resiliency and continuous availability. That is not the case with the Azure Resource Manager. The Resource Manager and control plane operations (requests sent to management.azure.com via REST API):

- Can distribute across regions as some services are regional.
- Can distribute across Availability Zones since locations in a region often have multiple availability zones.
- Need to worry about maintenance activity or the dependency of a single data center.

Considering that Azure Resource Manager is resilient and offers continuous availability, an administrator can manage the infrastructure through declarative templates rather than scripts. It is easier to deploy, manage, and monitor resources over time as a group rather than individually. Furthermore, when you need to redeploy anytime during the development lifecycle, the resources remain consistent when placed in Azure Resource Manager, whereas that is not the case if the administrator deploys the templates on their own. For example, should you need to deploy a resource based on another dependency, it is relatively easy to define a specific order using Azure Resource Manager to predefine the deployable order. Addressing a repeatable conditional order is not easily supported when a resource is standalone.

Azure Role-Based Access (RBAC) is natively integrated into the Azure so that Azure Resource Manager can inherit any role-based access controls given to a service when it comes to applying access control to services. Another benefit to using the Azure Resource Manager is the ability to tag resources across an entire subscription as a logical organizing technique. By following many of these techniques and tactics, it is possible to simplify an organization's billing by viewing costs using resource groups and sharing tag naming conventions.

Chapter Review

Chapter 2 is considered a framework chapter for the upcoming chapters. It provides you with vital Azure concepts, terminology, and architectural basics. The chapter begins by introducing you to the Azure user experience from a very high level. Using the Azure Portal enables a user to access all the features and functions needed to deploy Infrastructure and Platform as a Service offering successfully. You also can use the Azure Cloud Shell and Windows Power Shell if you prefer to complete activities using a command-line utility.

You must familiarize yourself with two important concepts for the exam: the Azure support plans and subscriptions. You do not need to have a paid support plan to access the knowledge base and documentation available at http://portal.azure.com. However, should your organization require any form of one-on-one support with a technical representative, Microsoft offers plans starting at $29.00 (Developer) to $1,000.00 (Professional Direct). The main difference among the support plans is that support will reach out to a customer on a ticket. Additionally, support offers basic architectural guidance on more advanced support plans.

As for subscriptions, Microsoft provides a variety of subscription types. Consumers can procure Azure for no cost at the Free level initially. However, after utilizing the $200.00 credit, which is active for 30 days and exceeds the Free Service Cap, a user is charged for excess service consumption under the Pay-As-You-Go plan. At the end of one year, a user will automatically transition to the Pay-As-You-Go plan. There are also special plans available for students and enterprise customers. You can procure Azure through several channels, including resellers and partners.

Building out every Azure resource from the ground up can be quite an uphill task for a cloud administrator. Microsoft Azure has its marketplace, known as Azure Marketplace, to download prebuilt, Azure-optimized resources such as virtual machines for a user to download to their accounts. Some resources may be free so long as you pay for the storage and bandwidth. Other resources require you to procure a license before usage in Azure. To access the Azure Marketplace, users can go to https://azuremarketplace .microsoft.com/.

From an architectural perspective, these are the key takeaways that you should remember for the exam:

- Every instance or service you create in Microsoft Azure is called a resource. These are items, including virtual machines, databases, or storage instances.

- A resource group is a way to bring together a collection of resources. A resource group acts as a container for like-kind Azure resources such as web apps, databases, and storage accounts that are deployable and managed.

- Each time a resource is deployed, a subscription and billing account must also be in place. A subscription helps Microsoft identify the cost of a resource created by a user, team, or project at a granular level.

- Management Groups help a cloud administrator manage access, policy, and compliance for one or more subscriptions. A secondary-level subscription will automatically inherit the conditions applied to a higher-level subscription.

- Azure regions are areas with a distinct geographical boundary. Each region is often at least 300 miles apart from one another.

- In Azure, a geography is typically a country or a defined area within a country that contains at least two local regions.

- There are two region types: recommended and alternate. A recommended region is one that provides the greatest service offerings given it can support Availability Zones. Alternate regions extend Azure's capabilities for data recovery in a geographical boundary. Alternate regions coexist in the same regions as recommended regions. A key difference, though, is that alternate regions do not support Availability Zones.

- Three types of services are available in a given region: foundational (always available), mainstream (generally available with some limitations), and specialized (on-demand, based on specific conditions).

- Within each of the geographies, you will find several data centers. A data center is a physically standing building with a complex computing infrastructure in a region that maintains its power, cooling, heating, network, water supply, generators, and network capacity.

- To ensure a system continually operates, Microsoft Azure operates its data centers operating in regional pairs. A regional pair is a relationship between Azure regions in the same geography. If one region were to experience a disaster, natural or otherwise, services in the secondary region would kick-in as that is the failover instance.

- Availability Zones are unique physical locations within a region that consists of a series of self-operating data centers. Should one datacenter fail, another data center within the same region will take on failover responsibility. All data centers within an Availability Zone are in the same geographical region.

Finally, the chapter closes by discussing automating resources utilizing the Azure Resource Manager. The Azure Resource Manager is a deployment and management service that allows an Azure cloud administrator to create, update, and delete resources in a provisioned account. Unlike the standard deployment of an Azure resource, utilizing Azure Resource Manager provides resilience and continuous availability. An administrator can manage the infrastructure through declarative templates instead of scripts.

Questions

1. Which of the following best describes the concept of geography?

    A. A regional parameter that is bound to another region within a 300-mile distance.

    B. A location within a region made up of one or more independent data centers equipped with power, cooling, and networking capabilities.

    C. A set of data centers deployed within a defined perimeter connected through a dedicated regional low-latency network.

    D. An area of the world containing at least one Azure region.

2. How does a user access the Azure portal?

    A. http://portal.microsoft.com/azure

    B. http://portal.office.com

    C. http://portal.azure.com

    D. http://cloud.microsoft.com

3. Where can a cloud administrator go to find pre-built solutions to expedite virtual machines online?

    A. Azure Marketplace

    B. Azure App Store

    C. Microsoft Partner Portal

    D. Microsoft Learn

4. Which of the following best describes a deployment and management service allowing Azure cloud administrators to create, update, and delete resources in a provisioned account?

    A. Azure Resource Monitor

    B. Azure Resource Manager

    C. Azure Region Manager

    D. Azure Region Monitor

5. Answer the following question by selecting Yes or No to these three questions.

	Yes	No
Any user can select US DoD East to host their virtual machine environment.	◯	◯
The regional pair for US DoD East is East US.	◯	◯
The regional pair for US East is US West.	◯	◯

    A. No, Yes, Yes

    B. No. No. Yes

    C. Yes, Yes, No

    D. Yes, No, No

6. How long does a user have access to a Free Azure account features before one must pay for services under a Pay-As-You-Go plan?

    A. 30 Days

    B. Free Forever

    C. 1 Year

    D. Until the $200 credit is spent

7. A company requires 24/7 support for their custom applications running on Microsoft Azure. Besides, they may want to speak to an architect by phone or Microsoft Teams to review their new Platform as a Service deployment. Which service plan must the company purchase to retain these services?

    A. Basic

    B. Developer

    C. Standard

    D. Professional Direct

8. A customer with a BASIC account can still submit a support ticket for an Azure Cloud issue?

    A. True

    B. False

    C. It depends on the type of Microsoft license you subscribe to.

    D. There is no such thing as a BASIC Account.

9. Answer the following question by selecting Yes or No to these three questions.

	Yes	No
A user can sign up for a Student plan with a .com email address.	◯	◯
A user can sign up for a new Azure Free account without a credit card.	◯	◯
A user can only utilize Azure services with an Azure subscription and billing account.	◯	◯

    A. No, Yes, No

    B. No, No, No

    C. Yes, No, Yes

    D. No, No, Yes

10. Which of the following are reasons to have multiple subscriptions? (Select two.)

    A. Different organizational structure

    B. Manage resource allocation

    C. Better manage security

    D. Better discounting options

11. What is an alternate utility integrated within the Azure Portal a user can access to complete cloud-based support actions?

    A. Windows PowerShell

    B. Azure Cloud Shell

    C. Azure Sentinel

    D. Azure ExpressRoute

12. What contains web apps, databases, and storage accounts that are deployable and managed in Azure?

    A. Resource groups

    B. Resource pairs

    C. Availability Zones

    D. Management groups

13. Azure SQL and Azure Cosmos DB are considered what type of service in an Availability Zone.

    A. Mainstream

    B. Foundational

    C. Specialized

    D. These services cannot operate in an availability zone.

14. Review the following statement. Look at the italicized text. Indicate if the statement requires any corrective actions.

The only category where all services are available in both recommended and alternate regions is *Mainstream*.

    A. Specialized

    B. Foundational

    C. Basic

    D. The current answer is accurate.

15. Review the following statement. Look at the italicized text. Indicate if the statement requires any corrective actions.

A *Free Account is a consumption-based* account whereby you are billed for the resources utilized. At the end of each billing cycle, you or your organization will receive an invoice for one or more subscription based on the resources consumed during a given period.

    A. No changes are required.

    B. Reseller account is a reservation-based account.

    C. Enterprise account is a consumption-based account.

    D. Pay-As-You-Go is a consumption-based account.

Answers

    1. D. This describes geography.

    2. C. It is the only address that directly takes a user to the Azure portal. While a user will be directed to an Azure website by going to http://portal.microsoft.com/azure and http://cloud.microsoft.com, which is reflected in answers A and C, answer B takes a user to the Microsoft 365 login.

    3. A. Marketplace is a location where prebuilt Microsoft and partner solutions are available for rapid deployment, already hosted on Azure. A user can download the template onto their environment for consumption based on the solution provider's terms and conditions.

4. **B.** Azure Resource Manager is a deployment and management service that allows cloud administrators to create, update, and delete resources in a provisioned account. One might use features such as access controls, locks, and tags to secure and organizatize resources after deployment with Azure Resource Manager. Keep in mind that within the Resource Manager, you'll find numerous templates that define one or more resource to deploy to resource groups, subscriptions, management groups, or tenants. The template might be used as a way to deploy resources using a schedule or incidentally.

5. **B.** No. Only select users associated with federal, state, and local agency credentials can host a virtual machine on a Government hosting environment such as DoD East.

   No. The regional pair for US DoD East is US DoD West. The pair must be a complementary pair to the DoD or Gov instance. East US is not complementary.

   Yes. The regional pair for US East is US West.

6. **C.** In contrast, Microsoft gives users the first 30 days to spend $200.00 toward Azure cloud premium features. All Free account features are available for up to one year before an account is automatically converted to a Pay-as-You-Go account.

7. **D.** This is the only support option where Microsoft will offer a company architectural support and 24/7 Severity A/B/C support.

8. **A.** Users can still submit a support ticket, even with a basic account. There may be a requirement to increase account limits or inform Microsoft of performance issues for a service. Therefore, submitting a ticket is still a feature enabled for all users. It does not matter what type of account you have, the support type listed is offered to all customers. A basic account is the most fundamental account offered by Microsoft.

9. **D.** No. A user cannot sign up for a Student subscription plan with a .com e-mail address. The only way student plans are made available is with a verifiable .edu account.

   No. A user cannot sign up for a new Azure Free account without a credit card. Signing up for an account requires a payment method an e-mail address.

   Yes. The only way a user can utilize Azure services is by establishing a subscription associated with a billing account.

10. **A, B.** Users prefer multiple subscriptions when many organizations exist, cause a variety of resources to be billed to an account. Instead of billing resources to a master account, differentiating the organization structure and better managing the resources against an individual bill will help each team, project, or cost center fully realize their spending. Since cloud computing spend is based on consumption, multiple subscriptions will help to mitigate billing concerns in an organization.

11. **B.** Azure Cloud Shell is an integrated utility in the Azure Portal.

12. **A.** Resource groups bring together resources in a single group. A resource group acts as a container for like-kind Azure resources such as web apps, databases, and storage accounts that are deployable and managed.

13. **B.** Azure SQL Database and Azure Cosmos DB are Foundational Services. These core database resources do not fall in any other category.

14. **B.** Foundational is defined as services that are available across all recommended and alternate regions. The services are deemed generally available or will be available within 12 months of new foundational services availability. On the other hand, mainstream indicates that services are available in a recommended region within 12 months and considered generally available. All these services are delivered in a demand-driven capacity only in alternate regions only.

15. **D.** The only logical account is Pay-As-You-Go, as this is the only consumption-based account listed.

CHAPTER

Azure Resources

In this chapter, you will learn to
- Identify key compute, storage, and database services in Microsoft Azure
- Configure foundational services such as Azure Virtual Machine, Azure Container Instances, Azure Kubernetes Services, and Windows Virtual Desktop
- Evaluate Azure network options, including virtual networks, virtual network gateways, virtual network peering, and Azure ExpressRoute

In the last chapter, you learned how to organize and manage core resources and solutions across Azure's global enterprise infrastructure. Organizational and geographic distribution is just one part of familiarizing yourself with Azure. Whether you are building a cloud environment from scratch or utilizing preexisting assets available in the Azure Marketplace, you must build a baseline infrastructure before you deploy cloud solutions. To do so requires compute, databases, storage, and networking resources, which are the backbone of the Azure Cloud. The chapter reviews each of these resource types at length to prepare you for the AZ-900 exam.

An Introduction to Compute Resources

Microsoft Azure is broken down into service groups. Among the most important groups are those associated with compute resources, which cover storage, database, and networking. Azure offers users many options to build and deploy applications, from the underlying infrastructure to a communication backbone. Microsoft Azure allows for infrastructure to scale on demand in a variety of scenarios. You may want to deploy virtual machines with a core operating system, creating an Infrastructure as a Service (IaaS) baseline or containerize applications using Platform as a Service (PaaS)–based support. If there is a need for unique storage or database features, one can provision such capabilities within the virtualized environments. As you begin exploring this chapter, keep in mind that Microsoft Azure offers a variety of pricing options from pay-as-you-go, to enterprise licensing arrangements, to prepayment commitments. You should consider how much you need and how long you will utilize a service as you select your technology options.

Azure Virtual Machines

To the everyday computing user, with the press of the power button on a desktop or laptop computer, an operating system loads with all their computer files. The user goes about doing everyday tasks, be it surfing the Internet, actively using software applications, listening to multimedia files stream, or allowing for files to remain stored on the device, as a means of backup, to complete. However, the hard drive on a computer has clear limits. There is no way to scale beyond the physical confines of the computer storage limits. In other words, you cannot create a computer within a computer! What happens if you wanted to run multiple operating systems—would it be possible? Is it possible for you to grow and expand your storage footprint effortlessly? These are some of the common challenges an end user might face if they rely exclusively on their computer to manage operational activity. How is it, then, that one can overcome these massive technical limitations? The use of virtual machines, also called images, is the solution.

A virtual machine is a standalone file that can be stored on your local computer or in the cloud in isolation from any other system. There is absolutely no interaction whatsoever with a host operating system. This means that any activity that a user completes on the virtual instance will have no bearing whatsoever on the computer the virtual instance operates on. Sounds too perfect to be true, right? You can create test and development environments without harming another system. If the test system is compromised by an accidental virus or error created by programmatic code, the host system remains safe. It does not matter if there is one or multiple virtual environments running on the same computer—all systems still run independently.

When virtualized environments run multiple operating systems side by side, the infrastructure requires the use of a software application called a *hypervisor*. A hypervisor allows for the management of many image instances to run concurrently, while a desktop or cloud compute environment employs a single operating system. The virtual environment presumably standardizes on a configuration that indicates a virtual hardware standard, including CPU, memory, hard drive storage, network interface, and other core capabilities that operate in lockstep with the operating system. Your virtual hardware maps to real hardware on a physical machine somehow, whether it is in the cloud or the computer on your desktop. Regardless, the main objective is to cut cost, expand the footprint capacity, and reduce the environmental impact through power consumption.

An Azure Virtual Machine is the deployable cloud solution to handling on-demand scalable computer resources in the Microsoft ecosystem. A user chooses the virtual machine environment they require when needing more control over compute capacity. Before creating a virtual machine in Microsoft Azure, a user should consider several factors, such as what tasks they will perform, the purpose of the application that will sit on the image instance, what ancillary applications will be needed to support the primary applications, and what a patching regimen may look like. Even though the virtual machine is not actually a real computer, you are still responsible for maintaining the instance as if it were a full-fledged operating environment. Table 3-1 describes the three scenarios where an Azure environment could be used.

Environment	Use Case
Development and Test	The most affordable and practical way to create a secondary virtual instance with a specific configuration. Using this option is appropriate when you are looking to test code or try out an application before launching into a production environment.
Production	When demand fluctuates and there is a need for scaling rapidly, you may want to consider putting the application in the cloud. This is referred to as production mode. Consider this the "sweet spot" for Microsoft Azure because you are running your operation when you need it and shutting it down when it is not necessary. You scale based on demand.
Data Center	Consider a virtual machine an extension of your storage footprint. The virtual machine may also act as an extension of your organization's network, albeit a secondary system or another storage appliance.

Table 3-1   Azure Environment Types

Azure Virtual Machine Design Configuration

A good programmer does not just dive right in and start coding. They plan out all the elements that will be required to execute the code flawlessly. The same should be true for the cloud professional as they embark upon configuring a virtual machine instance in Microsoft Azure. You have options to consider when you are building out an infrastructure in Azure. Some are necessary; others are nice to have. Table 3-2 addresses some of these considerations.

Area	Consideration
Resource Group	What is the logical container that you intend to place your virtual machine instance in related to your Microsoft Azure group instances?
Size	• Storage requirements are critical. Will your system be transactional in nature or dormant? Does your instance include a database or host a standalone self-contained application with little user interaction? • The size of a virtual machine is determined by the workload you intend to run. Consider compute power, memory, and storage capacity as part of these factors. Azure offers end users packaged configurations, as well as the ability to scale up and out to best suit a user's need to grow.
Data Residency	Where your virtual machine will be located can make a significant difference. Do you intend to store your data in a single location or across multiple regions?
Network Infrastructure	Three network infrastructure considerations: • **Virtual network** Will the instance be part of a virtual network? • **Public IP address** Will the instance have a public IP address to support public-facing user access or be available to only a limited number of users? • **Network interface** Will the virtual machine instance require communication with other public networks?
Operating System	You have the option to select from numerous operating systems that best suit your virtual instance. Options may include Windows OS, Linux, or CentOS.

Table 3-2   Virtual Machine Considerations

While this list is just a sampling of considerations you will need to address at the onset of virtual machine configuration, these are significant, nonetheless. Any time you decide to set up a virtual machine in Microsoft Azure, you will be asked to make numerous configuration decisions that will have an influence on performance and cost of services.

 TIP Creating an Azure Virtual Machine requires having an active Azure account. To create an active Azure account, go to https://www.azure .microsoft.com/en-us/free/.

Configuring an Azure Virtual Machine

To create a new Azure Virtual Machine instance, you will need to log in to the Microsoft Azure Portal using your Azure account. The address you want to go to is https://portal .azure.com. There are two methods to create an Azure Virtual Machine. The first option is creating a virtual machine based on a preexisting application configuration from the Azure Marketplace. A second alternative is creating a bare image that you install an application onto using a preconfigured instance that is only provisioned with the necessary storage, networking, and operating system essentials. You will configure the latter instance in this section. In Figure 3.1, you will notice in the Azure Dashboard various options to choose from under Featured Services. Links to those services can also be found under the column on the left.

1. Click Virtual Machine (Figure 3-1).

2. Select the Add Button, and choose Virtual Machine (Figure 3-2).

3. A page will load allowing you to begin configuring the virtual machine.

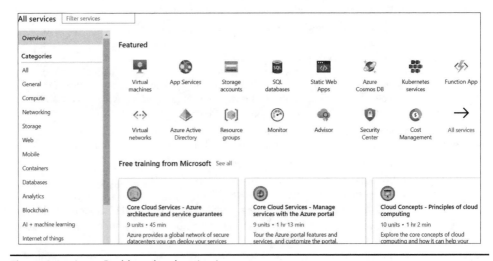

Figure 3-1 Azure Dashboard and navigation

Figure 3-2   Select Add Virtual Machine.

You have many options to select from, which include Basics, Disks, Networking, Management, Advanced, Networking, Tags, and Review + Create. For ease of ensuring that all steps are covered, follow the guided wizard. Start with completing all the steps under Basic in Figure 3-3. Then, configure the following items:

- **Subscription**   You may have one or more subscriptions (Enterprise Agreement, Pay-As-You-Go).

- **Resource Group**   Which bucket will all your objects be housed in for the purposes of billing?

- **Virtual Machine Name**   Enter the name of your virtual machine instance.

- **Region**   Select the geography/country where the virtual machine will be hosted.

- **Availability**   Select if you would like the image to be stored in an Availability Zone or Availability Set.

- **Spot Instance**   When you are looking to implement a development instance, you may choose to implement spot instances to support unused capacity for a particular region. Should there no longer be any availability for the VM, it becomes deallocated. Pricing is not fixed like a standard instance. It varies based on available capacity.

- **Size**   Based on two measures: vCPU and memory. The price increases based on higher vCPU and memory capacity. Memory tends to be the more expensive variable of the two.

- **Authentication Type**   Password (requires username and password) or SSH (requires username, SSH public key source, and key pair name).

- **Public Inbound Ports**   Either None or Allow Selected Ports (SSH, HTTP, HTTPS).

If your intention is to use a basic virtual machine configuration, click the Review + Configure button on the bottom-left area of the screen once you have completed the configuration of all the options listed. The one action that you will have the option to select at the end is the storage capacity.

Should you want to refine configuration options such as the disk type, the networking configuration, virtual machine operations (including boot diagnostics), host operations, and tags to the virtual machine, you will want to interact with each of the interfaces separately.

To configure the disk, click Next : Disks at the bottom of the Basics screen (Figure 3-3).

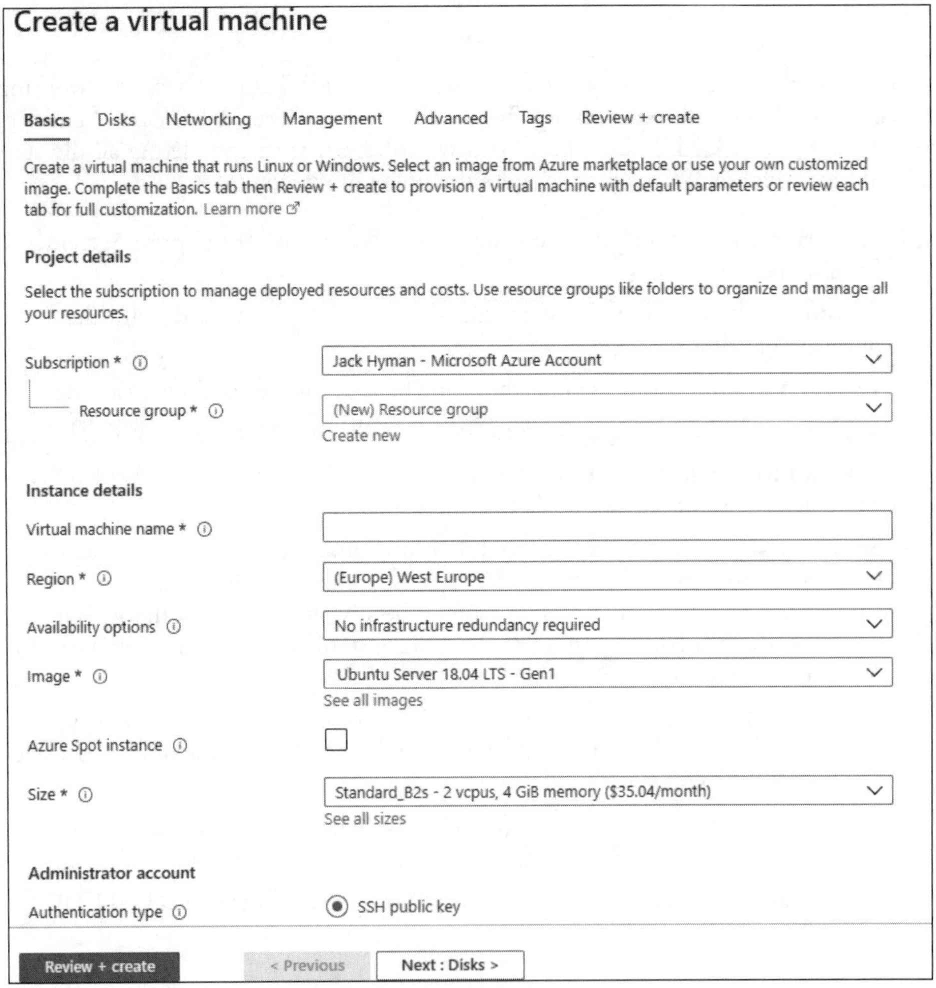

Figure 3-3   Basic virtual machine configuration interface

On the Disks screen (Figure 3-4), you will be asked to configure the following:

- **OS Disk Type**   Select from Standard HDD, Standard SSD, or Premium SSD.
- **Encryption Type**   Select from Encryption At Rest, Encryption At Rest With Customer-Managed Keys, or Double Encryption With Platform-Managed And Customer-Managed Keys

On the bottom of the Disks screen, if you select Advanced, you can choose the disk type: Managed or Ephemeral. *Managed disks* are ideal when you are looking for top-notch performance, reliability, scalability, and access control. Users should consider unmanaged disks when they intend to manage their own storage account or virtual hard drive (VHD). An *ephemeral disk* is created on a local virtual machine. So long as the storage is not used, you do not incur cost with this storage type. Upon completing the configuration of the disks, move onto the next screen by selecting Next: Networking.

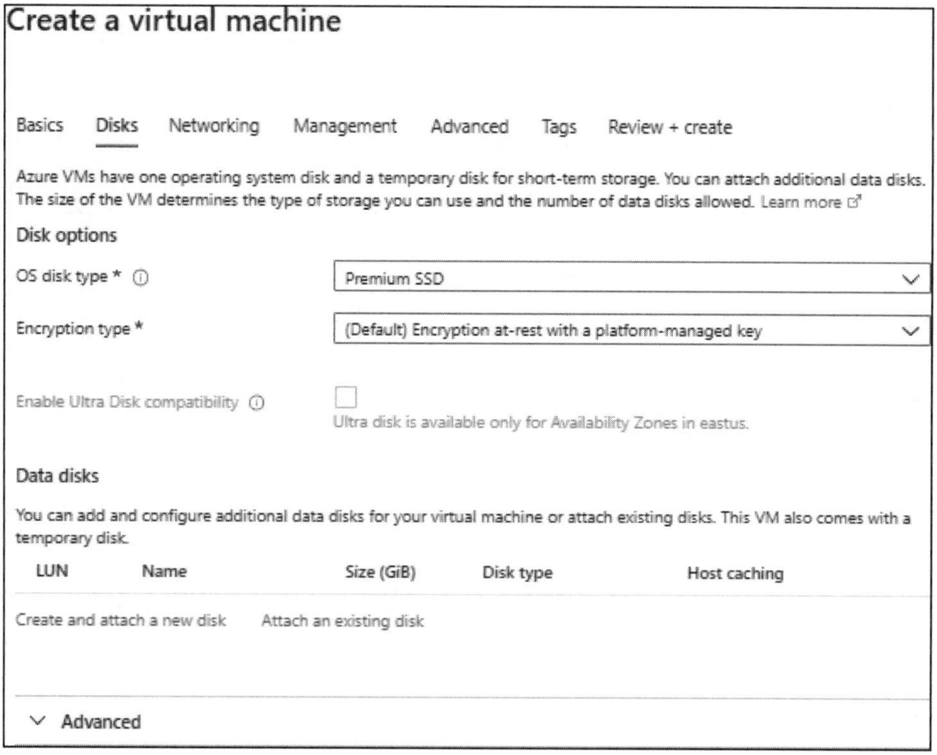

Figure 3-4   Disks interface setup for virtual machines

Configuring the network interface (Figure 3-5) requires that one understand the necessary network configurations for public and private network connectivity consumption. Addressable areas that will be necessary to configure include

- Virtual Network
- Subnet
- Public IP
- NIC Network Security Group
- Public Inbound Ports
- Select Inbound Ports (based on Public Inbound Ports)
- Load Balancing

Figure 3-5 Network interface

Upon selecting the appropriate items for the networking interface connectivity that enable either public or private connectivity, go to the bottom of the page and select Next: Management.

When you select this button, the next step in the configuration process under Management (Figure 3-6) requires you to set up Monitoring, Identity Auto-Shutdown, and Backup configurations. Configurations under this page include

- Boot Diagnostics
- Enabling OS Guess Diagnostics
- Setting System Assigned Managed Identity
- Enabling Auto-Shutdown
- Enabling Backup

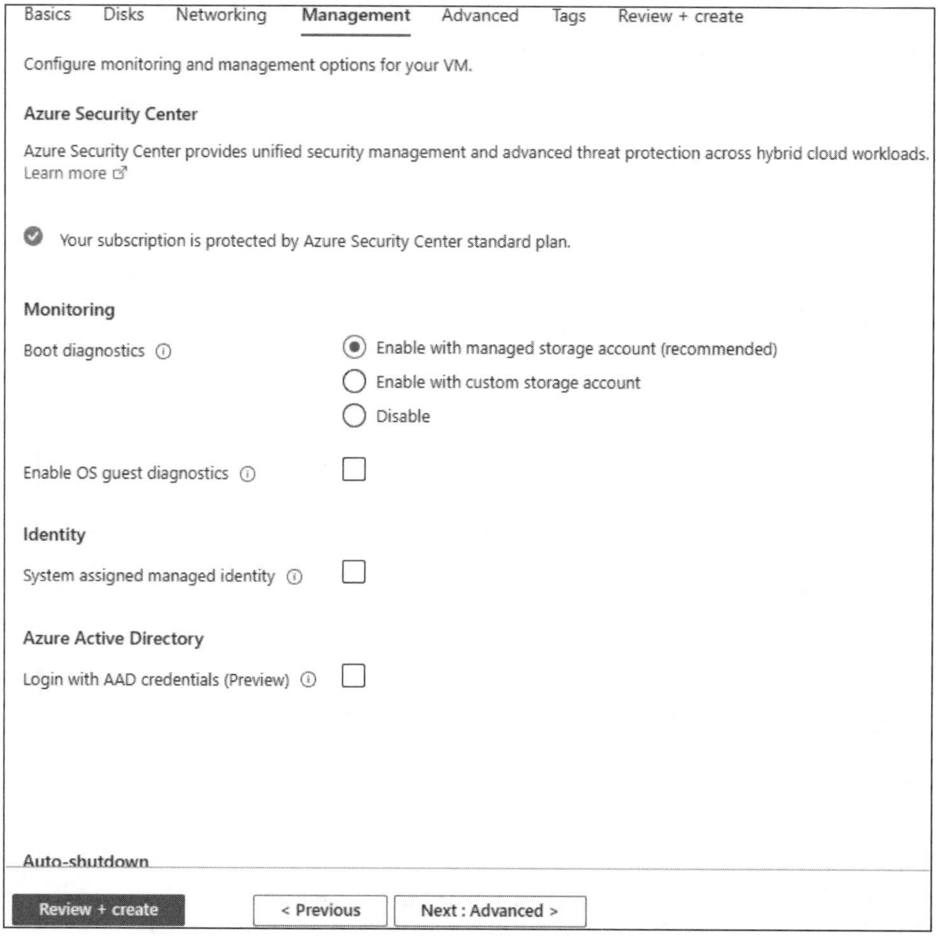

Figure 3-6   Management interface setup for virtual machines

Once management selections are chosen, you will click the Next: Advanced button on the bottom right. You are then presented with the Advanced interface (Figure 3-7). The purpose of this interface is to add configurations, agents, scripts, or applications via virtual machine extensions or cloud-init that are already not configured using standard parameters. Once you complete any ancillary configurations, click the button Next: Tags on the bottom right.

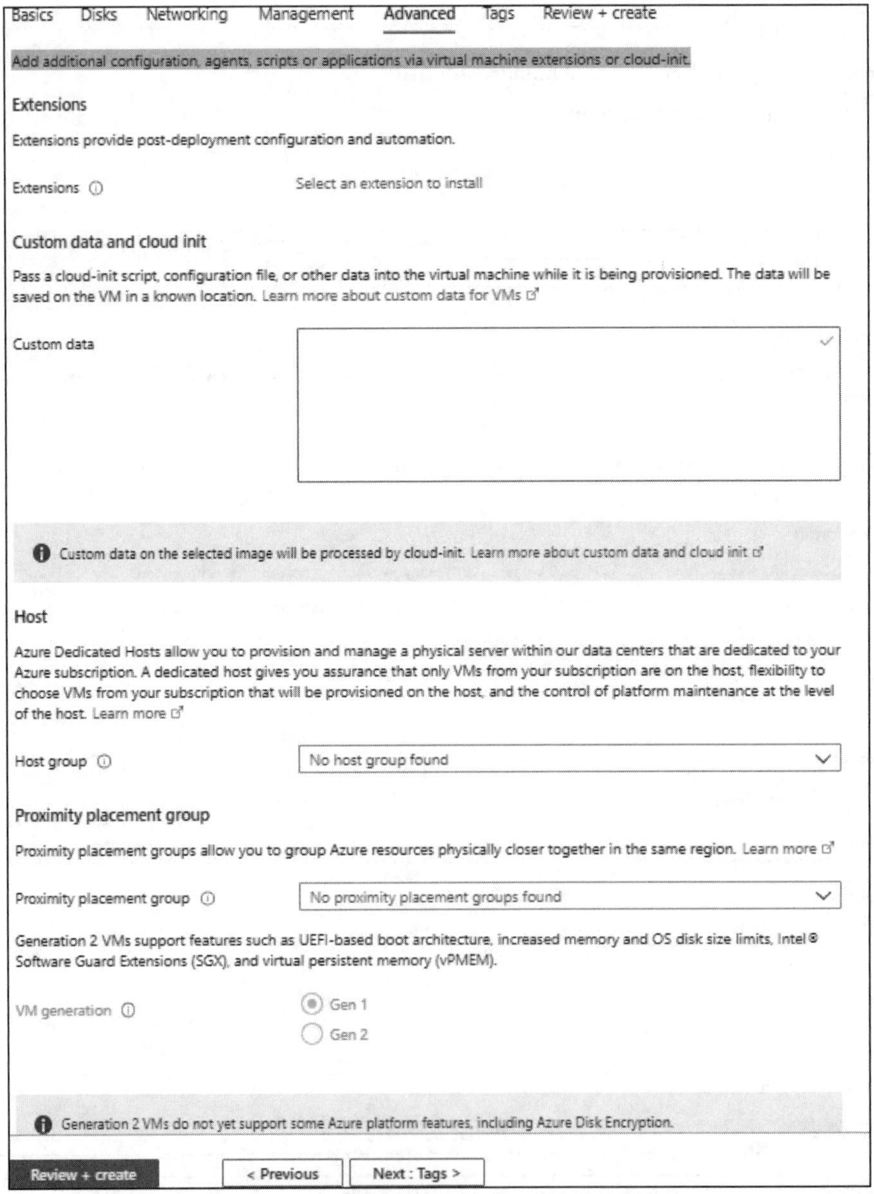

Basics   Disks   Networking   Management   Advanced   Tags   Review + create

Add additional configuration, agents, scripts or applications via virtual machine extensions or cloud-init.

Extensions

Extensions provide post-deployment configuration and automation.

Extensions ⓘ   Select an extension to install

Custom data and cloud init

Pass a cloud-init script, configuration file, or other data into the virtual machine while it is being provisioned. The data will be saved on the VM in a known location. Learn more about custom data for VMs ⬀

Custom data

ⓘ Custom data on the selected image will be processed by cloud-init. Learn more about custom data and cloud init ⬀

Host

Azure Dedicated Hosts allow you to provision and manage a physical server within our data centers that are dedicated to your Azure subscription. A dedicated host gives you assurance that only VMs from your subscription are on the host, flexibility to choose VMs from your subscription that will be provisioned on the host, and the control of platform maintenance at the level of the host. Learn more ⬀

Host group ⓘ   No host group found   ⌄

Proximity placement group

Proximity placement groups allow you to group Azure resources physically closer together in the same region. Learn more ⬀

Proximity placement group ⓘ   No proximity placement groups found   ⌄

Generation 2 VMs support features such as UEFI-based boot architecture, increased memory and OS disk size limits, Intel® Software Guard Extensions (SGX), and virtual persistent memory (vPMEM).

VM generation ⓘ   ⦿ Gen 1
                                      ◯ Gen 2

ⓘ Generation 2 VMs do not yet support some Azure platform features, including Azure Disk Encryption.

Review + create   < Previous   Next : Tags >

Figure 3-7   Advanced interface setup for virtual machines

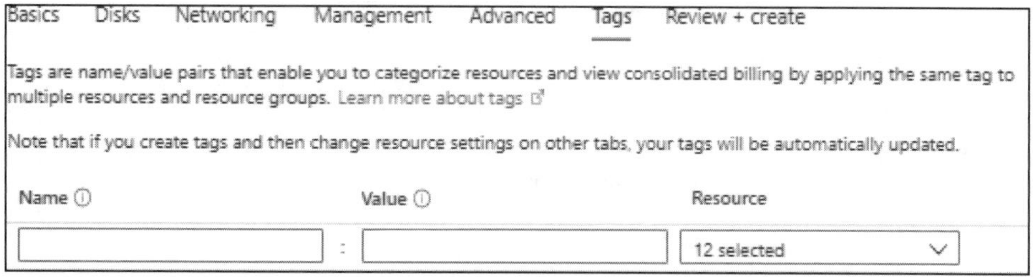

Basics   Disks   Networking   Management   Advanced   Tags   Review + create

Tags are name/value pairs that enable you to categorize resources and view consolidated billing by applying the same tag to multiple resources and resource groups. Learn more about tags ☐

Note that if you create tags and then change resource settings on other tabs, your tags will be automatically updated.

Name ⓘ		Value ⓘ	Resource
	:		12 selected ⌄

Figure 3-8 Tagging setup for virtual machines

Tagging, as seen in Figure 3-8, when creating an Azure Virtual Machine is designed to manage name/value pairs. More specifically, tagging enables a user to categorize resources and complete activities such as conduct billing management by applying a structure to resources. When you create a tag, any time a change is made to a resource setting, all changes made to other tags will automatically get updated. After all tagging is completed, select Next: Review + Create, which allows you to review a summary of all submitted configurations.

On the Review + Create interface, a user can review a snapshot of virtual machine configuration, including a complete breakdown of costs for the services they will consume for their virtualized environment. If all configurations are acceptable, click the Create button on the bottom left side (Figure 3-9). The Create button will trigger the execution of a customized virtual environment. A screen will notify you that your deployment is in process (Figure 3-10). Once the deployment is complete, a new screen appears providing you with a confirmation of the subscription, resource group, and deployment details associated with the virtual machine environment (Figure 3-11).

Billing and Virtual Machines

Once you create a virtual machine, the billing clock starts that very second. You might be puzzled and ask why? You are probably thinking, "I am not consuming Azure compute utilization capacity." You may not even be accessing the image more than once a month. This may all be true. However, if the virtual instance is powered up and you agree to pay for a large image at the onset of the configuration, you should be prepared to get a large invoice at the end of the billing cycle. So long as your instance is running and the default settings are configured, you will continue to pay perpetually.

To stop billing for a virtual machine, you must click the Stop button at the top of the toolbar, found in Figure 3-12. Azure will pause the virtual machine instance in its current state. Billing will cease. You will not be able to access the virtual machine while idle, but you also will save yourself from spending unnecessary funds. Even when you stop the operational state of the virtual machine, you still pay for the underlying storage. Therefore, you will still be billed for some form of infrastructure utilization, just not to the extent you would should your virtual machine instance be running.

There are some important networking considerations to address when stopping a virtual machine instance. Assuming you configured the virtual machine with a static IP address, your instance will remain the same. However, if you selected a dynamic address,

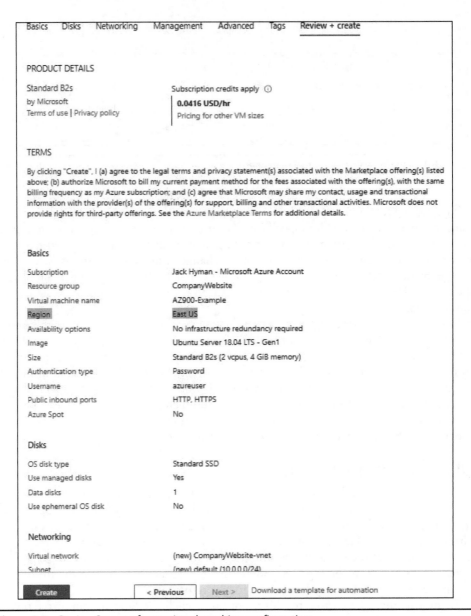

Figure 3-9 Review Screen of your virtual machine configuration

upon restarting the virtual machine, your address will change. Bear in mind that you may stop the virtual machine, but that does not mean that all resource costs are frozen. Since the IP address is still allocated to your instance, you will still incur a charge for the address, the managed disk, and other allocated resources. The only thing you are not paying for is the operating virtual instance being active.

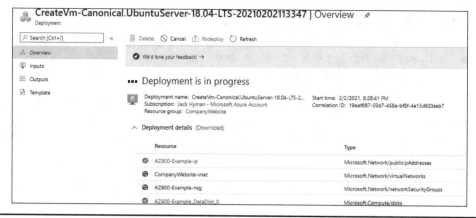

Figure 3-10 Deployment in process interface

Figure 3-11 Deployment of virtual machine complete

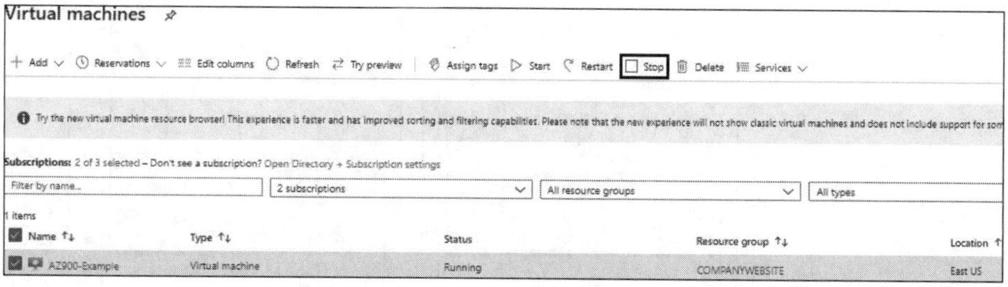

Figure 3-12 Stopping a virtual machine

Availability Options for Virtual Machines

Depending upon the capacity requirements needed across one or more virtual machines, workloads may require high throughput, performance, and redundancy to support virtual machine operations. There are numerous options in Microsoft Azure to achieve high availability, as described throughout this section.

The first option is *Availability Zones*. An Availability Zone expands virtual machine control to maintain the availability of applications and data on a virtual machine. Since an Availability Zone is a physically separate zone within an Azure region with distinct power sources, network, and cooling, the virtual machine environment in each zone can be replicated to best support the applications and data against loss. Assuming the virtual machine is replicated, if one zone is compromised, the replicated application and data in another zone are automatically made available in another zone.

A second alternative is a fault or update domain. *Fault domains* are logical groups of underlying hardware that share a common infrastructure such as power sources and network switches, similar to what you might find in an on-premises data center. Whenever the logical grouping requires maintenance, the domains can be updated taking the *update domain* approach by rebooting. Using this approach ensures that at least a single instance of an application remains operational in the Azure environment, even during a periodic maintenance event. It does not matter what the sequence of the maintenance is, but only one update domain can occur at a time. Figure 3-13 presents a fault and update domain residing in an availability set.

Availability sets are the third option when considering high availability. Representing another form of logical grouping that allows Azure to support application redundancy and availability with the potential of 99.95 percent SLA guarantees, an availability set requires two or more VMs to ensure operational reliability. There is no charge for maintaining the set itself. The only cost incurred is for maintaining each VM instance created. For example, a single virtual machine using a Premium SSD will incur a specific charge. In the availability set, the virtual machine is automatically distributed across the domains. Should there be potential physical hardware limitations and failures, there is limited impact to physical

Figure 3-13
Availability set
with two fault
domains and
three update
domains

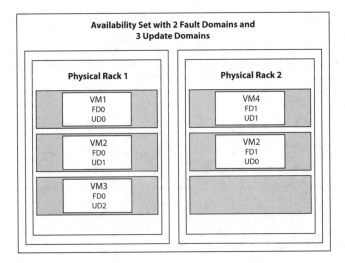

hardware disruption. It is important to remember that only virtual machine instances with managed disks can be created using managed availability sets. You must have at a minimum two or three managed disk fault domains per region to successfully operate in each region. If this is the case, an availability set will update across domains automatically.

Scale sets allow you to create and manage a load-balanced set of virtual machine instances. You can create or decrease the load in response to a defined schedule. Different from Availability Zones is the fact that scale sets can accommodate high availability through central configuration and update management across two or more virtual machines. For a scale set to work, it must have a minimum of two virtual machine instances, which also ensures 99.95 percent SLA terms. Like other high-availability architecture options, you only pay for the virtual machine instances created.

 EXAM TIP It is easy to get confused remembering the difference between an Availability Zone and a scale set. Remember, with a scale set, the virtual machines can be deployed across multiple update and fault domains to maximize availability. Such a design also ensures resiliency against data center outages and unplanned maintenance events. Virtual machines in a scale set can be deployed into a single Availability Zone. The Availability Zone is merely a potential distribution for virtual machines across physically distinct locations.

Azure App Service

Azure App Service provides PaaS options that support HTTP-based web application hosting, REST APIs, and mobile back-end support. If the end goal is to develop a standalone application in a native program language such as .NET, Java, PHP, or Python while also focusing on limited maintenance, App Service is ideal. You can run and scale an application within a Windows- or Linux-based virtual machine environment with strong security, load balancing, autoscaling, and automated management. Unlike with virtual machines, App Service offers DevOps capabilities, including continuous deployment, using Azure DevOps and GitHub. Staging environments, custom domains, and TLS/SSL certificates can also be applied to App Services for strong integration abilities. Like other Azure compute resources, you only pay for what you utilize based on the Azure App Service plan that you run your applications on.

Figure 3-14 illustrates the conceptual nature of an App Service architecture. The diagram simplifies how an App Service works whereby an Azure Load Balancer distributes traffic to a virtual machine housed within the App Service *front end*. An App Service front end enables the distribution of traffic to a specific web app. The virtual machine environments run inside an App Service plan, which is a logical container that houses one or more virtual machines running web apps.

App Service Plans

When configuring an App Service plan (Figure 3-15), you must identify a combination of factors: region, number of virtual machine instances, size of instance, and pricing tier selected. The factor that influences features for App Service most is the pricing tier, as seen in Table 3-3.

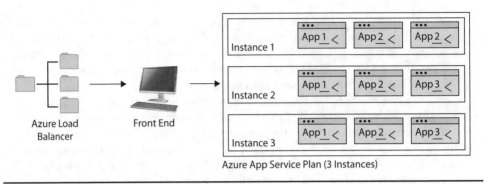

Figure 3-14 High-level App Service architecture model

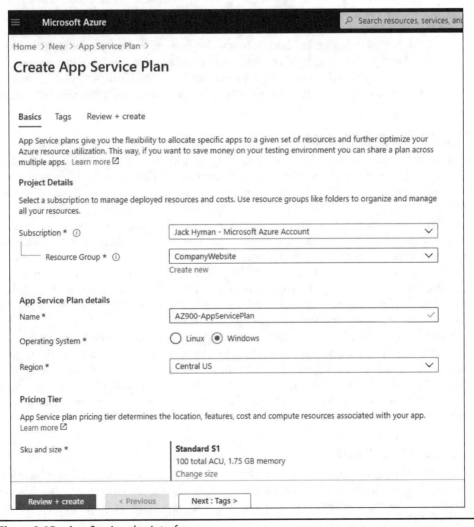

Figure 3-15 App Service plan interface

Tier	Features
Shared Compute: Free/Shared	There are two base tiers to run apps on: free or shared. With both options, you can run apps on the same Azure Virtual Machine as other App Service apps, which may be shared with other Azure customers. Because there is tiered allocation of CPU utilization against an app across many resources, scalability is limited.
Dedicated Compute	There are five dedicated tiers: Basic, Standard, Premium, PremiumV2, and PremiumV3. The primary difference is the number of virtual machine instances you can implement and scale out concurrently. Higher tiers allow for greater scale-out.
Isolated	The Isolated tier is the only option where you can run a dedicated Azure Virtual Machine on a dedicated Azure Virtual Network. All features are isolated on the network on top of compute resources dedicated to your apps. If your application requires maximum scalability, the Isolated tier is your best option.

Table 3-3   App Service Plan Tiers

Creating a Web App

Users have two options when they create a web app. The user can create a web app using an existing App Service plan or utilize a new plan for an app. Regardless of choice, web apps in an App Service plan run on a virtual machine. If you want to ensure reliability, consistency, and isolate your app from other system functions, a best practice is to contain a web app by creating a new App Service plan and containing the app within the virtual machine environment. You have a choice between creating a preconfigured virtual machine runtime stack or running an application using a dedicated container such as Docker. Should you choose to leverage a preconfigured stack, Microsoft Azure offers multiple versions of a given app service. Figure 3-16 illustrates how you can go about configuring a Web app. Additionally, Figure 3-17 provides you a sampling of some runtimes available for web apps.

Benefits of Azure App Services

When determining what solution is best to build a custom application, you should take a few factors into consideration. An organization that wants to forego managing infrastructure, security patching, and scaling is best suited for using Azure App Service versus other alternatives. The benefits are as follows:

- **Programming Language, API, and Integration Options**   You can quickly deploy and scale an app using almost any programming language, integrate with most APIs, configure an app within any container, or contain an app inside a Windows- or Linux-based virtual machine.

- **Enterprise Grade Security**   Organizations mandated to meet rigorous security and compliance requirements need not worry about achieving this through self-management, as an Azure App Service environment is fully managed.

- **Connectivity Options**   Integration with a virtual network in either isolated or dedicated mode in conjunction with a rigorous security and compliance posture that covers Security Operations Center (SOC) and Payment Card Industry (PCI) Compliance is only available under App Service because it is a PaaS.

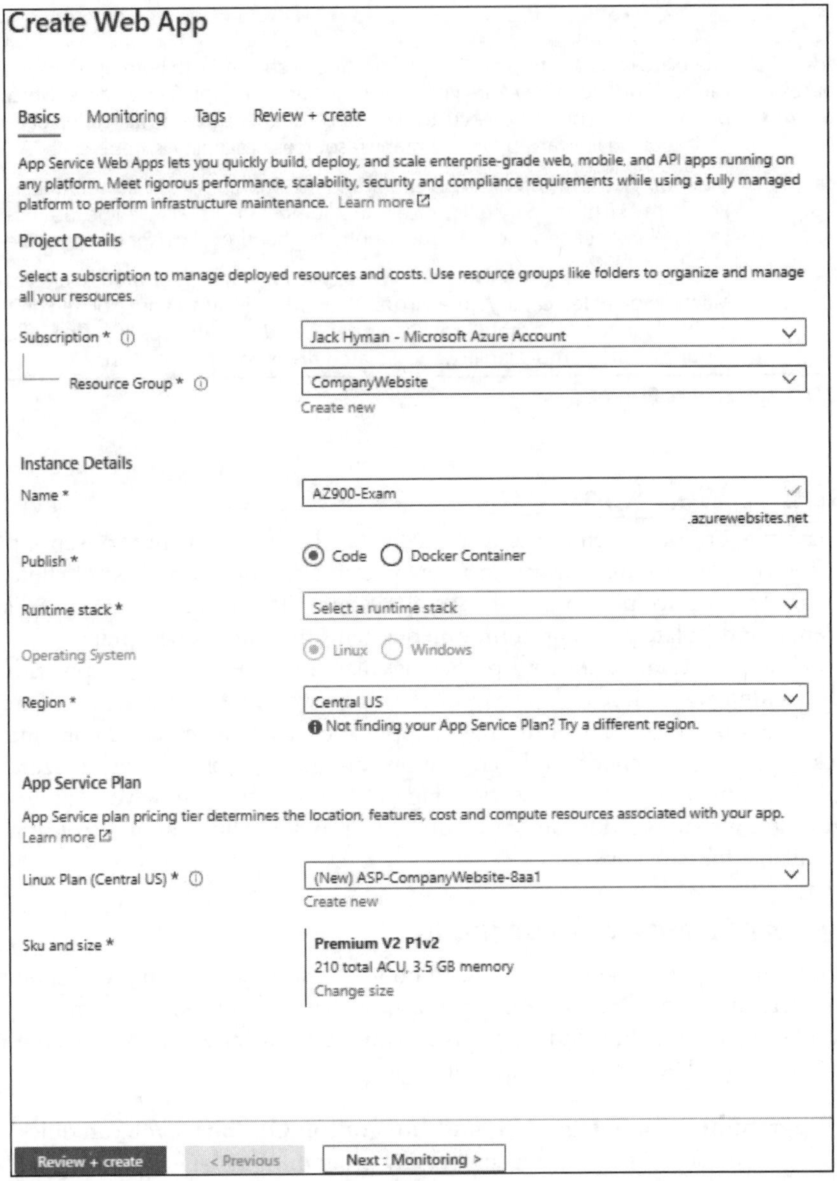

Create Web App

Basics   Monitoring   Tags   Review + create

App Service Web Apps lets you quickly build, deploy, and scale enterprise-grade web, mobile, and API apps running on any platform. Meet rigorous performance, scalability, security and compliance requirements while using a fully managed platform to perform infrastructure maintenance. Learn more ☑

Project Details

Select a subscription to manage deployed resources and costs. Use resource groups like folders to organize and manage all your resources.

Subscription * ⓘ   [Jack Hyman - Microsoft Azure Account   ∨]

     Resource Group * ⓘ   [CompanyWebsite   ∨]
                           Create new

Instance Details

Name *   [AZ900-Exam   ✓]
                                                              .azurewebsites.net

Publish *   ◉ Code   ○ Docker Container

Runtime stack *   [Select a runtime stack   ∨]

Operating System   ◉ Linux   ○ Windows

Region *   [Central US   ∨]
            ❶ Not finding your App Service Plan? Try a different region.

App Service Plan

App Service plan pricing tier determines the location, features, cost and compute resources associated with your app. Learn more ☑

Linux Plan (Central US) * ⓘ   [(New) ASP-CompanyWebsite-8aa1   ∨]
                               Create new

Sku and size *   **Premium V2 P1v2**
                  210 total ACU, 3.5 GB memory
                  Change size

[Review + create]   [< Previous]   [Next : Monitoring >]

Figure 3-16   Web app configuration interface

- **Scale and Availability**   Development options are available at a global scale, with high availability whether the organization requires a dedicated environment, DevOps optimization, connectivity to SaaS platforms, or a hybrid compute model.

App Service allows for more control over the operating system or security settings. If your organization is interested in implementing a microservice architecture, the *Azure Spring Cloud Service* or the *Azure Service Fabric* is more appropriate. The Azure Spring

Figure 3-17
Runtime options
for web apps

Cloud Service provides users with managed services that support full autonomy of running microservices on Azure using Spring-boot or Steeltoe, with minor code changes. On the other hand, if your application requires scaled distribution and the main objective is to package, deploy, and reliably manage microservices or containers, not just standalone App Service, using *Azure Service Fabric* will be more appropriate for your organization.

Azure Container Instances

When you are looking for a way to run event-driven applications in isolation with the support of a managed, serverless environment, your best compute choice is Azure Container Instances (ACI). With ACI, you can run Docker containers on-demand in a managed, serverless Azure environment. Azure Container Instances is PaaS-based.

The reason why containers are a solid option is their flexibility in allowing organizations to move applications between environments, especially in the cloud. Containers help alleviate the burden of transporting environments by creating an image of an application. The image includes all the components necessary to run the application in isolation, such as a database engine, a web server, security, and the operating system infrastructure. You can deploy the image to any environment that supports the use of containers. Once the image is moved to the new environment, it can be enabled so long as a container runtime is installed on the environment. Azure supports DC/OS, Docker, and Kubernetes runtimes.

Your organization should consider the use of containers when there is a need to enforce a strong security posture first and foremost. Since a container operates in an isolated environment with its own network backbone, storage, and operating system, other containers running in the same machine environment are not able to access any data on one system unless the image explicitly allows for interaction between both environments.

Creating an Azure Container Instance

One of the reasons you would consider using ACI is because it requires minimal configuration, being a serverless PaaS-based technology. To create a new container instance, go to the search bar at the top of the screen, enter **Container Instances**, and select Container Instances (Figure 3-18).

You will then create an Azure Container Instance following these instructions:

1. Click the New button (Figure 3-19).

2. The Create A New Container Image screen appears, as shown in Figure 3-20, which requires a user to configure the following:

   - **Subscription** Under the ACI, you are associating the Azure subscription with the container server. By selecting a subscription, you also associate how resource usage is reported and services are billed.

   - **Resource Group** Resource groups are buckets that allow a user to associate objects (resources) within the container under the same lifecycle, permission, and policy set to a named group.

   - **Container Name** A unique isolated instance to house the application in a managed, serverless setting, the Azure Container should be different from the image name.

   - **Region** What geography should the resource be deployed from?

   - **Image Source** If you create your own image, it must be stored in an Azure Container Registry. If you plan on using a pre-built image, follow the prompts with the QuickStart image by selecting an image pre-built by Microsoft under Image. Should you plan on utilizing Docker Hub or another registry, you must point to the location and select if the image is a public or private image.

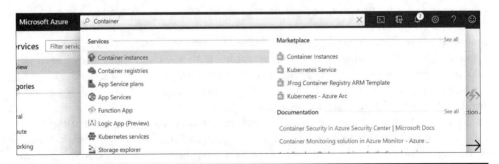

Figure 3-18 Searching for Container Instances

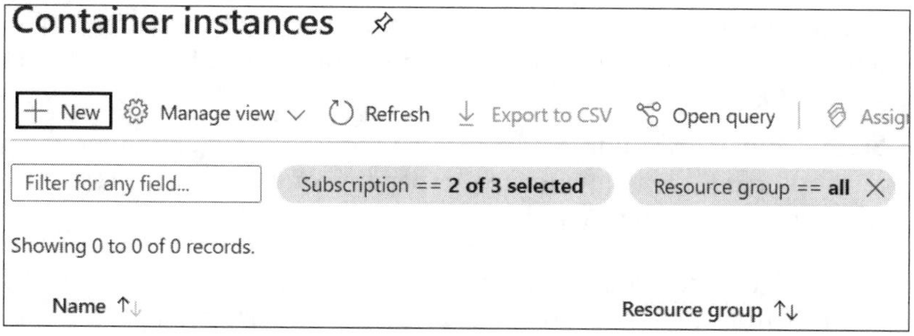

Figure 3-19   New Azure Container Instance button

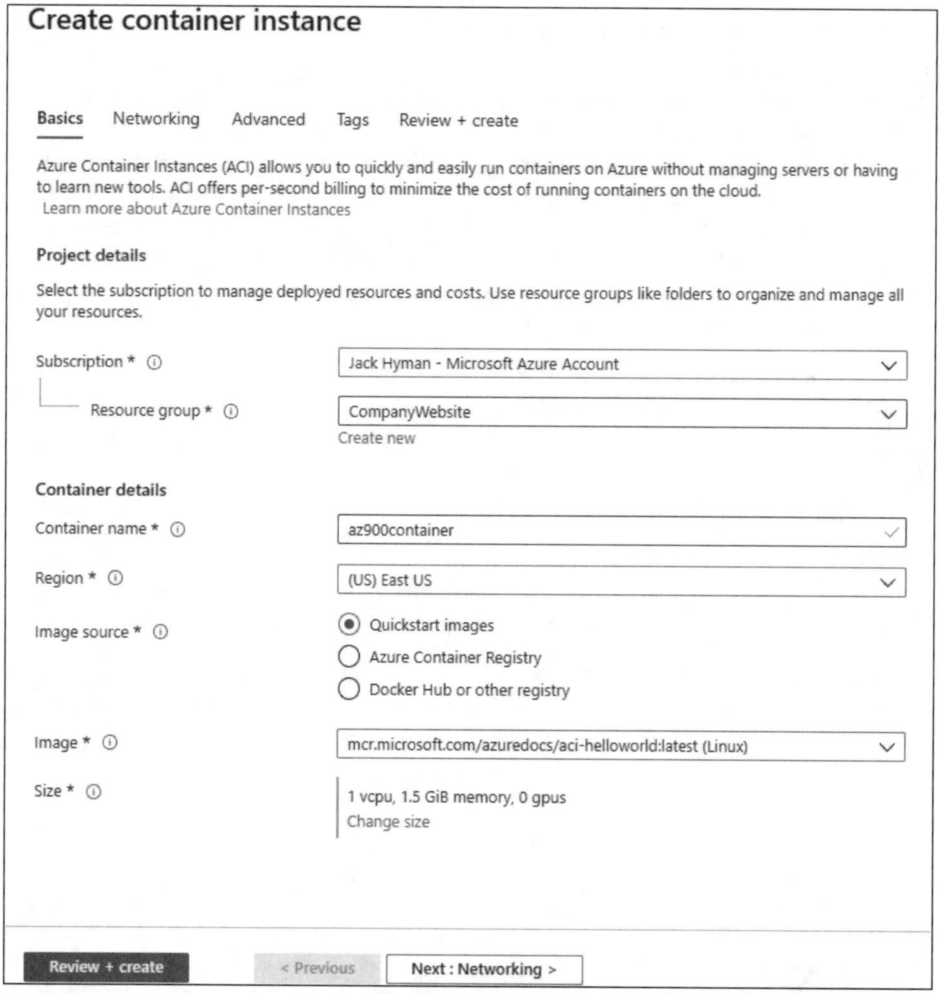

Figure 3-20   Azure Container Instance creation interface

- **Image** Depending on what your image source is, you would select an option from this menu for the most appropriate image based on operating system (OS) type.

- **Size** Containers require you to select a baseline configuration of CPU, memory, and GPU requirements. Depending on the region and technical requirements, availability varies.

Once you configure each of the fields, proceed to the next page by clicking Next: Networking on the bottom-right side. You must configure the Networking settings to ensure the container is available for either public or private consumption (Figure 3-21). Unless specific advanced settings are required, you can click the Review + Create button on the bottom of the Networking Configuration Interface page. On the following page, you will be asked to confirm the settings you have selected to create the ACI (Figure 3-22). Click Create once you have reviewed all options.

EXAM TIP Azure Container Interfaces only create resources you need, which provides cost savings, unlike a VM, where you are always paying for an underlying infrastructure unless the instance is stopped. For example, if your ACI app is running a machine with two CPUs and 4GB of memory and your total daily utilization is 30 minutes, you will only be billed for 30 minutes at the end of the calendar month. Therefore, if you are asked a question regarding virtual machine instances and container instances, the main differences are cost and resource allocation.

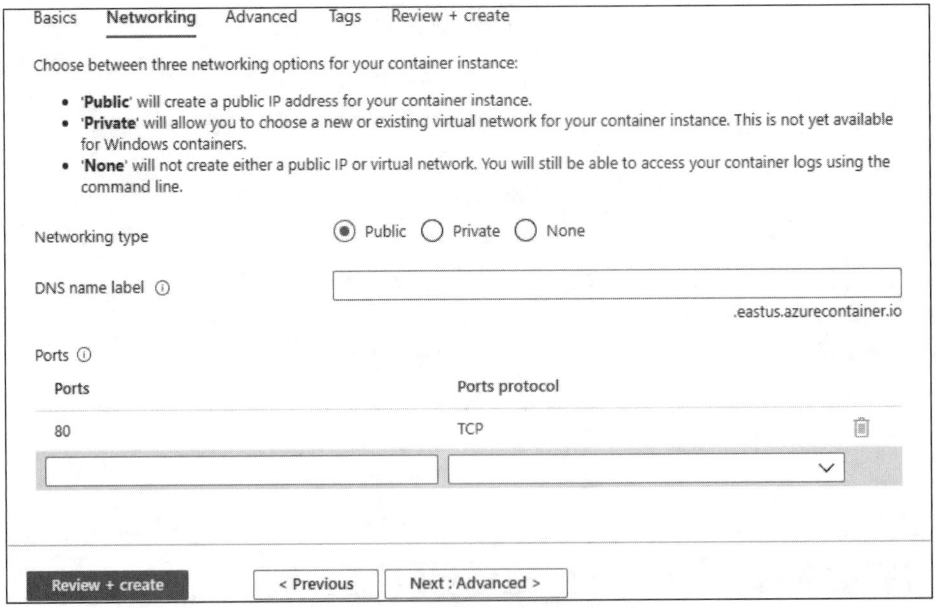

Basics **Networking** Advanced Tags Review + create

Choose between three networking options for your container instance:

- **'Public'** will create a public IP address for your container instance.
- **'Private'** will allow you to choose a new or existing virtual network for your container instance. This is not yet available for Windows containers.
- **'None'** will not create either a public IP or virtual network. You will still be able to access your container logs using the command line.

Networking type   ⦿ Public   ◯ Private   ◯ None

DNS name label ⓘ   [   ]

                                              .eastus.azurecontainer.io

Ports ⓘ

Ports   Ports protocol

80   TCP   🗑

[   ]   [⌄]

[Review + create]   [< Previous]   [Next : Advanced >]

Figure 3-21   Network configuration settings for Azure Container Instances

Create container instance

✓ Validation passed

Basics   Networking   Advanced   Tags   **Review + create**

Basics

Subscription	Jack Hyman - Microsoft Azure Account
Resource group	CompanyWebsite
Region	East US
Container name	az900container
Image type	Public
Image	mcr.microsoft.com/azuredocs/aci-helloworld:latest
OS type	Linux
Memory (GiB)	1.5
Number of CPU cores	1
GPU type (Preview)	None
GPU count	0

Networking

Networking type	Public
Ports	80 (TCP)

Advanced

Restart policy	On failure
Command override	[ ]

Tags

Create   < Previous   Next >   Download a template for automation

Figure 3-22   Review ACI configuration pre-creation

While the use of Azure Container Instances may sound appealing, there are several things to consider. First, the architecture is intended for simple applications. ACI is not optimal when you intend to have heavy application usage, because scalability is limited. Instead, Azure Kubernetes Service (AKS) is better suited for enterprise-grade, transactional serverless applications.

Azure Kubernetes Service

When you or the organization you work for is looking to establish a more robust solution for managing containers, including orchestration management, *Azure Kubernetes Service (AKS)*, is the best approach to take, since Microsoft handles the technical burden. AKS handles monitoring at all times, including when containers need to scale up or down. Given AKS is a PaaS platform, Kubernetes delivers containers using *pods,* which means all containers are grouped together because they are alike. Each container within a pod shares the resources with one another. If resource management is a concern, it should not be, because Kubernetes offloads any resource constraints through sharing restrictions seen in other types of multicontainer settings.

Resources in one pod container are not able to be shared within a container in another pod, though. Each Kubernetes pods runs in a *node,* also referred to as a worker. Each instance must have its own container runtime to operate. An example container runtime is Docker. To operate efficiently, nodes must also operate different services so that Kubernetes can manage the pods. In this case, there will be multiple nodes for a given Kubernetes instance under the control of a master node, also referred to as the *Kubernetes master.* The combination of all environment components, including the master and nodes, is called an Azure Kubernetes Cluster.

To create an Azure Kubernetes Service, locate the Kubernetes Service icon or search for Kubernetes Service. Then, once you have landed on the Kubernetes Service page, click the Add Kubernetes Cluster button (Figure 3-23). You will need to go through the Create Kubernetes Service interface (Figure 3-24) and enter the required fields across each of the tabs, including Basic, Node Pool, Authentication, Networking, Integrations, Tags, and Review + Create, to complete the AKS setup.

Figure 3-23 Add Kubernetes Cluster navigation screen

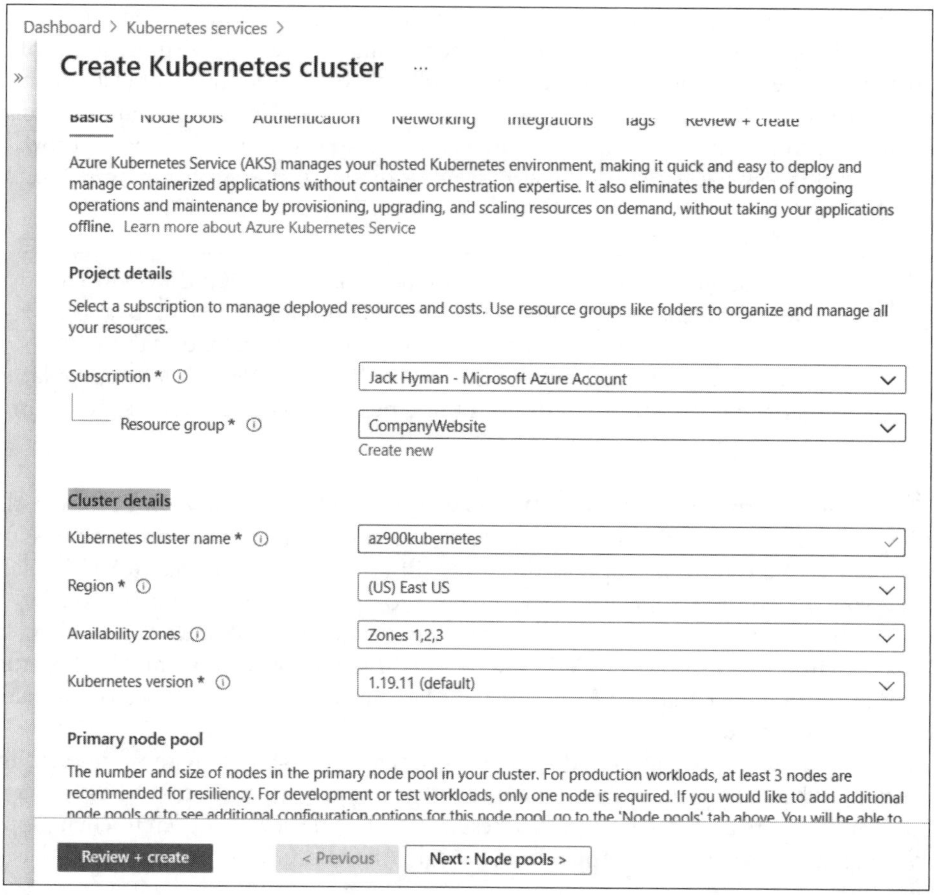

Dashboard > Kubernetes services >

Create Kubernetes cluster ...

Basics   Node pools   Authentication   Networking   Integrations   Tags   Review + create

Azure Kubernetes Service (AKS) manages your hosted Kubernetes environment, making it quick and easy to deploy and manage containerized applications without container orchestration expertise. It also eliminates the burden of ongoing operations and maintenance by provisioning, upgrading, and scaling resources on demand, without taking your applications offline. Learn more about Azure Kubernetes Service

Project details

Select a subscription to manage deployed resources and costs. Use resource groups like folders to organize and manage all your resources.

Subscription * ⓘ

| Jack Hyman - Microsoft Azure Account | ∨ |

Resource group * ⓘ

| CompanyWebsite | ∨ |
Create new

Cluster details

Kubernetes cluster name * ⓘ

| az900kubernetes | ✓ |

Region * ⓘ

| (US) East US | ∨ |

Availability zones ⓘ

| Zones 1,2,3 | ∨ |

Kubernetes version * ⓘ

| 1.19.11 (default) | ∨ |

Primary node pool

The number and size of nodes in the primary node pool in your cluster. For production workloads, at least 3 nodes are recommended for resiliency. For development or test workloads, only one node is required. If you would like to add additional node pools or to see additional configuration options for this node pool, go to the 'Node pools' tab above. You will be able to

| Review + create | | < Previous | | Next : Node pools > |

Figure 3-24   Create Kubernetes Service interface

Windows Virtual Desktop

When your organization prefers to control desktop and app virtualization by hosting all services on the cloud, they can create virtualized desktop environments. For Azure users, this service is called *Windows Virtual Desktop,* a PaaS-based offering. What makes Windows Virtual Desktop on Azure so attractive is the ability to deploy and scale capabilities rapidly with ease.

In the past, organizations used to deploy Microsoft 365 business productivity or a homegrown application by licensing an application. Then, the organization would deploy the application on each machine, making it quite inefficient and highly insecure to support business operations. A business would need to deal with data sprawl, given no two systems were configured alike, partially because operational inconsistencies and a litany of security constraints exist. Maintenance would be difficult for even the best IT support professional. That is why many businesses have shifted their ability to manage their workforce's compute capabilities to the cloud using desktop virtualization.

With desktop virtualization, a business can install an operating system, as well as the critical applications, on a centralized server. Using the desktop virtualization infrastructure features, the end user can access the full host of features from almost any form factor they desire, assuming it can connect to the Internet. Not a single application is downloaded to the end user's desktop—everything is accessed via a web-based browser, even though the user experiences the virtual environment as if the software were local to their desktop.

 TIP Do not confuse Windows Remote Desktop with Windows Virtual Desktop. Remote Desktop allows a user to remotely connect to an end-user's computer via a public or private connection so long as there is a trusted relationship between both users. Windows Virtual Desktop replaces fat-client (desktop-based) computing by putting all compute resources in the cloud.

It may sound easy to provision a Windows Virtual Desktop (WVD). However, the process can be quite complex at first, as it does require some advanced configurations initially. While Microsoft does support the entire infrastructure, given that WVD is PaaS-based, you are required to create a WVD tenant to operate. A WVD tenant consists of a collection of one or more host pools. A host pool is made up of one or more identical virtual machine instances within Windows Virtual Desktop environments. Each virtual machine instance is a dedicated Azure Virtual Machine instance that has been configured for Windows Virtual Desktop.

Upon completing a configured tenant, you can add users from the Azure Active Directory, where they can access all operating systems in each tenant and assignment permissions. Users have the option to access a WVD using several different client apps, including Windows, macOS, Apple iOS, Google Android OS, or through a web-based client browser.

Spotlight: Azure Reservations

Each of the storage options mentioned so far may offer end users significant cost savings if you or your organization is willing to make a long-term commitment to procuring cloud services from Microsoft.

Users on a pay-as-you-go plan that commit to Microsoft Azure long term, agreeing to a one- or three-year purchase of cloud services, can receive discounts on resources used. Reservations can significantly reduce your compute cost by as much as 72 percent compared to a pay-as-you go plan. Organizations are provided a discount at the time of resource purchase. A company can pay up-front for the purchase of their resources or pay monthly. A reservation is a billing discount—there is no effect on your system's runtime state or performance. Of note, you can only get a reservation discount on Microsoft Azure–based products, not third-party products. Azure reservations can be purchased from the Azure Portal at portal.azure.com.

Suppose your organization procures Azure Cloud Services. The organization prepays for all those services in advance for three years. However, there is overutilization of the reserved resource. Since you are no longer charged under the pay-as-you go plan, you have not been charged up to this point. You have paid for your services up-front or cyclically. Yet should there be an overage, your form of payment will then be charged the difference.

Should there be a need to make changes to a reservation, the person who initially purchased the reservation, an account administrator with privileges to billing responsibilities, an individual with access to an Enterprise Agreement, or someone who acts as the Microsoft Customer Agreement Billing Administrator can all make reservation modifications.

During the life of a reservation, it is not uncommon to want to evaluate utilization so that you can see just how much budget has already been spent from the original commitment. Users with view permissions can view their billing details using the Azure Portal, using the Cost Management features for each individual resource where a commitment has been made against a resource. Should an organization no longer require the user of a reservation or want to trade a reservation for another product, Microsoft allows exchanges up to US$50,000 in each 12-month period. However, the scope of the refund exchange is across all reservations with Microsoft.

EXAM TIP Remember, not every resource or service is covered by a reservation. The key products covered by a reservation include virtual machine, database and storage products, and a limited number of software plans.

An Introduction to Storage Resources

Numerous types of storage are available in Microsoft Azure. When you intend to use storage classes against code such as a REST API, offerings considered include blob, table, and queue storage. Such storage is commonly used with PaaS cloud instances. In a Platform as a Service environment, storage supports existing code-based frameworks, web, and mobile applications; microservices; and serverless applications. Likewise, when the need is specific to dedicated or shared storage, virtual machines, or networks running on Windows or Linux, disk or file offerings should be considered. IaaS is synonymous with VM and virtual desktop appliances. Table 3-4 provides an overview of these storage types.

On the exam, when it comes to storage-specific resources, you are only required to know about container (blob) storage, disk storage, and file storage. The section on database resources covers all content specific to table storage. Queue resources are not covered on the AZ-900 examination but covered here for the purposes of awareness.

Container (Blobs)	Tables	Queues	Disks	Files
• Highly scalable, REST-based cloud object storage • Block blobs: Sequential file I/O • Page blobs: Random-write pattern data	• Massive NoSQL autoscaling • Store dynamic data based on load • Scale to PBs of table data • Key/value lookups are fast	• Cloud-based reliable queue services • Decouple and scale components • Message visibility timeout • Update messages to protect against poor queue data	• Persistent disk for all Azure IaaS VMs • Based on page blobs (object storage) • Different types of storage available (premium, SSD based, high IOPS, low latency)	• Fully manages file shares, but in the cloud • Maps to a standard file system structure that has a semantic design • Often associated with legacy apps
Platform as a Service (Frameworks, Web /Mobile, Microservices, Serverless)			**Infrastructure as a Service** (Storage, VM, Networking)	

Table 3-4   Types of Storage in Microsoft Azure

Azure Container Storage

You may hear the phrases "container storage" and "blob storage" used interchangeably in the context of Microsoft Azure. A container is the organization of blobs or objects in a collection. Think of a container like a directory or file system with objects. When you create a storage account in Microsoft Azure, an unlimited number of containers can be created inside a storage account. The container can also store an unlimited number of blobs. With Azure, blob storage is optimized to handle unstructured data, or data that does not adhere to a specific format, such as you would find in a spreadsheet or a relational database table. When architecting storage design, consider blob storage when your organization is looking to save objects such as

- Images and documents
- Standard business productivity files
- Multimedia files
- Log files
- Backup, disaster recovery, and archiving

A user can access blobs in a storage container using either HTTP/HTTPS, the Azure REST API, Azure PowerShell, Azure CLI, or through an Azure Storage client library. Supported languages include .NET, Java, Node.js, Python, Go, PHP, and Ruby.

Type of Blob	Purpose
Block Blob	Best for storing text and binary data. Current block blob limits are 4.75TiB. Microsoft has continued to test large block blob data sizes up to 190TiB, depending what pricing tier is being utilized.
Append Blob	Best for logging data from virtual machines. Made up of blocks like blob data; however, these are optimized for append operations.
Page Blob	Stores virtual hard drive (VHD) files and disks for Azure Virtual machines. Can handle up to 8TiB in size.

Table 3-5   Types of Blob Storage

Container storage consists of three components: the storage account, the container, and blobs. A *storage account* is a unique namespace where a user may place data in Azure. Regardless of what is stored in Azure, every object has a unique address associated with the storage account name. Combining the account name and the storage blob endpoint results in the final address where a user can access items in storage. If you were to name a storage account `cloudcostorageact`, the endpoint for the blob that all users would access online would be `http://clourcostorageact.blob.core.windows.net`.

A container is a way of organizing a blob. There are three types of blobs: block, append, and page blobs. Table 3-5 explains the differences among the three blob types.

Once a user creates a blob, there is no way to change its type. You can only commit operational actions such as write or append to the blob. Blob changes are committed immediately. Every time a change is made, a version identifier, called an *eTag*, is associated with the blob. The eTag acts as a form of version control for a blob. As for duplicating blob data in its entirety, it is possible to create a complete duplicate of all blob types, also known as a *snapshot,* for the purposes of historical integrity.

EXAM TIP   You will likely find most questions on the AZ-900 exam that deal with storage focus on blob and table storage. Make sure you know what type of storage is appropriate for a given cloud architecture, especially container-based storage.

Azure Disk Storage

Virtual machines on Azure require managed disks. In Azure, managed disks are block-level storage volumes that are fully managed by Microsoft Azure and used by a virtual machine infrastructure. Like an on-premises server, managed disks are virtualized or cloud-based. When you are ready to provision disk storage, the configuration requirements are standard, requiring the type of disk and size of disk. A user can select from a variety of disk types: ultra-disk, premium solid-state drive (SSD), standard SSD, and standard hard disk drive (HDD). Each disk type is aimed at a specific customer use case, as seen in Table 3-6.

	Ultra-Disk	Premium SSD	Standard SSD	Standard HDD
Purpose	Enterprise applications, intensive workloads, top-tier databases	Production workloads, performance-sensitive activity	Web servers, lightly used applications, web-based applications, dev/test environments	Backup/recovery, noncritical storage
Maximum Disk Size	65,536GiB	32,767GiB	32,767GiB	32,767GiB
Maximum Throughput	2,000 MB/s	900 MB/s	750 MB/s	500 MB/s
Max IOPS	160,000	20,000	6,000	2,000

Table 3-6   Comparison of Disk Types

Managed disks support 99.999 percent availability. Every managed disk type provides users the option of replicating data, which includes high durability. Should one disk fail, the remaining replicas offer persistency of data and tolerance of data failures. Managed disks in Microsoft Azure offer many benefits unique to virtual machine instances. Features to consider include

- **At-Scale Virtual Machine Instances**   With managed disks, you can currently create up to 50,000 virtual machine disks of a given type in a subscription per region. Additional growth is possible using virtual machine scale sets.

- **Integration with Availability Sets**   Managed disks are integrated in an Availability Set so that the disks are isolated from one another, which ensures operational failures are mitigated across multiple disks.

- **Integration with Availability Zones**   High-availability requirements are also necessary in some instances for managed disks. In those cases, managed-disk Availability Zone support is available. Because Availability Zones are specific to physical Azure regions, the data centers will be equipped with their own end-to-end infrastructure, not being reliant on another region. When resiliency is important with mission-critical data, three separate zones should be active in an enabled region.

- **Granular Access**   Managed disks support Azure role-based access control (RBAC), assigning specific permissions to a managed disk to one or more users to only allow specific operational activities such as to read, write, delete, and retrieve a shared access signature (SAS) for a given managed disk. You control the full range of roles and responsibilities a person can have access to when setting disk access.

- **Disk-Based Roles**   There are three main disk roles in Azure: the data disk, the OS disk, and the temporary disk. These can either be persistent for data disks; temporary and local, meaning not persistent; or local, but custom defined.

- **Encryption**   Two types of encryption are available for managed disks: server side and Azure Disk Encryption. Server-side encryption offers encryption at rest so that you can meet your organization's security and compliance mandates. By default, server-side encryption is enabled for all managed disks, snapshots, and images, assuming support is available within the region for the disks. Azure Disk Encryption is specifically designed for IaaS virtual machines running OS and data disks.

Snapshots and Images

It may be confusing to understand the difference between a snapshot and an image, especially when having to deal with managed disks. With Microsoft Azure, there is a very clear difference.

An *image* is a full copy of a virtual machine instance at a moment in time. The instance includes all the disks attached to the virtual machine, which means the data is also on those disks. When you create an image, you can create a copy of the managed disks. Treat a *snapshot* like a picture: a moment in time.

If an organization needs to make regular backups of data, they will use a snapshot approach to do this. Why? It is all about money. Suppose your organization starts with a 100GiB drive's worth of data. The organization schedules a weekly backup. During the first weekly snapshot, 100GiB worth of data are captured. On the second snapshot, though, the incremental difference—the change in data—is only 5 GiB. In this case, the second snapshot will be 5GIB. Microsoft will only invoice the organization for the 105GiB worth of storage, not 200GiB. Had the organization created a weekly image, their storage requirement would exceed 100GiB per week.

Azure File Storage

For the small- to medium-sized business, or even personal user, having a robust Microsoft Azure account may be a bit much if the sole need is to have an affordable, simple way to securely store data in the cloud versus on-premises. It is not uncommon for organizations to want to shift their data from a data center to the cloud. Azure Files offers a fully managed file share service in the cloud using either the Server Message Block (SMB) or Network File System (NFS) protocol. Like computer hard drives, depending on the protocols, mounting options vary. Azure Files SMB support is available for Windows, Linus, and macOS, whereas NFS file support is limited to Linux and macOS. A key differentiation, though, is that with the SMB protocol on Windows servers, one can utilize Azure File Sync. Azure File shares can be mounted by clients in Azure Virtual Machines or from on-premises workstations. Businesses who are looking to sync and cache their files between an on-premises Windows server while maintaining local access will find Azure Files to be their best storage alternative.

 TIP   You must provision the Azure Files sync with the Azure Marketplace. You are given one free storage sync service per month. There is a nominal charge for additional connections.

Tier	Description
Hot Access	Should be used by frequently accessed applications. These are applications that have many read/write actions. The costs associated with the tier are highest, but access costs are lower.
Cool Access	Appropriate for data not accessed frequently by applications, but the expectation is that data will be stored for a minimum of 30 days. Use cases may include media files, backup and recovery data, and short-term log files. The cost of using the cool access tier is lower; however, access and availability are reduced. The service-level agreement is reduced. Additionally, when a user must access data, there is a charge.
Archive Access	Intended for limited usage once data is put in storage. While the storage price is the cheapest, the trade-off is that a user should not access their data for a minimum of 180 days to maintain optimal pricing. Users who decide to procure archive tier storage must also accept the retrieval charges, which can be exorbitant for large data volumes. The archive tier use case is common for compliance data, auditing data, and long-standing backups.

Table 3-7   Storage Tiers

Storage Tiers

Azure blob storage is a three-tier system: hot, cool, and archive. Each tier supports a different stage in the data lifecycle, offering a different price point and appropriate use case where storage should be used. Across all three storage tiers, 99.9 percent availability is guaranteed for the hot and cool tiers. The archive tier does not commit to a 99.9 percent guarantee. Similarly, when it comes to acquiring data from the moment a request is made, the hot tier and cool tier will respond in milliseconds. Because the archive tier data needs to rehydrate (access the data), it takes hours before the first bit of data will transfer from one system to another. Should you choose archive storage, another option to consider is the hydration period. Does your organization want to consider high-priority rehydration, which comes with a premium price tag, or standard rehydration? Table 3-7 illustrates the differences among the three tiers.

To select the appropriate storage account tier for you, there are a number of factors to consider over the long-term horizon: expected storage growth, data access costs, transactional activity, geo-replication data transfer needs, outbound data, and anticipated access tier changes.

An Introduction to Database Resources

All Microsoft Azure database resources are Platform as a Service. There was once a time that Microsoft offered a desktop database (Access) and an enterprise-class database (SQL Server) only. Those days are long gone. Today, Microsoft, through its Azure platform, offers customers a suite of offerings. Azure options include a fully managed relational option, NoSQL, and in-memory database. These options include proprietary and open source alternatives too. Microsoft recognized that its customers' needs vary, as the modern application developer has infrastructure management needs that do not fit a single profile. Scalability, availability, and security needs vary on a case-by-case basis. Table 3-8 compares key features among the different databases you will need to know

Product	Description
Azure SQL Database	Microsoft's modern yet classic enterprise relational database service for the cloud that offers serverless computer options, hyper-scale storage capabilities, and artificial intelligence (AI)–powered and automated features to support performance.
Azure SQL Managed Instances	Microsoft allows an organization to migrate all SQL workloads to Azure while maintaining legacy compatibility. Organizations can enjoy the benefits of a fully managed service while also recognizing the evergreening of Platform as a Service options.
Azure Database for PostgreSQL	A user can build scalable, secure, and fully managed enterprise-ready apps on the open source PostgreSQL database platform. There is the option to scale out using a single-node instance with high performance. Alternatively, a user can migrate a PostgreSQL instance and Oracle-based workloads to Azure.
Azure Database for MySQL	Deliver high availability and elastic scaling to open source mobile and web apps with a managed community MySQL database service, or migrate MySQL workloads to the cloud.
Azure Cosmos DB	The NoSQL option available for Azure, a user can build applications with guaranteed low latency and high availability across multiple geographies. It is possible to migrate Cassandra, MongoDB, and other workloads to the cloud as well using Cosmos DB.

Table 3-8   Select Azure Database Options

for the AZ-900 exam. Databases that will not be discussed directly include SQL Elastic Pools, Virtual Clusters, Elastic Job Agencies, SQL Managed Instances, Data Factories, SQL Server Stretch Databases, and Azure Database Migration Services. While you may see references to Azure Synapse Database (formerly SQL Data Warehouse), you do not need to be familiar with the details in the context of the database, as we will discuss this in a later chapter.

 EXAM TIP   It is not uncommon on the AZ-900 exam to have a series of questions asking to validate the best-fit database given a use-case scenario. Make sure you familiarize yourself with the product level differences, as the exam will present these nuances subtlety.

Azure SQL Database

Azure SQL Database is a PaaS offering. For nearly two decades, Microsoft has been a leader in relational database management technology with its popular enterprise SQL Server product. Now, the product is available for cloud consumption, not just for on-premises consumption. By having Microsoft fully manage the platform, all that a user is responsible for is data itself, not the maintenance of the infrastructure.

SQL Server databases are relational databases, although Microsoft does support non-relational database solutions in Azure. What is the difference? A relational database is one that maintains a structure where data is organized in tables. Each of these tables has a relationship with one another, sharing at least one dependency. Nonrelational databases are document oriented and have no meaningful structure.

Relational Database Design in Azure SQL Server

With relational databases, a schema contains data that always maps to an ID. The ID number may be associated with a name, date, phone number, and e-mail address. Each time a new record is added to a table, there is consistency in that the schema must adhere to a structure. If the format of the data does not comply with the field structure, the schema will not accept the entry. A SQL Server database will often contain many tables related to one another. Using queries, a user can make a request to find a specific piece of data from one or more of those tables by joining related tables together. In Figure 3-25, you see there are two tables: Customer Table and Invoice Table.

Notice that each customer has a unique Customer ID in the Customer Table that is mapped to the Invoice Table. The combination of these two columns is the relationship that binds the two tables together, creating a join. By placing the Customer ID in both tables, a user can query the database and identify information from both tables. Some fields may contain duplicate data, though. That is perfectly OK and to be expected. So long as the unique fields, the Customer ID (also known as the primary key) and the matching key in the Invoice Table (the foreign key), are unique, the system maintains its integrity.

Azure offers three deployment options: Single Database, Elastic Pools, and Managed Instances. Table 3-9 explains the differences between Single Database and Elastic Pools instances. The next section will elaborate on Managed Instances.

 EXAM TIP Watch out for words on the exam. Two words that many test takers take for granted are scalability versus autoscaling. These words are thrown around quite a bit, though they mean something very different in Microsoft Azure. Autoscaling means to scale automatically based on a set standard. Dynamic scalability references manual scalability without any downtime. Single databases are best served by dynamic scalability, whereas elastic pools are better served by autoscaling.

Azure SQL Databases are cloud-native stable versions of the Microsoft SQL Server database engine. When Microsoft releases new features for SQL Server, it will first release

Customer Table

Customer ID	Username	Date	Email
X4581D	Jsmith2	1/1/2021	Jsmi***th@gmail.cm
X4582D	Jesmith3	1/1/2021	Jesm***th1@hotmail.com
X4583D	emsmith1	1/2/2021	Iame***1@smith.com

Invoice Table

ID	Transaction ID	First Name	Last Name	Phone Number	Item ID	Item Description
X4581D	1001	Joe	Smith	212-555-1212	ITM-12S	Azure Book
X4582D	1002	Jen	Smith	212-555-1213	ITM-23X	Pencils, 25/Pk
X4583D	1003	Emma	Smith	646-555-1212	ITM-12S	Azure Book

Figure 3-25 Example Relational Database Table

Database Type	Description
Single Database	Fully managed, isolated instances, which are appropriate when you have modern cloud applications and microservices requiring a robust data source. Single databases are isolated from one another, with guaranteed compute, memory, and storage requirements. The cost to host a database is also significantly greater, since the database is a dedicated resource because this is not a shared resource with another Azure resource. Dynamic scalability is feasible with single database instances, which includes using the SQL Server hyperscale service tier, allowing for fast backup and restore capability.
Elastic Pools	A collection of single databases utilizing shared resources such as CPU and memory capacity, elastic pool utilization can vary based on capacity demand. The key difference between a single database and elastic pool is that one can assign resources by databases in a pool, allowing for maximum cost savings and allocation. When it is necessary to dynamically scale elastic pool resources up and down, a user can easily do so based on necessary capacity and speed at a moment's notice.

Table 3-9 Difference Between Single and Elastic Pool Databases

capabilities for the SQL Database and then for Server, which means you as a user get the latest enhancements without having to deal with any infrastructure overhead across any of your databases.

Not every organization needs to procure a SQL Server database infrastructure at the same size and scale. There are three distinct purchasing models to choose from: vCore, DTU, and serverless. All three options offer fully managed services with built-in high availability, backups, and maintenance operations. However, the way resources are allocated varies.

- The *vCore pricing* allows for users to select the number of vCores (CPU), memory, speed, and storage. Users are also able to select if they want to utilize Azure Hybrid Benefits to recognize costs savings should they decide to procure SQL Server for a long-term commitment. vCore is best suited for extensive workload capacity.

- *DTU pricing* provides users a more affordable approach to the three Azure Service tiers: compute, memory, and I/O resources. Each tier provides a different mix of resources to best fit your technical profile needs. DTU is best suited for scalable database needs.

- *Serverless pricing* is only appropriate under certain conditions. The serverless model will scale compute capability based on workload demand. You are billed only for compute capacity used per second. When the database is not in use and is paused—hence a state of inactivity—you are not charged. However, if any processes are running, even one, you will be charged. Consider the following, though: the serverless compute tier can automatically pause databases during periods when your storage is billed but the database is inactive. That means if the database is inactive but other forms of storage are being used, you will not be charged twice.

You may already notice that determining how pricing and availability for a database service is configured can be quite complex. One last element for Microsoft Azure SQL is service tiers. There are three tiers available that can greatly affect the pricing of your database deployment. The service tiers are

- **General Purpose/Standard**   Intended for common workloads. These are most appropriate for lightweight compute and storage needs where the specific focus is dev/test, not production-sensitive needs.

- **Business Critical/Premium**   Intended for online transactional processing (OLTP) applications with high-volume activities and low-latency input/output (I/O) rates. This service class offers high resilience by utilizing replica isolation.

- **Hyperscale**   Designed exclusively for massive OLTP database processing with autoscaling fluid storage and compute capacity. Hyperscale is not available for managed instances currently.

Azure SQL Database offers many other advanced features, which you are not required to know for this exam, such as extensive monitoring and alerting, availability support, built-in intelligence, automatic performance monitoring and tuning, advanced security and compliance, native threat protection, data encryption, auditing, advanced querying processing tools, and a bevy of integration tools. Should you want to explore further, consider evaluating the course curriculum for the DP-300 exam Administering Relational Databases on Microsoft Azure.

Azure SQL Database Managed Instances

With so many database vendors on the market today, it is not uncommon when an organization decides to move its workload to the cloud that it also requires a migration strategy for its database environments. For those customers that require a straightforward migration from an on-premises or third-party environment to Azure, they can select an Azure SQL Database managed instance. These are database instances that are fully compatible with SQL Server on-premises. Since the objective is to integrate with an isolated VNet, which also has a private IP address, your database server will be able to connect to the Azure VNet without much effort. Minimal configuration is required to lift and shift databases to Azure. As noted earlier, managed instances are only supported at the General Purpose and Business Critical service tiers.

TIP   While Azure SQL Database and SQL Managed Instance share a common code base with the latest version of SQL Server, there are still some differences among the two products that remain significant. As the product evolves, Microsoft lists these changes at https://docs .microsoft.com/en-us/azure/azure-sql/database/features-comparison.

Offering Type	Description
Single Server	The Single Server option is a fully managed database service requiring minimal customization. The server platform can handle patching, backups, high availability, and security management with minimal user configuration. Intended for 99.99 percent availability on a single Availability Zone, this instance type is best suited for cloud-native applications not requiring granular patching schedules or custom MySQL configuration settings.
Flexible Server	Like the Single Server option, Flexible Server is fully managed but provides a more granular experience. This offering provides more control over server configurations and customization settings compared to a Single Server deployment. Flexible Server allows a user to opt for high availability within a single availability and across multiple Availability Zones. That is not the case in a Single Server architecture. Cost optimization controls are built-in with Flexible Server, such as the ability to start and stop an instance, burstable SKU limits, and controls to limit continuous compute workload capacity. If the objectives are for zonal-redundant high availability or managed maintenance windows are necessary, Flexible Server is the better of the two offerings to consider.

Table 3-10   Azure Database for MySQL Offering Types

Azure Database for MySQL

Azure Database for MySQL has adopted the relational database capabilities of the open source MySQL community offerings. Like other database services, Azure Database for MySQL is a PaaS-based offering. There are two Azure Database for MySQL offerings: Single Server or Flexible. The two offering types are described in Table 3-10.

Both are fully managed Database as a Service offerings that can handle mission-critical workloads. Managed databases also offer predictable performance and dynamic scalability with key security and management control differences. Both offerings are currently based on the MySQL Community Edition (available under the GPLv2 License) database engine. Three different versions are available under the current community edition: 5.6, 5.7, and 8.0.

 TIP   Throughout the chapter, you have noticed that all database services are referenced as Platform as a Service. There are exceptions to this rule! When a database such as MySQL Server is part of a managed virtual machine on the Azure Cloud platform, the database is then considered an Infrastructure as a Service offering.

Azure Database for PostgreSQL

Azure Database for PostgreSQL is another Azure relational database PaaS-based option. The open source database system was originally available for those needing database support on Unix or Linux environments. However, given the combination of being able to implement the database using virtualization, as well as the growing open source community, platforms such as macOS, Linux, OpenBSD, and Windows can now take advantage of utilizing the relational database platform. PostgreSQL is an enterprise-class database solution, as it supports complex operations where many users are involved.

The most significant difference between standalone PostgreSQL and Azure Database for PostgreSQL is that Azure Database for PostgreSQL is managed. Azure manages the database for the user without them having to worry about the server, database security, and core administrative tasks. Azure Database for PostgreSQL supports high availability for strong scalability with 99.99 percent SLA support. Consistent with other Azure relational databases, you have the choice of single-zone or zone-redundant high availability to ensure performance optimization and advanced security. Pricing is in line with other relational database solutions in the Azure database portfolio. There are options for Basic, General Purpose, and Memory Optimize options, which means if you add CPU, memory, or storage capacity, your price will increase.

Azure Cosmos DB

Azure offers both relational and nonrelational database options. Azure Cosmos DB is a globally distributed, multimodal nonrelational (NoSQL) data alternative for data management and application development. Users can elastically scale an instance based on throughput and storage across one or more Azure regions worldwide. One of the features that make Azure Cosmos DB stand out is its fast single-digit-millisecond data access performance. The platform works across numerous popular APIs, such as MongoDB and Cassandra. Microsoft's expansive service-level agreement, with a guaranteed 99.999 percent availability for Azure Cosmos DB, ensures an organization that throughput for latency, availability, and consistency affords automatic and instant scalability.

Unlike other database alternatives offered by Microsoft Azure, Cosmos DB supports schema-less data, because a NoSQL database does not require a relational database design. At the same time, you can build a highly responsive, always-available application to manage highly dynamic data that is stored in the database, which can be updated and maintained by one or more users anywhere around the world. Since Cosmos DB is distributed, data storage is possible across one or more regions.

When you deploy Azure Cosmos DB, you will be asked to configure parameters that will determine performance metrics such as speed, development readiness, service-level agreement terms, and your preferred deployment topology. In Table 3-11, specific parameters are identified.

Benefits of Using Azure Cosmos DB

There might be questions on the exam asking you to consider the key differentiators that Cosmos DB offers compared to other Azure database offerings. When it comes to deployment and mission criticality, you should remember the following:

- **Operational Capabilities** Cosmos DB is a nonrelational NoSQL database option that can run its most critical workloads in any Azure region in the world with SLA-backed speed, availability, throughput, and consistency up to 99.999 percent. Should an organization require production-ready business continuity with multimaster replication and enterprise-class security that support global compliance along with end-to-end encryption, Cosmos DB is the best database choice.

- **Analytics**   Cosmos DB offers an enterprise organization near-real-time analytics and AI capabilities for operational data, reducing the time to produce insights. The platform also seamlessly integrates with Azure Synapse Analytics (formerly Azure SQL Datawarehouse).

- **IoT Device and Data Service**   Cosmos DB is the best database solution when you have a diverse, unpredictable workload, such as Internet of Things (IoT) datasets requiring massive data ingest and querying performance. Other reasons to consider Cosmos DB include constant data streaming or data analysis, with the need to have changes in data feeds for real-time data insights delivering high-performance customer experiences, product recommendations, dynamics pricing, and inventory recommendations (i.e., the next best action support). If your organization is looking for a database solution that enables fast data personalization across high volumes of data in milliseconds, supporting low-latency data across multiple data centers around the world (geo-redundancy), then Cosmos DB is your only alternative.

Capability	Description
Speed	Cosmos DB offers burst capability with instant limitless elasticity. The database platform allows for fast reads and multimaster writers across one or more geographies. A user can configure speed parameters in Cosmos DB by enabling geo-redundancy and multiregional writes.
Development opportunities	Cosmos DB offers SDKs for popular languages. There are also APIs for SQL, MongoDB, Cassandra, and Gremlin and non-ETL–based analytics platforms. The configuration can be completed by selecting one of the options under the API menu.
Service-level agreement support	Cosmos DB guarantees business continuity up to 99.999 percent availability and enterprise-level security for those organizations selecting production-ready, provisioned throughput.
Deployment options	Cosmos DB is fully managed. It also offers a cost-effective serverless database option, which can scale instantly to meet an enterprise's application needs. Again, some of the features such as geo-redundancy, production throughput, account type, capacity mode, and location all contribute to the best deployment options for Cosmos DB.
Appropriate for data-rich, analytics-driven applications	Microsoft has built into the Azure Cosmos DB platform the use of Jupyter Notebooks. A user can configure the option for Notebooks on setup by turning it on or off. Notebooks are available for all API- and ETL-based data modeling options listed in Cosmos DB to increase the ability to visualize and interact with large datasets. Developers, data scientists, and analysts can use the industry-standard Jupyter Notebook platform to run interactive queries; explore and analyze data; visualize data; and build, train, and run machine learning/artificial intelligence (ML/AI) models inside Azure.

Table 3-11   Azure Cosmos DB Features

An Introduction to Networking Resources

Azure core networking services offer numerous capabilities that can be utilized independently or concurrently. For the AZ-900 exam, Microsoft core network resources are limited to connectivity services, which consist of connecting Azure resources and on-premises resources to Azure features such as Virtual Network (VNet), VPN Gateway, Peering Services, and ExpressRoute. While there are other services in the Microsoft Azure connectivity catalog, those are not covered on the exam. In later chapters, you will learn about other areas of networking connectivity, such as application protection, application delivery, and network monitoring. Each of these areas play an integral role in securing, managing, and fortifying the IaaS and PaaS backbone for Microsoft Azure.

Azure Virtual Network

Azure Virtual Network, commonly referred to as VNet, is the building block to any private network in Microsoft Azure. A VNet enables many Azure resource types. Whether it is Azure Virtual Machines, which can communicate with one another, creating connections to the Internet, or supporting connections to on-premises networks for hybrid connectivity, VNet mirrors traditional network connectivity, which you would expect to operate in a data center environment. The only difference is that Microsoft handles operational maintenance activities such as scale and availability versus the organization being responsible for these tasks. Table 3-12 explores the different communication options a user has with Azure Virtual Network.

To optimize network traffic, you may want to filter network traffic using specific virtual network options, such as *network security groups* or *network virtual appliances*. With network security groups, your security groups can contain multiple inbound and outbound security rules, allowing you to filter traffic to and from resources. Filtering occurs by source and destination IP address, port, or protocol. On the other hand, network virtual appliances are virtual machines that perform the network function itself, which may include a firewall.

 EXAM TIP   Keep in mind that Azure approaches traffic management in a few different ways, using either route tables or Border Gateway Protocol routes. Both methods allow traffic to be routed between subnets, connections between virtual networks, and support between on-premises networks and the Internet.

VPN Gateways

At some point, you will need to connect your VNet to another network, whether it is in Azure or elsewhere. It could be on-premises or within an Azure cloud instance. Under any condition, you will need to have a mechanism that allows you to connect over the Internet. To ensure your data is secure, you and your organization should establish a virtual private network (VPN) connection.

Communication Approach	Description
Internet	With Internet communication, all resources in a VNet can communicate on an outbound basis. Inbound communication with resources is assigned to a public IP address or through a load balancer. These options are also available for outbound connections.
Through a virtual network	Virtual networks allow for the deployment of Azure resources such as virtual machines, App Service environments. AKS, and virtual machine scale sets.
Through virtual network service endpoints	Should you need to extend the virtual network via a private address space, you can use the identity of your network connecting to any Azure service resource over a direct connection. Service endpoints enable a user to secure critical resources, with an emphasis on storage and database resources, to only an assigned virtual network.
VNet peering	If you can connect virtual networks to one another, you are in effect enabling resources on either side of a virtual network to communicate with one another via VPN peering. The network connection can be in the same or different Azure region.
Point-to-site virtual private network (VPN)	A VPN is a true point-to-site network, which means it establishes a network connection between a virtual network and a single computer. Any computer wanting to establish a connection with a virtual network must configure its own connection. This type of connection is ideal for those looking to make few modifications to their existing network infrastructure, since the connection is sent between your computer and the virtual network using an encrypted tunnel over the Internet.
Site-to-site VPN	A site-to-site VPN establishes a connection between an on-premises VPN device and a single Azure VPN Gateway, deployed to a virtual network. The connection allows for any on-premises resource that supports authorization to connect to a virtual network. Like a point-to-site VPN network, connectivity is encrypted through a tunnel over the Internet.
Azure ExpressRoute	A specific type of connection created by Microsoft Azure, it connects your network to the Azure ExpressRoute partner, a private network connection. Traffic remains private.

Table 3-12   Connectivity Options for Virtual Networks

Fundamentally, a VPN is a network technology that allows connectivity between a private network and a public network. For example, if you have ever connected to resources on your company's private network from your home computer, you have likely used a VPN connection that allows your home network to connect to your company's network.

Taking it one step further, a virtual network gateway consists of two or more virtual machines (VMs) deployed to a specific subnet. You connect the subnet to a gateway subnet. Each time you create a virtual network gateway, your instance will be associated with routing tables and run specific gateway services. By default, you are not able to configure a virtual machine that is part of a virtual network gateway.

You must configure a virtual network gateway to a specific type of virtual network. The gateway type determines how the gateway will be used and what actions will be taken. For example, you may have the type "VPN" for a virtual network. This can be distinguished from an ExpressRoute gateway, which uses a different gateway type.

Creating a virtual network gateway cannot be completed quickly, as it can take up to an hour to complete, depending on the compute resources associated with your instance configuration. Depending on the conditions you establish your virtual network gateway under, gateway virtual machine instances are deployable to a gateway subnet and will be configured with specific settings. Upon initiating the VPN gateway creation process, you will be able to create different tunnel types, including IPsec/IKE between the VPN gateway and another VPN gateway (such as VNET-to-VNET), or create a cross-premises IPsec/IKE VPN tunnel connection between the VPN gateway and your on-premises VPN devices, which are site to site. Other options may include creating a point-to-site VPN connection using Open VPN, IKEv2, or Secure Socket Tunneling Protocol (SSTP), which allows you to connect to a virtual network from any remote location.

Security and encryption are other critical aspects of VPN gateways that should be addressed. A virtual network gateway is used to send encrypted traffic to and from Azure networks and on-premises locations over the public Internet. You can also use a VPN gateway to send your encrypted traffic between Azure virtual networks over the Microsoft network. Each virtual network is limited to a single VPN gateway, although it is possible to create multiple connections to the same VPN gateway. A rule of thumb is that when creating multiple connections to the same VPN gateway, your VPN tunnels will need to share the available gateway bandwidth.

Virtual Network Peering

Another situation you may encounter is when you need to connect virtual networks with one another. Azure virtual network peering does just that. Once connected, the virtual networks appear as one connected network. Traffic between the two virtual machines is routed through Microsoft's network infrastructure using a dedicated IP address. Virtual peering allows for connections across Azure regions, also known as global peering.

There are distinct benefits to using virtual network peering, either in a local or global configuration:

- Peering offers low-latency, high-bandwidth connectivity between resources within different virtual networks.

- You can use resources for one virtual network to communicate with resources in another virtual network.

- You can transfer data between virtual networks across Azure subscriptions, including Azure Active Directory tenants, deployments models, and regions.

- You can peer virtual networks using Azure Resource Manager.

- You can peer a virtual network through Resource Manager to one using a deployment model.

- You should not experience downtime with virtual networks when creating any peering resources, even after peering is created.

When traffic is between peered virtual network resources, it remains private. The traffic between the virtual private network will be kept on the Microsoft backbone network. Therefore, no public Internet gateway or encryption is necessary to communicate for any virtual network.

Configuring a Virtual Peering Network

To configure a virtual peering network, you must have a virtual network established already (Figure 3-26).

You connect two VNets using the virtual network peering options by opening the Virtual Network interface. Then select Peerings (Figure 3-27) on the Azure menu panel. Once you select Peerings, the next page will ask you to click +Add on the right menu panel. Click +Add to add a virtual network peering connection (Figure 3-28).

You will fill in the necessary fields on the virtual network peering interface form on the Add Peering page to configure the VNet between the existing VNet and the new VNet you are about to create. Once all fields are filled in, click OK. You will be taken to a list of all available virtual peering network connections currently established (Figure 3-29).

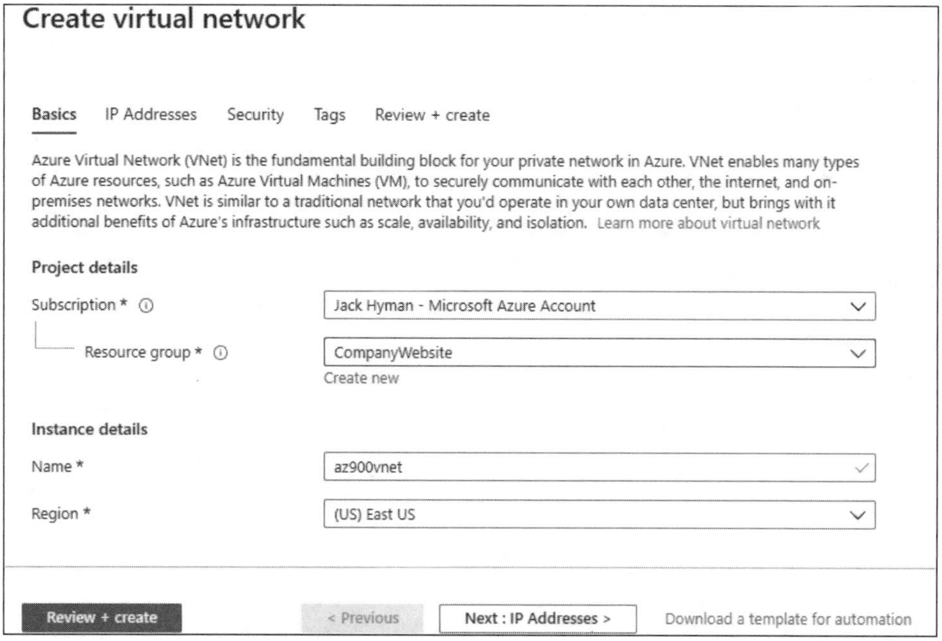

Figure 3-26 Virtual private network setup interface

Figure 3-27
Virtual network
page with
Peerings menu

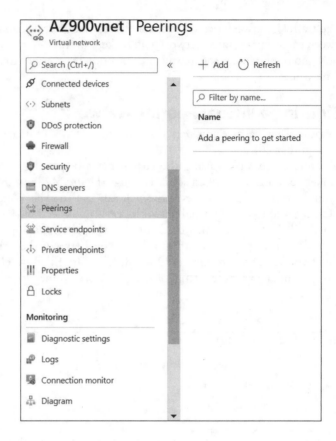

Figure 3-28
Adding a
Peerings menu
option

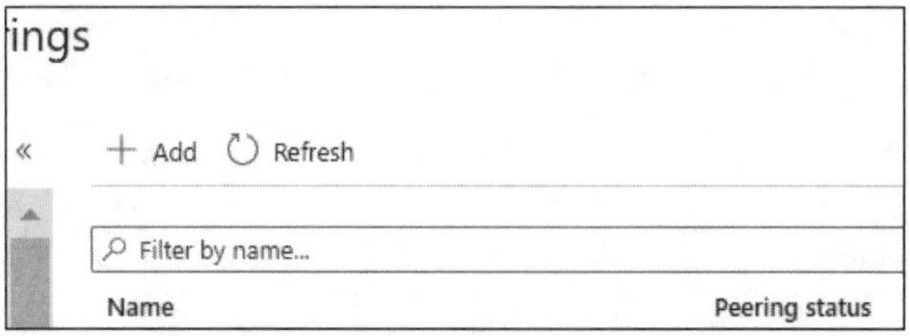

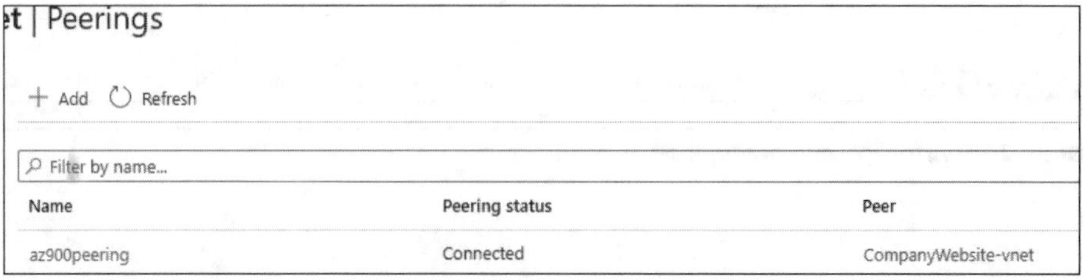

Figure 3-29   Virtual peering networks listing

Azure ExpressRoute

Ever know of an organization to complain about connectivity between their on-premises network to their cloud service provider? This problem is all too common. Microsoft recognized this issue with many of its enterprise clients who maintain a hybrid footprint whereby they needed to extend the network connectivity from an on-premises network into the Microsoft cloud data centers using a private connection. The solution is called *Azure ExpressRoute*. Users can establish connections between Microsoft cloud services such as Azure and Microsoft 365 to the on-premises environments and gain tremendous performance enhancements.

With ExpressRoute, you can connect from any IP VPN network using a connectivity provider via colocation. Since ExpressRoute connections are not bound to the public Internet, they are more reliable, provide more consistent speed, have minimal latency, and provide a greater tendency for hardened security.

Edge connectivity is established between your on-premises network to a Microsoft Enterprise Edge router (MSEE) with ExpressRoute. In most instances, the connection within the organizational data center is also edge-bound within the on-premises data center.

Reasons for Choosing Azure ExpressRoute

VPN users are bound by limited connectivity speeds with Microsoft Azure, as the maximum cap is 1.25 Gbps. For some industries, particularly where real-time data analysis is of the essence, you need more than just a VPN connection. While a VPN gateway can send traffic over the public Internet, performance is unpredictable. Organizations always need assurances for uptime support. Key benefits to consider include

- Layer 3 connectivity between on-premises and Microsoft cloud data centers.
- Connectivity across all regions, including those with a geopolitical focus.
- Global connectivity to Microsoft services across all regions, with additional capacity opportunities using ExpressRoute premium features.
- Dynamic routing to ensure SLA guarantees between your network and Microsoft. Support includes Border Gateway Protocol (BGP).
- Every peering location includes redundancy options for high reliability.

ExpressRoute Direct

A bit different from ExpressRoute is *Azure ExpressRoute Direct* because customers are given the opportunity to connect directly to Microsoft's global network using peering locations. Such locations are distributed worldwide. Users are provided with dual 100-Gbps connectivity, allowing for active-active connections. You would choose

ExpressRoute Direct if you were looking for massive data ingest into services like data-related storage, require physical isolation for cloud services because of regulation (e.g., banking, government, health care, insurance), or must have granular control over circuit distribution within a business.

Of all the differentiators, the most significant between ExpressRoute and ExpressRoute Direct is the options associated with the acquisition and consumption of bandwidth. With both ExpressRoute products, you can purchase circuits ranging from 50 Mbps to 10 Gbps. Connectivity, however, is dependent on what your hosting provider can support. Circuit bandwidth can increase and decrease fluidly without having to re-engineer your network connection. Also, given the unpredictability of data transfer and activity in an organization, Microsoft offers two primary billing models: Unlimited data, where you are charged a monthly fee based on bandwidth. For that scenario, inbound/output data transfer costs are inclusive. A second option is metered data charges. For this use case, while inbound data transfer is free, outbound data charges accumulate per GB. Data rates vary by region.

Azure Marketplace

In Chapter 2, you were briefly introduced to Azure Marketplace. This section covers Marketplace from a compute resource point of view. The Microsoft Azure Marketplace is an online store containing thousands of IT software applications and services that are distributed from third-party cloud service providers and Microsoft. In the Marketplace, there are many free application offerings, while other times, there are offers to find, try, and buy. Regardless of whether the offer is free or requires a paid subscription, you will still need to pay for the underlying infrastructure, which includes the storage capacity to host the service offering found in the Marketplace. The Marketplace offerings are not just limited to SaaS-, IaaS-, and PaaS- based options that are industry and technical area specific; you can also establish consulting relationships with Microsoft Solution Partners.

To provision a service offering from the Azure Marketplace, whether it is free or requires a subscription, you must have an active Azure subscription tied to a payment method. Customers can either pay using their credit card (under the pay-as-you-go plan) or utilize an invoice with an existing Microsoft purchasing agreement.

 TIP   A user can access the Azure Marketplace by going to https://azuremarketplace.microsoft.com/en-us/marketplace/ or via the Azure Portal at https://portal.azure.com and searching for Marketplace.

Figure 3-30 presents you with a list of offerings when a user clicks the Web navigation option Web on the left-hand side. Azure Marketplace breaks down the various product categories for ease of searchability. Users can also use the search option where it says Search The Marketplace to find a product or service offering, should it be available in the Marketplace.

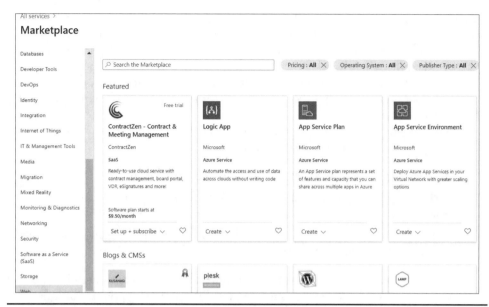

Figure 3-30   Reviewing all results under a category in the Azure Marketplace

Chapter Review

Chapter 3 covers the requisite knowledge to cap off topics pertaining to Azure compute resources. While not every compute capability is covered in the chapter per the Microsoft AZ-900 exam guidelines, the underlying infrastructure and networking specifics are quite robust. The chapter starts with an extended discussion on Azure Virtual Machines, an Infrastructure as a Service offering. Virtual machines (VMs) allow a user to manage the operating system configuration. Should a user need to protect their VM infrastructure, they have the option of utilizing Availability Sets with fault domains or update domains. Fault domains protect a virtual machine from a hardware failure, whereas an update domain provides protection from unexpected reboots. Should you need to expand the capacity of a virtual machine, consider using a scale set to autoscale a virtual machine instance horizontally.

Not every compute solution will require a user to manage the operating system and underlying infrastructure. For those looking to have Microsoft Azure manage the infrastructure on their behalf and simply host a web application, which is a Platform as a Service application, you would use Azure App Service. There are two options for running Azure App Service. You can have Service apps, which run inside an App Service plan. Based on the service plan, a specific number of virtual machines can operate following a set configuration. A second option is the use of containers. Containers allow one to create a virtual machine image of an application. The image would run inside the container as needed, resulting in a significantly lower operational cost compared to a virtual machine instance. When there is a need to manage several virtual machine instances without user intervention, Azure Kubernetes Service makes it easy to host a virtual machine cluster in the cloud. Another PaaS-based infrastructure option that Microsoft expects learners to know about covered in this chapter is Windows Virtual Desktop, which allows users to access all applications, including a complete operating system, using the Internet instead of a desktop from any device.

A common requirement for any infrastructure solution is storage. Azure has a variety of storage types. Key storage types covered include

- **Blob storage**   Ideal for unstructured data, including binary files.
- **Disk storage**   Appropriate if you are looking for a solution that acts as a replacement virtual disk.
- **File storage**   Allows you to have cloud-based storage for files you would likely have on your desktop otherwise.

Of all the storage types covered, the most prominent is blob, as it is heavily leveraged in PaaS applications, which include Frameworks web and mobile applications, microservices, and serverless applications. It can also be used as part of database application storage. There are three tiers of blob storage: hot, cool, and archive. Blob storage tiers are based on how long you intend to store and access the data.

Completing the discussion on storage options is an extensive review of database alternatives. While the exam does not require you to be familiar with every database alternative in the Azure platform, it does focus on key Microsoft, relational open source, and unstructured options. Microsoft has taken its flagship SQL Server product and enabled it for the cloud by creating Azure SQL Database and a managed instance version. Azure also introduced two popular open source database platforms as managed services: Azure Database for MySQL (based on the Community Edition of MySQL database) and Azure Database for PostgreSQL for hosting the PostgreSQL database. Microsoft has also placed significant emphasis on Azure Cosmos DB, its NoSQL database solution for unstructured data. All database solutions, unless hosted within a virtual machine environment, are considered Platform as a Service offerings in Azure.

The latter half of the chapter covers networking resources. The building blocks of Azure networking is Azure Virtual Network (VNet), which allows Azure to communicate with each other and the Internet. Users can add a public IP address to support inbound Internet connectivity, which can be useful if a website runs your VNet and you want users to access it publicly. When users require encrypted connections between Azure Virtual Network connections, be it between one another or on-premises, an Azure VPN gateway should be considered. Furthermore, if a user requires that the distribution of traffic be balanced across multiple virtual machine instances, one should use Azure Load Balancer. To configure two VNet connections to optimize communication, there are several options to consider. There is site-to-site, point-to-site, and VNet-to-VNet connectivity. When you are looking to connect two or more Azure VNets to each other without restricting bandwidth, the best option is to utilize virtual network peering.

A final solution that is unique to those that require high-bandwidth connections to Azure of up to 10 Gbps using a Microsoft Enterprise edge (MSEE) router is ExpressRoute. ExpressRoute offers network connectivity to internal-facing traffic only.

The chapter concludes by reviewing the Azure Marketplace. Marketplace can help you find compute-based templates for creating infrastructure and networking resources. Users can access Marketplace using the Azure Portal or directly the from Azure Marketplace website over the Internet. Some of the templates available in the Marketplace are created by Microsoft, while others are created by third-party solution partners. Regardless of who creates the templates and whether the resource is free or not, all Marketplace resources require a user have an active account to provision any service functionality. As Azure becomes more pervasive and integrates more capabilities, both within the Microsoft suite of products and that of third-party tools, such interfaces and integrations may change.

Questions

1. Review the following scenario and select the most appropriate response.

   A virtual machine, which is a *Platform as a Service* offering, requires end-user maintenance and support for specific operating system features and functions.

   A. Infrastructure as a Service

   B. Platform as a Service

   C. Software as a Service

   D. No correction required

2. Indicate if the following statements are true or false.

	True	False
You must have an active subscription to download items from the Azure Marketplace.	◯	◯
Even if a virtual machine instance from the Azure Marketplace is free, you must still pay for the storage instance.	◯	◯
The only place you can access the Azure Marketplace is from http://azure.portal.com.	◯	◯

   A. True, False, False

   B. False, False, False

   C. True, True, False

   D. False, False, True

3. Indicate if the following statements are true or false.

	True	False
Azure Virtual Gateway connects two Azure virtual networks together.	○	○
Express Route is best suited for customers looking for networking data connecting that supports massive data ingest into services like data-related storage, require physical isolation for cloud services because of regulation.	○	○
An example of a Virtual Network, a Point-to-Site network (VPN) represents a connection between a virtual network and a single computer.	○	○

    A. False, False, True

    B. False, False, False

    C. True, False, False

    D. True, False, True

4. Which of the following is a PaaS-based nonrelational Azure Database offering?

    A. Azure Database for PostgreSQL

    B. Azure Database for MySQL

    C. Azure Cosmos DB

    D. Azure SQL Server Managed Instances

5. When you are looking to implement a development virtual machine instance with excess storage in a particular region at a significantly reduced rate, what would you need to select during the configuration process of your virtual machine instances?

    A. Snapshots

    B. Images

    C. Scale sets

    D. Spot instances

6. You recently received an invoice from Microsoft indicating 720 hours of virtual machine usage. You were surprised, considering you only accessed the virtual machine twice the entire month. To avoid being charged for unnecessary usage, what must you do?

    A. Delete the VM each time you no longer need to use it.

    B. This must be an error. Request a refund.

    C. Stop the virtual machine instance.

    D. Select a different image from the Azure Marketplace.

7. Which of the following describes a virtual machine that can be deployed across multiple update and fault domains to maximize availability, which also ensures resiliency due to data center outages and unplanned maintenance events.

   A. Availability Zone

   B. Scale sets

   C. Virtual networks

   D. Virtual network gateways

8. Which of the following is not a configuration you must identify when setting up an app service plan?

   A. Region

   B. Number of virtual machines

   C. Size of instance

   D. SDK support

9. Which of the following are open source relational database platforms that Microsoft Azure supports as managed service offerings? (Select two.)

   A. Azure Database for PostgreSQL

   B. Azure Cosmos DB

   C. Azure SQL DB

   D. Azure Database for MySQL

10. Your organization requires a managed solution that can support its massive online transactional processing database solution. To ensure optimal performance, your team requires a solution that supports applications with high volume activities and low input/output rates. Autoscaling and fluid storage capacity are desired. Which service tier should you select?

    A. General

    B. Business Critical

    C. Hyperscale

    D. Free

11. Review the following scenario and select the most appropriate response.

    You must store data in storage for three years. Each year, you may need to access the data from *cool storage* from the previous year.

    A. No changes are necessary

    B. Hot storage

    C. Archive storage

    D. Database storage

12. You have a website with light traffic. Which type of disk storage is appropriate?

   A. Ultra Disk

   B. Premium SSD

   C. Standard SSD

   D. Standard HDD

13. There are three types of blobs, also referred to as containers. Which of the following is not one of those types?

   A. File blob

   B. Append blob

   C. Page blob

   D. Block blob

14. What are the differences between virtual machines and Azure Container Instances? (Select two.)

   A. Cost

   B. Resource allocation

   C. Disk type

   D. Operating system

15. You need to deploy an Azure virtual machine running Windows 2019. You need to ensure that the services running on the virtual machine are available if one of the assigned data centers fails. You deploy the virtual machines to two Availability Zones. Does that meet the goal?

   A. Yes

   B. No

Answers

1. **A.** A virtual machine is an Infrastructure as a Service offering. End-user maintenance and system support are required to continue to provide end-user support.

2. **C.** True. To utilize any Microsoft Azure Marketplace offering, even if it is free, you must install and configure the offering on an active account.

   True. Even if a virtual machine provided by a Microsoft Solutions Partner is provided complimentary, you must pay for the underlying storage infrastructure the virtual machine instance runs on.

   False. You can access the Azure Marketplace from the Azure Portal as well as from https://azuremarketplace.microsoft.com.

3. **A.** False. Azure virtual network peering connects two Azure virtual networks together.

   False. ExpressRoute Direct, not ExpressRoute, is best suited for customers looking for networking data connections that support massive data ingest into services like data-related storage and that require physical isolation for cloud services because of regulations.

   True. As a type of virtual network, a point-to-site network (VPN) represents a connection between a virtual network and a single computer.

4. **C.** Azure Cosmos DB is a NoSQL, nonrelational, PaaS-based Azure Database offering.

5. **D.** An Azure spot instance allows you to run a cost-optimized virtual machine in Azure when excess capacity is available in a particular region. Once capacity is no longer available, the instance is deallocated.

6. **C.** You will always pay for storage, as it is an underlying condition for managing a virtual infrastructure. That said, you kept the virtual infrastructure running, hence the excess operational costs.

7. **B.** A scale set is a virtual machine that can be deployed across multiple update and fault domains to maximize availability, which also ensures resiliency due to data center outages and unplanned maintenance events.

8. **D.** Except for SDK support, which is not a legitimate feature, all other choices are prerequisites for configuring an app service plan.

9. **A, D.** Azure Database for PostgreSQL and Azure Database for MySQL are both open source relational databases that Microsoft has enabled as a Platform as a Service offering in Azure.

10. **B.** Although you might expect the answer to be Hyperscale (C), based on the massive OLTP requirement, Hyperscale support does not align with managed instance support at this time. Business Critical/Premium Support does offer OLTP benefits for massive data processing.

11. **C.** Archive is appropriate under these conditions because the storage access will be limited to yearly. This is the cheapest access, given that the user will not access the data for a minimum of 180 days to maintain pricing.

12. **C.** While all storage types can be used for web storage, the most appropriate is Standard SSD. Standard SSD is appropriate for backup, recovery, and noncritical storage and is also useful for web servers, lightly used applications, and web-based applications.

13. **A.** File blob is not an actual file type.

14. **A, B.** By default, disk type and operating systems are two resource types that are allocatable. Therefore, cost and resource allocation are the correct answers.

15. **A.** Yes. There is redundancy from one data center to the next, given system protection, should one data center fail. The use case presented provides ample assurances.

Management Tools and Solutions

In this chapter, you will learn to

- Use Azure management tools to build, deploy, test, and validate cloud resources and project requirements
- Identify best-in-class Azure solutions for IoT, data analytics, AI and machine learning, serverless computing, and DevOps

In the last chapter, you learned about Azure core services. While you need to know these core tenets, there is a bit more that you must be familiar with when managing Azure as a developer or administrator. Azure offers both visual and command line–based management solutions to support the core implementation and operational activities. Additionally, Azure includes robust solutions to extend the cloud building blocks we've already covered by way of advanced solution capabilities such as Internet of Things (IoT), data analytics, artificial intelligence (AI) and machine learning (ML), serverless computing, and DevOps. These areas have several solutions that support automation and ease of operation for you, the cloud professional.

Azure Management Tools

The Microsoft Azure Cloud platform allows the system administrator and developer to manage resources so that they are secure, compliant, and operational using a combination of graphics-oriented and code-based editors. Some of the tools have been around well before Azure was founded in 2010, while others are foundational to the Azure Portal user experience. The selection of Azure management tools you should be aware of is found in Table 4-1.

As you review the next few sections throughout Chapter 4, the Azure platform offers many management tool offerings. The questions you need to ask yourself help determine the best tool for your use case. Consider the following:

- Does your team need to perform one-off management, administrative, or reporting actions? If that is the case, review the sections on Azure PowerShell or Azure CLI.

Azure Management Tool	Description
Azure Portal	Azure Portal is a web-based console that provides a visual user experience to all Azure solutions. The portal is the most common way for interactions with the Azure environment. Users can build, manage, and monitor all features, from simple web apps, subscriptions, billings, and even complex cloud deployments from their web browser. The Azure Portal is designed for resiliency, low access latency, and high availability because it is available in every data center.
Azure PowerShell	An extension of the legacy Windows PowerShell, which includes modules and cmdlets, the Azure PowerShell includes many of the same cmdlets so that a user can perform powerful common tasks on the Azure Cloud. The benefit is that the system administrator or developer can bypass having to go into the Azure Portal directly. PowerShell also supports the use of automated scripting for repetitive tasks to reduce administrative burdens.
Azure Command-Line Interface (CLI)	Azure CLI is a set of commands used to create and manage Azure resources. CLI, which requires a user to install a set of extensions, is available across Azure services.
Azure Cloud Shell	Combining the power of the browser-based experience with many PowerShell features, this tool provides more flexibility than PowerShell since it is machine and OS independent. Users can utilize Cloud Shell in Bash mode or PowerShell mode to complete tasks and activities inside a browser if they desire versus the portal.
Azure Cloud Advisor	Considered a personal cloud consultant across all Azure solution areas, the tool guides five core areas to ensure systems are optimized for cost-effectiveness, performance, high availability, and security. Recommendations are made to be proactive, actionable, and personalized based on your specific subscription and resource groups.
Azure ARM Templates	A JavaScript Object Notation (JSON) file defines the infrastructure and configuration for repeatable use.
Azure Mobile App	System administrators and developers can manage and monitor the health and viability of their Azure environment on-the-go with the Azure mobile app.
Azure Monitor	To ensure maximum operational availability, you can utilize Azure Monitor to ensure optimal uptime availability and performance of applications and services.

Table 4-1   Azure Management Tools

- Are you in the cloud management or administrative role looking to build templates for repeatable business operations? Head over to the section on ARM templates straight away.

- Will your team need a mobile solution once the cloud environment is ready? If you answer yes to that question, read the section on the Azure mobile app.

- Do you and your team need a way to repeatedly stand up one or more resources to ensure all dependencies are consistent? Again, the section on ARM templates is your best bet. You may look to the PowerShell and Azure CLI section to complete these tasks, but only if these are short, automated scripts, assuming validation is not required.

- If you plan on scripting and you or your team intend to use Windows or Linux administrative features, you only have two options: PowerShell or the Azure CLI. You could also use Cloud Shell should you want to complete the actions in-browser.

 EXAM TIP Make sure you understand the various use-case scenarios for management tools, as there are often at least two or three questions on the AZ-900 exam. Like many other IT vendors, Microsoft will use word subtleties to throw off candidates when crafting questions about tools that may appear obvious, but in fact, the question is a trick. An example: Cloud Shell incorporates both Bash and PowerShell using the browser-based experience. That is a true statement. Switching one word around, such as PowerShell and Cloud Shell, would make that inaccurate.

Azure Portal

By this point in the book, we have referenced the Azure Portal often. You already know that to complete any web-based activity, you must go to the URL http://portal.azure .com. You cannot just know that this is the web front end to all Microsoft cloud tools for the exam. You must be aware of what core capabilities are available depending on your level of access.

Azure Portal is the web-based unified console for all features and functions offered under the Microsoft cloud umbrella. Azure allows a user to manage all user subscriptions and cloud capabilities with a web-browser user interface (UI). Every feature that you may have assumed requires a command-line utility that can be completed using Azure Portal, whether it is to build, manage, or monitor resource activity in the cloud.

Azure was built for resiliency and continuous availability, given its global footprint. Each data center provides a consistent configuration in its respective geography to avoid system latency and performance failures. By offering this level of continuity, Microsoft assures virtually no downtime for maintenance operations.

The two most important aspects of the Azure Portal that you need to focus on are the Azure Portal menu and Azure Home page. These are the launchpads to all services, especially those covered in this chapter. As a subscriber to Azure, you will need to decide which page should be your default home page. The Azure Home page integrates all compute resources that are associated with your subscription. It could be App Services, Virtual Images, Key Vaults, or Resource Groups. The list of options is plentiful. To pick which page you would like as your default home, go to the Gears icon on the top right of the Azure Portal page (Figure 4-1). Then, you can select a few options:

- **Sign Out** After a session is idle, how long before a user should be logged out automatically.
- **Choose Your Default View** Home (a predefined view created by Microsoft) or Dashboard (a view customized by you, the end user).

Figure 4-1
Portal Settings
menu

- **Default Mode for Portal Menu** Docked (list of icons on the left-hand side always visible) or Flyout (drop-down menu–based design).
- **Theme and Contrast** Color scheme to help with the visibility of content across the portal user experience.

EXAM TIP For the exam, you should know how to navigate your way around key navigational areas. To accomplish these actions, you must become familiar with the Azure Portal menu (Figure 4-2) and Azure Services Home page (Figure 4-3). You can use the Microsoft-based home page or create your own Azure Dashboard-based home page (Figure 4-4).

You need to be most familiar with the menus, including Security Center, Cost Management And Billing, All Resources, and All Services. Under these four menu options, you gain access to most of the features within the Azure Portal. Other menu options are posted based on usage and known convenience.

Azure PowerShell

If you are familiar with command-line operations and are looking for a tool that supports cloud-based and native environment command operations, consider the use of Azure PowerShell. Leveraging lightweight commands known as *cmdlets,* a user can manage Azure resources from the PowerShell command line. Users may choose PowerShell over other command-line tools available within Azure because of its automation capabilities.

Figure 4-2
Azure Portal
menu

Figure 4-3 Azure Services Home page (selected by default)

Figure 4-4 Customized Azure Dashboard

Azure PowerShell is supported under version 5.1 and higher on Windows and 7.x and above on all other platforms.

 EXAM TIP PowerShell can run on Windows, Linux, or macOS. That said, the PowerShell `az model` uses the .NET standard library for core functionality. It runs on PowerShell version 5.x and higher. Only version 6.x and higher are cross-platform compatible, though.

The Azure PowerShell module requires installation before it is used. To execute the PowerShell client, you must run it locally as an Administrator in Windows or as a Superuser in Linux or macOS. Across all operating systems, you will need to execute a command line using SUDO privileges. To run the module, the command line is:

```
Install-Module -Name AZ -AllowClobber
```

Once an install is initiated, PowerShell verifies if existing modules are in place. The system will verify via command name if there are like-kind module names installed. Should there be modules with the same name, the installation will fail. By including the `-AllowClobber`, PowerShell is being told it has the authority to manage the environment for any commands that exist in place of other modules. Users who are unable to run PowerShell as an Administrator or Superuser can install the module using the following command line:

```
Install-Module -Name Az -AllowClobber -Scope CurrentUser
```

Once the installation is complete, you must log in to your Azure account by running the following command line:

```
Connect-AzAccount
```

Once you run the command line, a token will display in the PowerShell window. You will be asked to go to a device login window and enter a code to authenticate your PowerShell session. Do not close your browser window. Should you close your window, you will need to run the command-line process all over again. The URL that will appear is `http://Microsoft.com/devicelogin`.

Azure PowerShell: In-Depth

There are thousands of web pages, users' manuals, and books on Windows PowerShell and Azure PowerShell. The tool is very robust. For the AZ-900 exam, though, you only need to know that it is an Azure management tool and very elementary concepts. As you may have figured, cmdlets follow a standard naming convention. The convention is verb-noun. The structure is that the verb describes the action, and the noun describes the resource type. So, for example, you might see a verb such as `New`, `Get`, `Set`, or `Remove` and a resource type such as `AzVM`, `AzSqlDatabase`, or `AzKeyVault`. With Azure PowerShell, the noun will always start with `Az`, unlike Windows PowerShell. To learn more about approved verbs and nouns in Azure PowerShell, go to https://docs.microsoft.com/en-us/powershell/module/?view=azps-4.8.0.

 TIP If you are looking to learn more about the Windows PowerShell commands, including all the cmdlet options, you should review https://docs.microsoft.com/en-us/powershell/azure/. Utilizing a command line is not a major emphasis on the exam. You should simply be familiar with the basic command-line structure as well as the difference between Azure PowerShell and Azure CLI.

Azure CLI

There is little difference between Azure CLI and Azure PowerShell. The Azure CLI is also an executable program that a developer or systems administrator can use to execute commands in Bash. Like PowerShell, the command calls the Azure Rest API to perform the management task in Azure. You can run commands independently or combine them into a script. Once implemented into a script, you can execute scripts for setup and maintenance for basic resources or an entire environment. Like PowerShell, you can run CLI on Windows, Linux, or Mac via a web browser using Cloud Shell. The key difference for CLI is that the syntax is a combination of references, commands, and parameters.

TIP If you want to learn more about the Azure CLI reference types and status, go to https://docs.microsoft.com/en-us/cli/azure/reference-types-and-status.

Azure Cloud Shell

If you are looking for an interactive, authenticated, browser-based shell for managing resources in Azure, consider using Cloud Shell. You have the option of working in Bash or PowerShell mode. There are two primary options to access Cloud Shell: Direct Link at https://shell.azure.com or the Azure Portal by selecting the Cloud Shell icon (Figure 4-5).

A user can select either Bash or Power Shell mode. To select which mode you prefer, follow these steps:

1. Click the Cloud Shell button.

2. Select the button that corresponds to the mode preferred: Bash or PowerShell (Figure 4-6).

3. If you decide after you launch you would like to switch, you can go to the drop-down menu on the left-hand side and switch the mode (Figure 4-7).

In this example, you would switch from PowerShell to Bash mode. Since Cloud Shell is managed by Microsoft, you get popular command-line and language tools built into the Azure Portal experience. Users do not need to worry about secure authentication, as Cloud Shell provides instant secure authentication to resources through the Azure CLI and PowerShell cmdlets.

Figure 4-5
Selecting Cloud Shell in Azure Portal

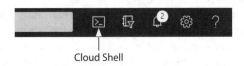

Cloud Shell

Figure 4-6
Select Bash or PowerShell.

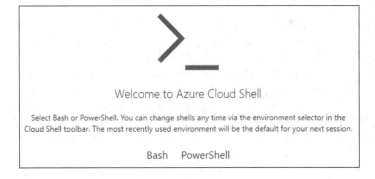

Welcome to Azure Cloud Shell

Select Bash or PowerShell. You can change shells any time via the environment selector in the Cloud Shell toolbar. The most recently used environment will be the default for your next session.

Bash   PowerShell

Figure 4-7
Select an
alternative
option in Azure
Cloud Shell.

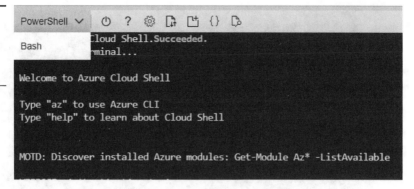

TIP The first time you use Azure Cloud Shell, you will be asked to create an Azure Storage Account. Any installations and settings established using Cloud Shell across any device will be stored using Azure Storage. You want to make sure that you select the appropriate account and resource group for the storage account during the initial execution of Cloud Shell.

Many of the commands that are available in Azure CLI are also accessible from Cloud Shell. If you are using PowerShell, you can call commands from the `az PowerShell` module. The navigation bar in Cloud Shell is limited to just going back and forth between Bash and PowerShell mode. You can reset power, seek help, adjust settings, and upload and download files to Cloud Shell using a graphical interface (Figures 4-8 and 4-9).

The next button in the list allows a user to open a new session. In this case, you will be asked to log in to the Azure Portal again.

Next to the Open New Session button, you will find a button that has two brackets. This button opens the Monaco Editor, a visual-oriented code editor. Based on the Visual Studio native .NET editor, the Monaco editor is built into the Cloud Shell as a

Figure 4-8
Cloud Shell
navigation

Figure 4-9
File menu for
Cloud Shell

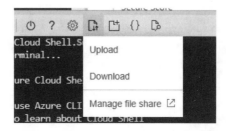

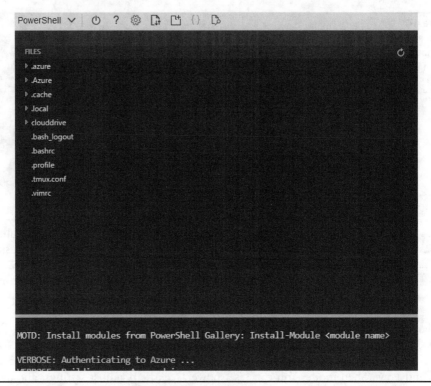

Figure 4-10   Monaco Editor and Web Preview button

lightweight equivalent. The very last button on the toolbar is the Web Preview button, allowing developers to preview custom applications they develop using Cloud Shell (Figure 4-10).

Azure Mobile App

While a cloud administrator cannot fully manage all cloud resources via their mobile device, Microsoft has created an app specific for Azure to accomplish four core tasks:

- Monitor the health and status of Azure resources
- Diagnose and fix issues using the Azure Portal or one of the command-line interfaces
- Run command-line operations to manage Azure-specific resources
- Manage security and encryption anytime, anywhere

Figure 4-11
Azure Mobile
account

Instead of managing resources such as a virtual machine or a web app from a desktop, users can manage these cloud resources from their smartphones or tablets. When a cloud administrator is alerted to system issues, they can check those alerts, view metrics, and take actions to fix common issues using Azure's guided wizards. More complex corrective measures, though, will still require a desktop. If a cloud administrator needs to start a virtual machine instance or web app or even connect to a virtual hard disk, all these activities can be accomplished directly from the mobile app. Example activities are presented in Figures 4-11 and 4-12.

Should a user prefer to run a command-line interface, the app offers the Azure CLI or PowerShell command available in the app. The Azure mobile app is available on both the Apple iOS and Google Android OS.

Azure Advisor

Managing cloud compute resources is not easy, especially when you have no control over some of the operating environment controls. That is why Microsoft created Azure Advisor, an automated cloud consultant to help resolve common deployment issues and provide

Figure 4-12
Azure Mobile
monitoring

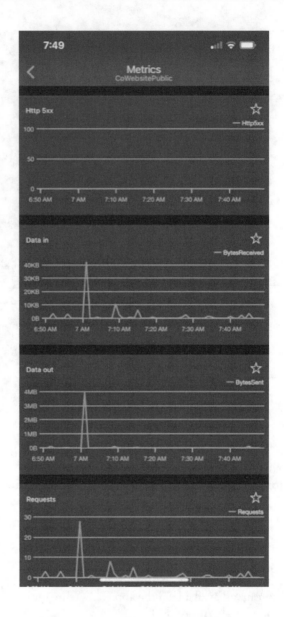

best practice guidance across all Azure deployments. You can analyze resource configurations and usage metrics. Based on the current environmental conditions, Advisor makes recommendations to improve the performance, reliability, security, cost management, and efficiency of Azure resources. To access Advisor, go to the Azure Portal.

1. Locate Advisor on the Navigation menu or search for Advisor in the search bar.

2. Selecting Advisor will open a dashboard that looks like Figure 4-13.

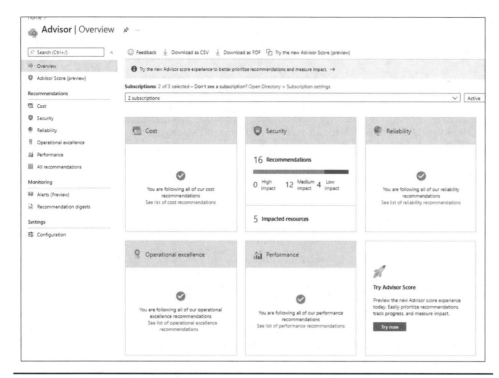

Figure 4-13   Azure Advisor dashboard

Azure Advisor dashboards display personalized recommendations for one or more subscriptions. You can apply filters to display recommendations for specific subscriptions and resource types too. The recommendations are divided into five categories:

- **Reliability**   Also known as high availability, this monitors the state of mission-critical applications running in Azure.
- **Security**   Helps detect threats and vulnerabilities leading to potential security breaches across resources.
- **Performance**   Guides how to improve the speed of resources within the environment.
- **Cost**   Guides current spend, forecasted spend, and ways to reduce spend.
- **Operational Excellence**   Ensures that process and workflow efficiency, as well as resource deployment best practices, are followed.

You can click any of the tiles to see a more detailed review of issues reported. In this case, immediately after installing a web app and virtual machine, 16 security issues require resolution. Figure 4-14 provides a snapshot of a few of those issues that you might find related to security. Furthermore, Figure 4-15 shows that when you click on one of the links listed as a recommendation, a detailed recommendation list is generated.

Figure 4-14   Detailed review of security issues in Azure Advisor

In this example, the recommendation is to update the PHP version of a web app created under the "Jack Hyman - Microsoft Azure Account" subscription, reflecting a medium-level security concern.

Not every recommendation needs to be acted upon. As the cloud administrator, you can postpone, exempt, or act on Azure Advisor's recommendations. If you choose to postpone a recommendation, you can do so for anywhere from a day to three months presently. Should you have recommendations to review, there is a way to complete an audit offline by downloading all CSV file issues.

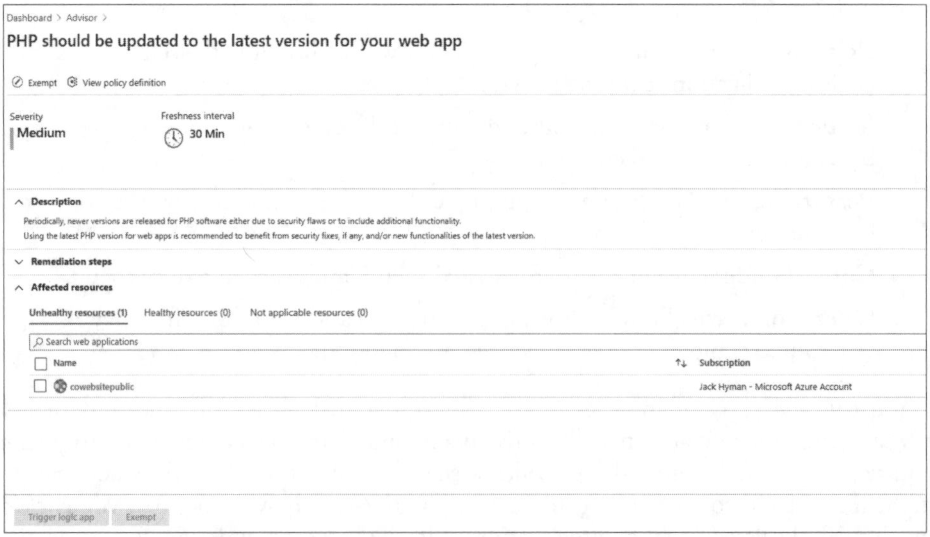

Figure 4-15   Specific issue detail page on single security issue in Azure Advisor

Azure Resource Manager Templates

Azure Resource Manager (ARM) was covered in Chapter 2 to distribute Azure resources efficiently. With so many organizations migrating to the cloud, there is a desire to find agile development approaches. Teams often look for deployment solutions that can support repeatability in their infrastructure, unifying operational processes. One method that organizations utilize to automate this process is to automate deployments. You define the infrastructure that requires deployment as part of the code defined in the project. Like application code, you store the infrastructure code in an Azure source repository. Version control would be instituted. Any team member can access the code as necessary if given permission.

These reusable templates are called ARM templates. ARM templates, a JSON file, are intended to define the infrastructure of a project environment. Templates leverage a declarative syntax. As part of the template, you state what needs to be included in the deployment while avoiding programmatic code to create repeated deployments many times. The templates do not require the ordering of operations, since the Resource Manager orchestrates the deployment of interdependent resources in the appropriate order. Resource Manager also supports parallel deployments to complete a deployment far faster than a serial output with ARM templates.

ARM template files can be broken up into smaller components, thereby creating reusable components. These template files can be linked together at deployment time. Files can also be nested inside other templates.

Testing Validation, Compliance, and Deployment Methods

On the AZ-900 exam, you may find questions regarding testing and validating ARM templates. As you review, remember these key points:

- ARM templates support the use of both PowerShell and Bash scripts.

- To test, you want to make sure you follow recommended guidelines by utilizing the ARM template tool kit (arm-ttk), a PowerShell script downloadable from GitHub.

- Before deploying, your templates should be evaluated utilizing what-if operations, which constitutes a preview change.

- Any time a template is deployed, it will require passing built-in validation. Only after a template fully passes validation will an ARM template be deployed.

- ARM templates support the use of Azure Policy, a code framework to automate governance. If you intend to use Azure Policy, remember that policy remediation is completed on noncompliant resources if you deploy using templates.

(continued)

- You can take advantage of Deployment Blueprints to meet ARM template regulatory and compliance standards. These templates are pre-built for various architecture conditions.

- If continuous deployment and continuous integration (CI/CD) tools are an integral part of your business, consider integrating ARM templates in your practice. ARM templates can help automate release pipelines for application and infrastructure needs, including updates.

- Combining Azure DevOps and ARM template capabilities, it is possible to quickly scale in conjunction with Azure Pipelines projects.

Azure Monitor

Azure Monitor collects metrics based on conditions that you determine across Azure resources and services in a single interface. Alerts are not bound to the Azure Portal, either. Notifications can be sent to a device or a specified channel, assuming an address is defined. To access Azure Monitor, follow these steps:

1. Go to the Navigation menu and click the navigation monitor, a single blade in the Portal Navigation (Figure 4-16).

2. If this is your first time using Azure Monitor, you must configure the environment to support your metric series and scope of choice. In this case, we will be configuring a resource under the CorporateWebsite Resource Group, which can be found under the Subscription - Jack Hyman Microsoft Azure account.

Figure 4-16
Azure Monitor
blade

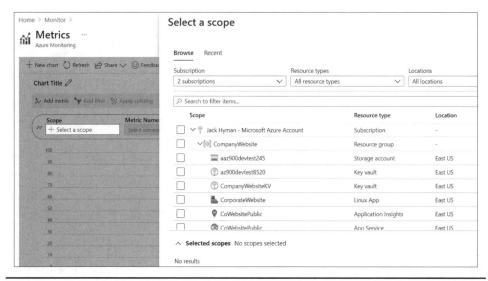

Figure 4-17 Select resources to monitor in Azure Monitor.

Once you select a resource, you are presented with a list of metrics related to that resource (Figure 4-17), from which you can select given items you have already created in your Azure environment. To create a chart-based metric, you will notice that the only item that needs to be modified is the Metric selection. In this case, you will notice the selection of CPU Percentage (Figure 4-18).

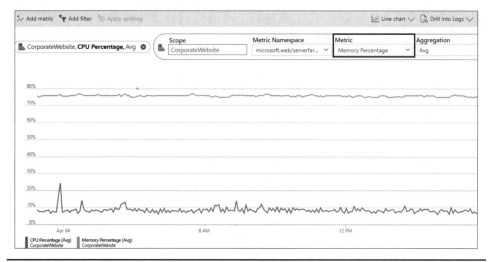

Figure 4-18 Metric menu drop-down in Azure Monitor

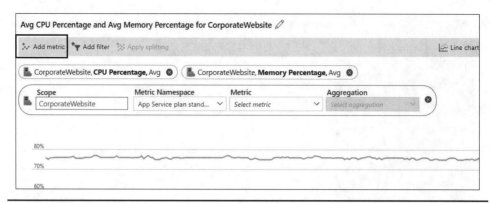

Figure 4-19   Azure Monitor output on CPU Percentage and the Add Metric button

Once you select CPU Percentage, the chart update will appear. Should you want to add more metrics, repeat the steps by selecting the Add Metric button, shown in Figure 4-19. You can see the button to click in the newly created chart.

TIP   When creating metrics, add like-kind metric measures. For example, if you are going to measure CPU Percentage, a complementary measure is Memory Percentage. What is the common measure? Percentage! Common units of measure will appear together on a chart. Otherwise, you will not be able to view aggregate results on a chart. Figure 4-20 shows an example of two measures appearing on the same chart with a like-kind unit of measure.

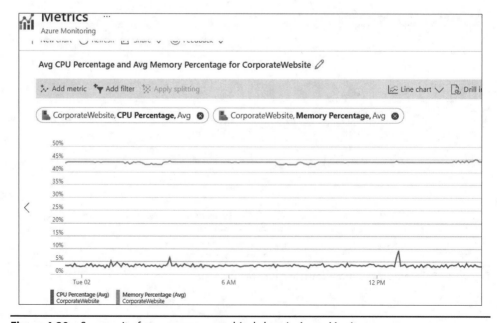

Figure 4-20   Same unit of measure on a graphical chart in Azure Monitor

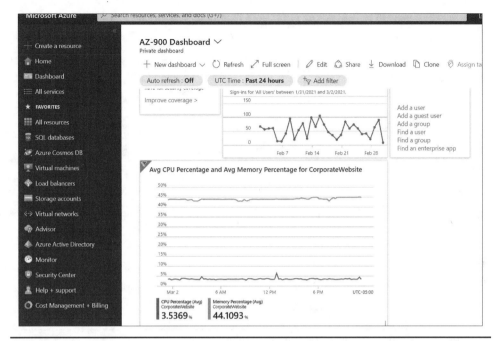

Figure 4-21   Metric created in Azure Monitor found on the Azure Portal dashboard

If you find that you have built a strong metric candidate, select the Pin To Dashboard button on the right side of the screen. You will be asked if you want to keep the metric as a private candidate (for yourself) or share it with all members of your team. In this example, you will keep it private. The metric should be posted to the AZ-900 dashboard created under Azure Portal in this chapter. Click Pin. The result appears on the AZ-900 dashboard, as seen in Figure 4-21.

Creating graphical alerts is not a system administrator's or organization's only option to monitor performance. Azure Monitor Alerts can also be configured to alert you of critical events or even performance events in the environment that breach specific thresholds. These event notifications can be sent using numerous communication channels, including e-mail or SMS text messages. You could even set up an Azure Function or Logic App. Like graphic-based metrics, you must create rulesets. If the rule is met, an alert performs an action. There are two ways to create a ruleset: from one of the graphics-based charts or from scratch by clicking New Alert Rule (Figure 4-22).

Upon clicking New Alert Rule, you will be prompted to select a resource (Figure 4-23).

Figure 4-22
Creating a
new rule alert

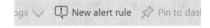

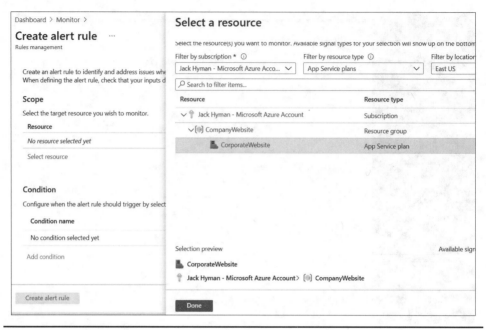

Figure 4-23   Selecting a resource for a new alert rule

Then, you will need to set the condition for the alert. Click the link Add Condition. Select the signal requirements. Again, you see the condition set is CPU. Additional conditions are set as seen in Figure 4-24, based on dynamic activities occurring every hour and the number of violations. In this instance, four violations (not seen) trigger an action. Specific conditions that can be set for this example include the operator, aggregation type, threshold, dimension logic, frequency, and violation triggers. Depending on the parameter, configurations vary.

Azure Service Health

Ensuring your resources are healthy is an important part of business, especially when an outage has the potential to affect operational availability. Azure offers a suite of tools to help you maintain the health of cloud resources, which are a combination of incremental services: Azure Status, Service Health, and Resource Health. To access Azure Service Health, go to the All Services Menu and select All. Then find the option under General titled Azure Service Health (Figure 4-25).

Azure Status is responsible for keeping users abreast of service outages in Azure through the Azure Status page (Figure 4-26). The page is a global map of the health of all Azure services across every Azure region. When looking to find out if there is an outage anywhere globally, this is the best place to start for incident and maintenance management.

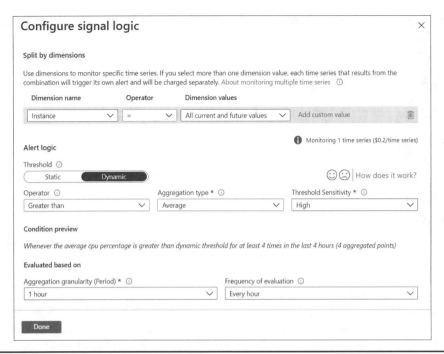

Figure 4-24 Configuring an Azure Monitor Alert

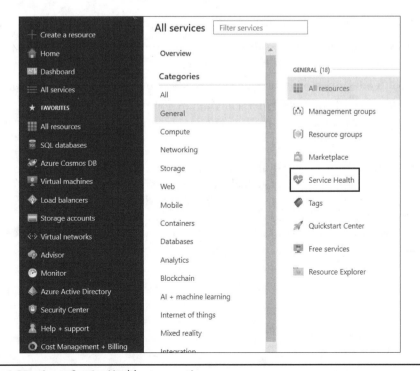

Figure 4-25 Azure Service Health menu option

Figure 4-26   Azure Status page under Azure Service Health

Service Health provides a personalized view of the Azure services across regions that are currently in use. Unlike Status, an overview of global resources, the Services page is specific to the regions and resources you are utilizing. Events can be tracked up to 90 days (3 months). Four metrics are evaluated: service issues, planned maintenance, health advisories, and security advisories. Figure 4-27 offers you a preview of a health advisory. Specific capabilities for the four metrics include

- **Service issues**   Issues with Azure that should be addressed immediately.
- **Planned maintenance**   Maintenance notifications provided by Microsoft that can affect the system availability of services.
- **Health advisories**   Changes in services and resource states requiring your attention. Examples include upgrades, depreciation, and migrations.
- **Security advisories**   Notifications tied to resource violations or security alerts on system availability of Azure resources.

Resource Health offers an administrator a review of specific health data on cloud resources such as app services or virtual machine instances (see Figure 4-27). Resource Health, which can be used with Azure Monitor notifications, helps you realize the state of your resources in intervals as small as a minute. You can quickly assess if there are issues caused by the Azure platform or configurations directly tied to an administrative error.

Figure 4-27 Example of Resource Health

Azure IoT Solutions Overview

The IoT is a system of interrelated, Internet-connected devices that collect data over networks, usually wireless, without any human interaction. The data collected from these networks is often across edge and cloud platforms where devices connect, monitor, and collect relevant pieces of data from billions of assets. This data can be from any security solution, operating system, mobile device, sensor, or standalone data and analytics system to help businesses build, deploy, and manage applications. When discussing Azure IoT, consider how these services work together across three components: things, inputs, and actions. To make these things, inputs, and actions work in harmony, numerous solutions help facilitate operations. For the AZ-900 exam, you will need to know about three IoT solutions: Azure IoT Hub, Azure IoT Central, and Azure Sphere.

Azure IoT Hub

The Azure IoT Hub is a managed service hosted in Azure Cloud. The service supports bidirectional communication. You can virtually connect to any device using the IoT Hub. This is possible because there is a reliable and secure communication connection between the environment, the IoT devices, and the back end of the cloud-hosted solution. Messaging patterns supported include device-to-cloud telemetry, file upload from devices, and request-reply methods to control your devices from the cloud.

IoT Hub monitoring can help you maintain the health of your solution by tracking events such as device creation, device failure, and the connection of your device. When you are building out applications that must scale using IoT Hub, consider the purpose of the application and the application patterns of the industry. Use cases associated with IoT Hub include industrial manufacturing equipment, health care monitoring, or infrastructure asset checking.

IoT Hub can scale to millions of devices. When it comes to configuring and pricing IoT Hub, you need to address several factors, such as the number of events per device and your solution scale. These two factors translate into the tier of IoT Hub that you will utilize and the product pricing. The two tiers are basic and standard:

- **Basic Tier** Appropriate for collecting data for devices and analyzing it centrally.
- **Standard Tier** Appropriate for remote device configuration or distributed configuration built-in workloads.

The first measurement that one must evaluate when considering tier and pricing is data throughput. This measure can vary daily. The traffic on a per unit basis changes. There is device-to-cloud messaging, cloud-to-device messaging, and identity registry operations. As seen in Table 4-2, the sustained throughput and send rate vary based on the IoT Hub's tier edition.

Scaling your solution is an important factor to consider as you plan an IoT Hub implementation as well. The Basic tier solutions typically support unidirectional communication from devices to the cloud. In contrast, the Standard tier supports bidirectional communication capabilities, which means a broader range of features, including security and communication capabilities offerings, as seen in Table 4-3. Of note, an IoT Hub can only support one data throughput edition within a tier at a time. You can, however, mix several of the same data throughput editions within the same tier for many devices in each IoT Hub. As an example, you can have many S2 units within a Basic tier, but not S2 and S3.

IoT Hub offers a free edition for testing and development purposes only. It offers all the features of the Standard tier with a very limited allocation of messaging. A complete listing of the feature is provided in Table 4-4. As you can see, the key difference in pricing is how messages are transmitted per day and the size of the messages transmitted with the two tiers. You can upgrade from the Basic tier to the Standard tier without interrupting your existing operations at any time.

Tier Edition	Sustained Throughput	Sustained Send Rate
B1, S1	Up to 1,111KB/minute per unit (1.5GB/day/unit)	Average of 278 messages/minute per unit (400,000 messages/day per unit)
B2, S2	Up to 16MB/minute per unit (22.8GB/day/unit)	Average of 4,167 messages/minute per unit (6 million messages/day per unit)
B3, S3	Up to 814MB/minute per unit (1,144.4GB/day/unit)	Average of 208,333 messages/minute per unit (300 million messages/day per unit)

Table 4-2 Data Throughput Editions for IoT Hub

Capability	Basic Tier	Free/Standard Tier
Device-to-cloud telemetry	Yes	Yes
Per-device identity	Yes	Yes
Message routing	Yes	Yes
Message enrichment	Yes	Yes
Event grid	Yes	Yes
HTTP, AMQP, and MQTT protocols	Yes	Yes
Device provisioning service	Yes	Yes
Monitoring and diagnostics	Yes	Yes
Cloud-to-device messaging		Yes
Device twins		Yes
Module twins		Yes
Device management		Yes
Device-based streaming		Yes
Azure IoT Edge		Yes
IoT Plug and Play		Yes

Table 4-3   Comparison of Features in IoT Hub

Tier/Edition	Price Per IoT Hub Unit (Per Month)	Total # of Messages/ Day Per IoT Hub Unit	Message Meter Size
Basic Tier/B1	$10	400,000	4KB
Basic Tier/B2	$50	6,000,000	4KB
Basic Tier/B3	$500	300,000,000	4KB
Standard Tier/Free	Free	8,000	0.5KB
Standard Tier/S1	$25	400,000	4KB
Standard Tier/S2	$250	6,000,000	4KB
Standard Tier/S3	$2500	300,000,000	4KB

Table 4-4   Tier/Edition Pricing for IoT Hub

To configure an IoT Hub, follow these steps:

1. Go to the All Services Blade, then All, then Internet Of Things Blade.

2. Select IoT Hub (Figure 4-28).

3. Once the next screen loads, you will be asked to create a new IoT Hub. Upon filling in all the necessary fields on the Create New IoT Hub form (Figure 4-29), select the Management tab on the navigation area on the top of the form.

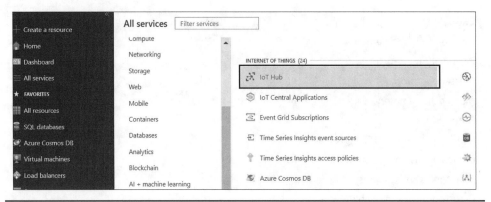

Figure 4-28 IoT Hub services navigation

4. You will want to pick the appropriate messaging tier to manage your messaging units and pricing based on your needed configuration (Figure 4-30). This menu determines your tier and edition requirements, as discussed earlier in this section.

5. If you are satisfied with your selection, move on to the Review + Create tab.

6. Click Create.

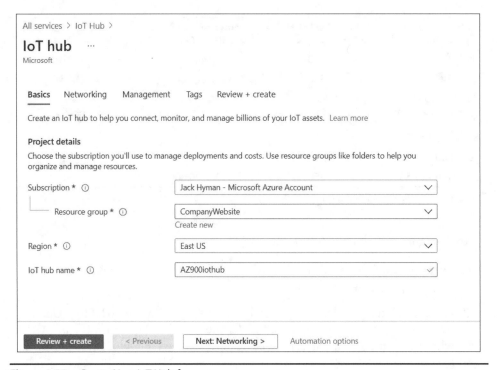

Figure 4-29 Create New IoT Hub form

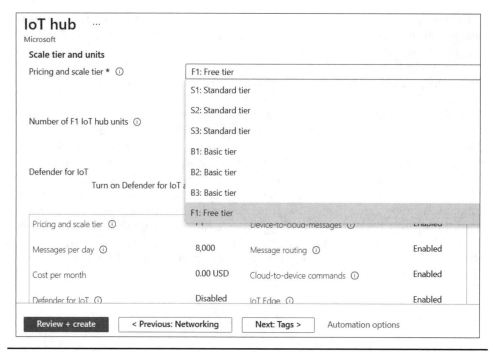

Figure 4-30　Messaging pricing and scale tier menu

7. Your IoT Hub deployment will be provisioned.

8. Upon being provisioned, you will add a new IoT device (Figure 4-31).

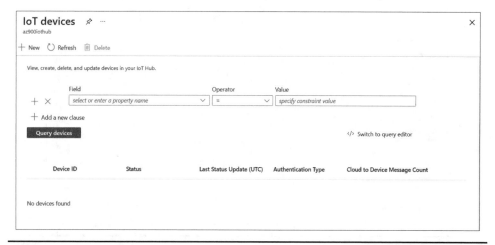

Figure 4-31　Add a New IoT device.

Each time you want to create a new device, you must know a few different parameters such as your device ID name, the authentication type, key parameters, and if you want to autogenerate keys to connect to IoT Hub. You must also decide if you prefer to connect the device to an IoT Hub. The authentication type dictates the requirements of the key parameters. Figure 4-32 demonstrates all the parameter options required to create a new device.

During the configuration, you'll notice that the Symmetric Key option requires a valid base-64 format with a key length between 16 and 64 bytes, whereas the X.509 Self Signed and CA options have specific certificate attribute requirements. The Symmetric Key requirements must be shared with the primary and secondary keys. On the other hand, an X.509 Self Signed option requires thumbprint authentication. Only the X.509 CA Signed option automatically connects a device to the IoT Hub without requiring a thumbprint or key credentialing. All three authentication type/key pair models require matching a parent device before creating a device can fully commit to a save. Once you save a configuration for one device, you can repeat this process for as many devices as necessary in the IoT Hub to communicate unidirectionally or bidirectionally between Azure and the IoT source.

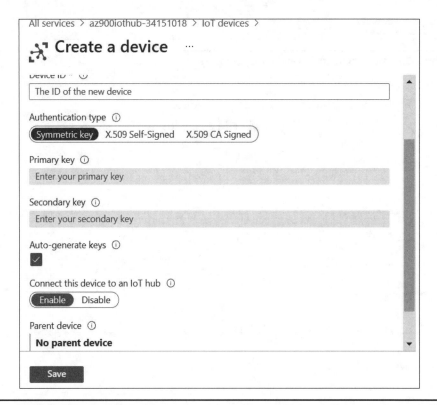

Figure 4-32 Device creation parameters

Azure IoT Central

In the last section, you learned how to create, manage, and deploy devices to support message-based communications using IoT Hub. To configure a device with IoT Hub requires a series of configurations, which may seem complex. When you are looking to monitor and collect data on all your IoT devices without configuring the IoT devices, you will want to use Azure IoT Central. Azure IoT Central helps reduce the burden and cost of all your lifecycle activities, such as developing, managing, and maintaining enterprise-grade IoT solutions. Instead, you can focus on data transformation exclusively. IoT Central and its centralized web UI enable users to monitor devices, create rules, and manage devices throughout the lifecycle. You can also act on the insights provided by IoT intelligence by responding to line-of-business application needs.

IoT Central has four personas. A persona is a user of the application environment. IoT Central is considered a SaaS-based solution compared to other Azure solutions, as you can plug-and-play your devices into the web experience to build a rapid, deployable connected device. The four personas are

- **Solution Builder**   Responsible for creating applications, configuring rules and actions, defining integrations with other services, and customizing the application for operations and device developers.

- **Operator**   Responsible for managing the devices connected to one or more applications

- **Administrator**   Responsible for administrating any task, including managing user roles and the permissions within the application.

- **Developer**   Responsible for creating the code that runs on the device or IoT Edge module connected to your applications.

Configuring an IoT Central Application Environment

Each time you want to set up a new device template, you must set up a new dedicated IoT Central application environment. Since each device template is intended for a new business use case, it is best to isolate each use case as a standalone instance. To set up a new instance, follow these steps:

1. Go to All Services, then All, then IoT Central Applications (Figure 4-33).

2. Select the link IoT Central Applications.

3. Click the New button.

4. Upon clicking the New button, a Create New IoT Application form appears (Figure 4-34).

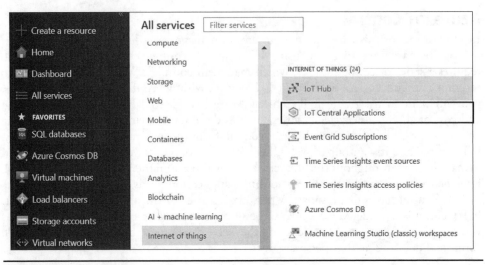

Figure 4-33 IoT Central Applications

5. You are asked to provide the following:

- **Resource Name**   Requires the name of the IoT application.
- **Application URL**   Enter address for the IoT Central application prefix.
- **Subscription**   Select where charges will be billed at the global level.

Figure 4-34
Create a new
IoT Central
application.

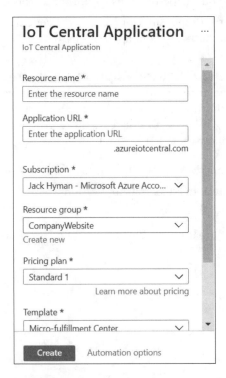

- **Resource Group** Select where all charges are billed at a project level.
- **Pricing Plan** Select a pricing tier based on need.
- **Template** Select a template type from the list.
- **Location** Defined based on configuration options selected in the previous options.

Once you have filled out all the necessary fields, click Create.

6. A new device template is created.

7. Click the URL on the following page once the resource is provisioned successfully.

Creating an IoT Central Application

IoT Central allows you to create custom, cloud-hosted IoT solutions for your organization. A typical solution will consist of an application that receives telemetry from a device, enabling you to manage the devices, or you can manage those devices running the custom code connected to the cloud-based application. Microsoft has created pre-built industry-focused templates for industries such as energy, health care, government, and retail. You also have the option to create your device template using web-based tools. When configuring your templates, you can set options such as business, device, and command properties. An example of what can be accomplished in both scenarios is seen in Figure 4-35 (pre-built) and Figure 4-36 (new template). The pre-built application template represents a configurable continuous monitoring health care environment, whereas the new device template allows a user to create a configurable device template. Available pre-built templates are listed in Figure 4-37.

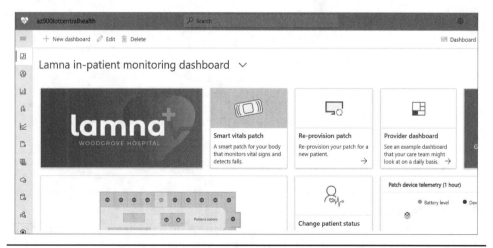

Figure 4-35 Creating an IoT application using existing device templates for health care

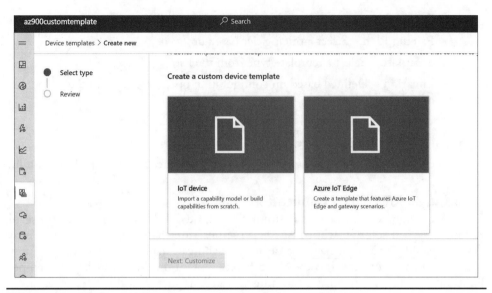

Figure 4-36   Creating an IoT application using new device templates

Figure 4-37
List of pre-built
IoT Central
templates

Manage Devices

In IoT Central, once a device is configured to work with a given template, you should monitor the device, assuming it is connected to an application. IoT Central allows for the provisioning of new devices, as well as the troubleshooting and remediation of issues. You can complete all these actions by defining custom rules and actions using data streams from the connected devices. The IoT Central operator can enable or disable the rules to the device at any time. It can even add further automation should it be required.

As new devices come online or perhaps devices are deprecated, scaling the environment becomes an important part of maintaining the environment. You can't just assume self-management is enough when you connect devices in the cloud, though. Some level of administration and structure is required. Devices and the environment they are managed in must also remain connected, healthy, and compliant at all times for IoT Central to report the status of the devices properly.

Dashboards

Dashboards offer a personalized user experience to monitor device health and telemetry. You can start with pre-built application templates or create your own based on the persona requirements, which are often tailored specifically to the operator's needs as the first line of defense. Dashboards can be shared or kept private, much like those deployed for the general Azure Portal experience.

Rules, Actions, and Jobs

Custom rules based on the device state and telemetry help identify problematic areas. You can configure specific actions that require notifying those devices and data sources that require corrective measures. Jobs allow you to update devices by setting properties or calling commands independently or in bulk. Most of what operators and administrators do as part of managing applications falls under these responsibilities.

Third-Party Integration

Since IoT Central is a SaaS-based platform, you can transform IoT data into business intelligence insights. Those quantifiable insights can be used as data analytics outcomes. Three outputs often produced from third-party sources include rules, data export, and public REST APIs.

Azure Sphere

Being connected to the Internet at any time has its advantages and disadvantages. For example, if you ever wanted to check in on your pets using that web camera inside your home, there is surely an advantage to being connected using an IoT device. On the flip side, there are those with ill intentions who are looking to gain access to your device no matter how secure it might be. An Internet security breach is like someone bypassing the door lock at the front door of your home.

Like every other device, IoT devices have the application software and a micro-operating system. The only difference is that the programs are focused and tightly integrated on the chipset. These programs have a specific purpose. All programs are susceptible to viruses and can be compromised. Given that there is little standardization across the IoT industry for how applications operate, even though they are all stored on an embedded chip, Microsoft realized a major business and security vulnerability to IoT-based applications.

Azure Sphere fills in the business void by providing a highly secure application platform for Internet-connected devices. The platform is composed of securely connected crossover microcontroller units, also referred to as MCUs. The platform is built on top of a custom

Linux-based operating system and a cloud-based security posture specifically designed for continuous, renewal security that is consumable for mobility-based devices exclusively.

The Sphere Security Service ensures that MCUs are secured. Whenever there is an OS update, all applications that run on the MCUs are updated, assuming they are properly connected to a live network connection. Since all IoT devices are network-enabled, any time a security update must be rolled out to a user, it is done automatically. So long as the network infrastructure is secure, as is the network communication bridge between devices, the environment will always be up to date with the most current operating system and security configurations offered by Microsoft.

Data Analytics Solutions

Data aggregation is difficult, especially when you have many systems that may not talk to one another. There is no denying that big data has created new business challenges. Not all data systems can easily pass data to and from each other without requiring solutions that can extract, transfer, and load (ETL) the data from one system to another. Whether the data you are trying to evaluate is structured or unstructured, Microsoft Azure has a data analytics solution that can help you analyze your data.

The Microsoft portfolio of data analytics solutions includes numerous tools that support big data analysis and analytics management. In the next several sections, you will become familiar with key technologies on the AZ-900 certification.

Azure Synapse Analytics

Data warehousing and enterprise analytics are synonymous with one another. Data warehousing allows an organization to store a large volume of data. The organization can query and analyze that data based on transactional sources for business intelligence (BI) and data mining purposes. Whether the data is raw or highly curated, using a data warehouse allows an organization to support enterprise analytics evaluation at a massive scale. In the past, organizations have had to glue together many big data applications, including data warehousing technologies, to create data pipelines that work across relational systems. For the enterprise, managing these systems is difficult to build, maintain, and secure.

Azure Synapse Analytics offers an integrated analytics service to bring together the data across data warehousing and big data systems. Built on core enterprise SQL Server technologies, you can stitch together a combination of SQL Data Warehousing, Spark tools for big data, Azure Pipelines offerings for data integration and ETL management, and integrate other data-driven solutions available to Azure. Options include Power BI, Cosmos DB, AzureML, MariaDB, and PostgreSQL, to name a few.

You would consider using Azure Synapse Analytics if you are looking for a distributed query solution for T-SQL, enabling data warehousing and virtualization to handle streaming data and machine learning. Unlike other data analytics offerings in Azure, Synapse Analytics offers both a serverless and dedicated resource model. The reason for this has to do with pricing and consumption. To determine what model best fits your need, follow these guidelines:

- **Predictable Performance and Cost**   Create a dedicated SQL pool to reserve processing power for your stored data in SQL tables.
- **Unpredictable, Burst-Based Workloads**   Configure your systems to be always available using serverless SQL endpoints.

 EXAM TIP   You might see references on the exam to SQL Data Warehouse. Don't be alarmed. Azure Synapse is the new name for this legacy product. Yes, Azure Synapse adds more punch to the product; SQL Data Warehouse was focused exclusively on big data storage, whereas Synapse adds analytics and big data analysis features.

Azure Synapse requires the use of five different application components, which form an Azure Synapse cluster. The components are Synapse SQL, Apache Spark for Azure Synapse, Interop of SQL and Apache Spark with your Data Lake, integration with pipelines using Azure Data Studio, and a front-end interaction with Azure Synapse called Synapse Studio. Table 4-5 illustrates the features for each of the solutions within the Azure Synapse cluster.

Azure Synapse Cluster Capability	Description
Synapse SQL	The core component of Azure Synapse Analytics. This component is the big data analytics services enabling users to query and analyze data using the T-SQL language. Users can utilize a standard ANSI-compliant dialect within the SQL language directly from the SQL Server if off-premises or Azure SQL Database if cloud-based for data analysis.
Apache Spark for Azure Synapse	Apache Spark is an open source big data engine. Microsoft has seamlessly integrated the native features to support all capabilities with Synapse to handle data preparation, engineering, ETL, and machine learning tasks.
Interop of SQL and Apache for Data Lake	A shared Hive-compatible metadata system supports the creation of table definitions and files within the data lake. You can seamlessly consume Spark or Hive with Synapse. In addition, SQL and Spark can analyze numerous file types via file exploration such as Parquet, CSV, TSV, and JSON. Synapse offers a highly scalable environment for data between SQL and Spark databases.
Integration with Pipeline for Data Studio	Synapse offers the same built-in data integration as Azure Data Factory. You can integrate and ingest 90+ third-party sources. This also helps scale ETL pipelines without having to utilize a third-party environment beyond Synapse Analytics. The environment supports code-free ETL with data flow activities.
Azure Synapse Studio	Synapse Studio is the front-end user experience tool that allows data engineers to build, explore, orchestrate, prepare, and visualize the data using Azure Synapse Analytics. You can also write SQL and Spark Code in Synapse Studio to support all data responsibilities, including authoring, debugging, and performance optimization. Synapse Studio integrates with all Azure CI/CD process features.

Table 4-5   Features Included in Azure Synapse Analytics

HDInsight

If you are familiar with Apache Hadoop, then you will understand the concept of Azure HDInsight. You can create and manage clusters of computers using a common framework designed to perform distributed processing of big data tasks. Hadoop is not the only type of cluster supported by HDInsight, as noted in Table 4-6. Given that each of these solutions is an open source platform, it comes with open source components on clusters by default. As indicated by Microsoft, as of winter 2021, the list of capabilities includes Apache Ambari, Avro, Apache Hive, HCatalog, Apache Mahout, Apache Hadoop MapReduce, Apache Hadoop YARN, Apache Phoenix, Apache Pig, Apache Sqoop, Apache Tez, Apache Oozie, and Apache ZooKeeper. Use cases where HDInsight should be considered are large-scale ETL batch processing jobs, petabyte-plus-based data warehousing requirements using Synapse Analytics or third-party tools, streaming data requirements for IoT-based needs, machine learning, data science projects, and when you are trying to support a hybrid analytics architecture.

Developing new features with HDInsight requires the use of specific development tools. Supported development tools within the Azure environment include IntelliJ, Eclipse, Visual Studio Code, or Visual Studio Enterprise. These are tools to author and submit HDInsight data queries and jobs within the context of Azure.

Cluster Type	Description
Apache Hadoop	This cluster type leverages the MapReduce programming model, a popular open source framework that uses HDFS or YARN resource management. You can process and analyze batch data using parallel compute capacity.
Apache Spark	An open source framework that supports parallel processing and in-memory processing, which can boost system performance by combining big data analysis of applications.
Apache HBase	An Apache-based NoSQL database built on Hadoop provides random access, strong consistency, and data support for unstructured and semi-structured data. This is most appropriate for datasets that are billions of rows and millions of columns deep.
ML Services	Used for hosting and managing parallel, distributed R processes, the ML Services provide data experts access to scalable methods for analytics on HDInsight.
Apache Storm	Allows for the processing of large streams of data fast, with particular emphasis on computation systems. This solution is offered as a managed cluster.
Apache Interactive Query	In-memory caching solution for Hive queries.
Apache Kafka	Intended for streaming data pipelines and applications, Apache Kafka also supports publishing and subscription services for messaging.

Table 4-6   Cluster Solutions Available in Azure HDInsight

Azure Databricks

When you have petabytes of data stored in a data warehouse or data lake, it's often hard to extract and pull together a coherent message, especially when the data is unstructured. If the data is coming from many sources, the problems only mount for the data expert. Can you imagine having data come from sources beyond Azure and trying to build a complete data model that is meaningful for a data mining or machine learning solution? That's why you would use Azure Databricks. When you need to build data-intensive analytics applications, Databricks is a solution you would consider. But it is a bit more complicated than that. You have two environments to select from with Databricks in Azure: Databricks SQL Analytics and Databricks Workspace.

- **Azure Databricks SQL Analytics**   This is the platform for an analyst looking to run SQL queries on data lakes, create visualizations, explore query results from different perspectives, and build dashboards.

- **Azure Databricks Workspace**   When looking to support interactive collaboration between data experts, you would use Workspace. You can ingest various types of data in Azure through the Azure Data Factory, which is built into Databricks using batches or can stream the data using one of the other solutions such as Kafka, Event Hub, or IoT Hub. The data is then stored in an Azure storage container depending on the use case. The data is transformed across the multiple data sources into a single source of truth using Spark.

To get started with Azure Databricks, you need to create a new Databricks workspace, which means creating an instance of Azure Databricks. You do this by following these steps.

1. Go to All Services, then All, then Analytics.

2. Under Analytics, select Azure Databricks.

3. When you click Azure Databricks, a page such as the one shown in Figure 4-38 appears.

4. You will need to fill in the required fields to create a new Databricks instance.

5. Once you create the initial Databricks workspace, it will take a few minutes to deploy.

6. Upon configuration, you will want to launch the workspace.

7. Click the Launch Workspace button in the center of the screen (Figure 4-39).

8. You will be asked to log in to your account, which may happen automatically if you have an Active Directory account provisioned.

9. At this point, you will be presented with the Azure Databricks Portal (Figure 4-40). You can import and export data or create a notebook to start querying, visualizing, and modeling your data in Azure Databricks.

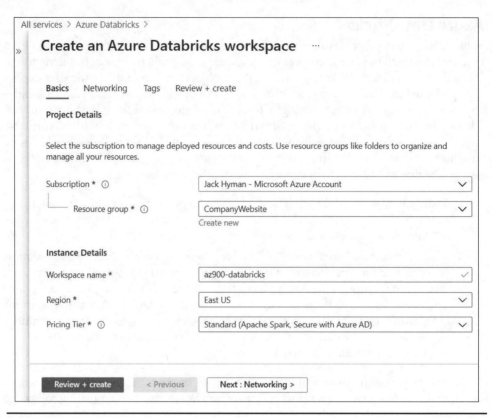

All services > Azure Databricks >

Create an Azure Databricks workspace ...

Basics   Networking   Tags   Review + create

Project Details

Select the subscription to manage deployed resources and costs. Use resource groups like folders to organize and manage all your resources.

Subscription * ⓘ | Jack Hyman - Microsoft Azure Account   ⌄ |

    Resource group * ⓘ | CompanyWebsite   ⌄ |
                            Create new

Instance Details

Workspace name * | az900-databricks   ✓ |

Region * | East US   ⌄ |

Pricing Tier * ⓘ | Standard (Apache Spark, Secure with Azure AD)   ⌄ |

[Review + create]   [< Previous]   [Next : Networking >]

Figure 4-38   Create a new Azure Databricks workspace

TIP   While you might think that Azure Databricks is associated with the company Databricks and Apache Spark, it is not. Microsoft built the entire Azure Databricks framework from the ground up as a service to run in Azure. Databricks by Apache is more focused on storage alone, whereas Microsoft's offering is focused heavily on analytics management.

Figure 4-39
Launch
Databricks
workspace

Launch Workspace

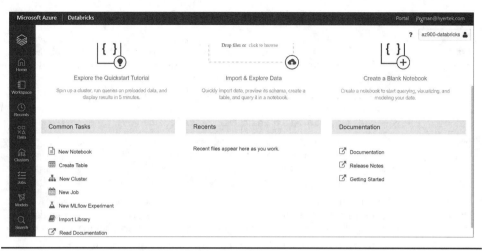

Figure 4-40   Azure Databricks Portal

Artificial Intelligence and Machine Learning Solutions

Microsoft offers numerous mission-critical products and services that can analyze images, comprehend speech, make predictions using data, and ingest data to evaluate the behavior of others. All these capabilities are native in the Microsoft Azure Artificial Intelligence and Machine Learning solutions area. With Microsoft Azure, you can quickly build, train, and deploy machine learning models using Azure Machine Learning or Azure Databricks. Over time, the more these models learn user behavior and the data they produce, the better these models respond accurately at scale and speed.

Azure Machine Learning

Before we begin discussing Azure Machine Learning as a platform, it is important to understand the technology's underpinning. At the root of Machine Learning is *artificial intelligence*, which is the capability of a computer to imitate intelligent human behavior. With AI, machines analyze images; comprehend emotions, speech, and interactions; and predict behaviors using data. When one references machine learning, it often includes artificial intelligence. Interestingly, another type of artificial intelligence called deep learning, a subset of machine learning, uses neural networks to train the machine. All three layers have one thing in common: they maintain one or more algorithms, which are a sequence of calculations and rules used to solve a problem or analyze data. Table 4-7 describes the differences among the three cognitive levels.

Azure Machine Learning is priced based on the resources consumed. So depending on the type of optimized resources used, such as compute, storage, or memory, the price will vary. This model aligns with other pricing methodologies applied with Infrastructure as

Cognitive Level	Definition
Artificial Intelligence	AI uses mathematical algorithms to support the creation of data models. Most models are predictive in nature. The algorithms use parsed data fields and learn from those found in the algorithms' patterns to create these models.
	Models are then used to make predictions based on validated sources, usually measuring performance metrics. A data expert can modify the scenarios as needed through model training. Models are modified over time.
Machine Learning	In Azure, machine learning combines data science techniques and solutions, allowing computers to use existing data to forecast trends and analysis. Using machine learning powered by low-code or no-code capabilities, Microsoft allows for apps and devices to become smarter using data analytic insights.
Deep Learning	Deep learning is a type of machine learning that can determine if predictive results are correct using algorithms to analyze data at scale. The scale that deep learning requires for analysis is far greater than that required for machine learning.
	Deep learning evaluates data with the use of artificial neural networks consisting of multiple layers of algorithms. Each algorithm layer looks at incoming data to perform specialized analysis. Additionally, each of the layers in a neural network and multiple neural networks can learn through data processing. Deep learning requires the most compute power of any machine learning and cognitive services solution offering.

Table 4-7   Difference Between Artificial Intelligence, Machine Learning, and Deep Learning

a Service offerings, such as virtual machines. Every time you run a model or utilize the Data Studio, a nominal charge is applied to your bill based on compute consumption requirements. Again, depending on the combination of resources utilized and demand required, pricing varies. If you know that you intend to utilize Azure Machine Learning heavily, consider getting a reservation to reduce your costs.

Like other applications in this chapter, Azure Machine Learning requires you to set up a dedicated workspace. A *machine learning workspace* is a centralized location to maintain all of your artifacts built with Azure Machine Learning. The workspace allows you to keep a history of all training assets developed over time so that you can constantly evolve the models you build. To create an Azure Machine Learning workspace, follow these instructions:

1. Go to All Services, then All, then Machine Learning.

2. Select the Machine Learning link.

3. Click the New button.

4. Complete the form to create a new Machine Learning workspace (Figure 4-41).

5. You will need to select the following on the Create New Workspace form:

   • **Subscription**   Select an account.

   • **Resource Group**   Select an account where machine learning resources will be invoiced.

All services > Machine learning >

Machine learning ...
Create a machine learning workspace

Project details

Select the subscription to manage deployed resources and costs. Use resource groups like folders to organize and manage all your resources.

Subscription * ⓘ   Jack Hyman - Microsoft Azure Account   ⌄

    Resource group * ⓘ   CompanyWebsite   ⌄
                        Create new

Workspace details

Specify the name and region for the workspace.

Workspace name * ⓘ   az900mlspace   ✓

Region * ⓘ   East US   ⌄

Storage account * ⓘ   (new) az900mlspace9025830096   ⌄
                              Create new

Key vault * ⓘ   (new) az900mlspace2363066784   ⌄
                              Create new

Application insights * ⓘ   (new) az900mlspace6998299735   ⌄
                              Create new

Container registry * ⓘ   (new) az900container   ⌄
                              Create new

[Review + create]   [< Previous]   [Next : Networking]

Figure 4-41   Creating a Machine Learning workspace

- **Workspace Name**   Enter the original new workspace name.
- **Region**   Select the location where the workspace will be used. It will default to where hosting is currently set for the subscription.
- **Storage Account**   Machine Learning resources must be saved to a storage account.
- **Key Vault**   Used to store secrets associated with sensitive information.
- **Application Insights**   Used to assist with the monitoring of data models.
- **Container Registry**   Used to register Docker images used in training and deployments.

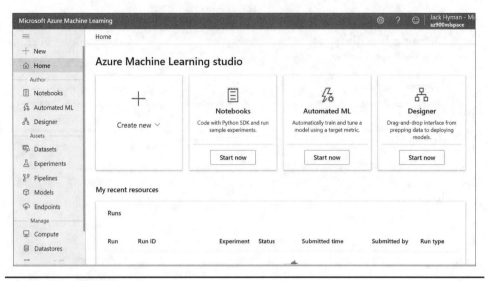

Figure 4-42   Machine Learning Studio user experience

6. Upon completing the form, click Review + Create.

7. The process will take a few minutes to provision deployable resources.

8. Once deployed, go to Resources.

9. You will now be taken to your Workspace page, allowing you to go to Machine Learning.

Users can use Azure Machine Learning Studio to build, train, evaluate, and deploy machine learning models. You will do so by creating individual templates. To access the Learning Studio, click Launch Studio.

You will be introduced to the Machine Learning Studio user experience (Figure 4-42). This is where you can combine no-code and code-first activities to support various data science platform experiences, depending on the type of projects needed. The key three project types you will find include:

- **Notebooks**   A code-based solution that allows you to code with the Python SDK and run sample experiments.

- **Automated ML**   A machine learning solution that automatically allows you to train and tune models using data metrics.

- **Designer**   Drag-and-drop interface from prepping data to deploying models.

There are three functional areas in Machine Learning Studio: Authoring, Assets, and Manage. Authoring (Table 4-8) provides you the ability to create the machine learning assets in Azure Machine Learning. Assets (Table 4-9) allows a user to support the rules, workflows, and job features in Azure Machine Learning. Manage allows users to create new data assets, link existing data, and better codify those data assets ingested in Azure Machine Learning (Table 4-10).

Authoring Capability	Description
Notebooks	Allows you to work with files, folders, and Jupyter Notebooks within the ML workspace.
Automated ML	Automatically trains and finds the best model based on the data available in your instance of Azure Machine Learning without writing code.
Designer	Works with your existing and graphical UI-based tools to create models rapidly. Coding requirements are minimal using Designer.

Table 4-8   Authoring Capabilities in ML Studio

Assets Capability	Description
Datasets	Datasets help you manage data for model training and pipeline creation.
Experiments	Experiments help you train and support those runs to build models.
Pipelines	Pipelines offer reusable workflows to train models at all phases in the lifecycle.
Models	Models are files that are trained to identify patterns over time.
Endpoints	Endpoints are an instance of your model that can be hosted in the cloud or connected with an IoT module based on device deployment.

Table 4-9   Asset Capabilities in ML Studio

Manage Capability	Description
Compute	Compute features help run experiments.
Datastores	Datastores attach to a workspace used to store data and feature specific connection-related attributes of the Azure Storage Service.
Data Labeling	Labeling allows for the creation, management, and monitoring of projects in support of data.
Linked Services	Linked Services connect other Azure services and assets together in a single location.

Table 4-10   Manage Capabilities in ML Studio

Cognitive Services

Azure Cognitive Services are cloud-based solutions that help users integrate machine learning–based intelligence into their applications. Built using REST APIs and client library SDKs, any user can add such features to their application without knowing basic programming skills about artificial intelligence or data science. The Azure Cognitive Services catalog comprises numerous AI services that allow an application to see, hear, speak, understand, think, and process decisions intelligently. The AZ-900 exam acknowledges five main pillars of cognitive solutions: vision, speech, language, decision, and search. Table 4-11 provides an overview of the Cognitive Service category, product name, and description of service.

Category	Name	Description
Vision APIs	Computer Vision API	Offers access to advanced cognitive algorithms for processing images and returning visual-based information.
	Computer Vision Service API	Supports the building of custom image classifiers.
	Face	Provides access to advanced face algorithms, including enabling face attribute detection and recognition.
	Form Recognize	Helps identify and extract key-value pairs and table data from documents. Outputs structured data into relationships within original files.
	Video Indexer	Extract insights using video files.
Speech API	Speech service	Adds speech features to applications like speech-to-text and speech translation.
Language API	Language Understanding (LUIS)	Helps users understand what they want in their own words.
	QnA Maker	Allows users to build a question-and-answer service from a semi-structured content solution.
	Text Analytics	Offers natural language processing over raw text, which includes support for sentiment analysis, key phrase extraction, and language detection.
	Translator	Provides machine-based text translation in near real time.
	Immersive Reader	Incorporates an immersive screen reading comprehension capability to integrate within any application.
Decision API	Anomaly Detector	Monitors and detects time series data abnormalities.
	Content Moderator	Provides monitoring for potentially offensive, undesirable, and risky content.
	Metrics Advisor	Allows for evaluating customizable anomaly detection on multivariate time-series data, including fully featured web portal applications.
	Personalizer	Chooses the best experience based on real-time behaviors and user selection.
Search API	Bing News Search	Returns a list of news articles queried based on user relevancy.
	Bing Video Search	Returns a list of video recommendations based on user relevancy.
	Bing Web Search	Returns a list of web search results based on user-relevant criteria.
	Bing Autosuggest	Allows you to send a search query term to Bing. Suggested queries are provided to the end user.
	Bing Custom Search	Allows you to create personalized search experiences for topics that you care about.
	Bing Entity Search	Allows you to return information about entities that Bing determines are relevant to a user's query.
	Bing Image Search	Allows you to return a display of images determined to be relevant to the user's query.
	Bing Visual Search	Allows you to provide insights about an image such as like-kind similar images and B2B product sources found in images.

Table 4-11   Cognitive Service Solution Options *(continued)*

Category	Name	Description
	Bing Local Business Search	Enables your applications to find contact and location information about local businesses based on search queries.
	Bing Spell Check	Allows you to perform contextual grammar and spelling checking.

Table 4-11 Cognitive Service Solution Options

Azure Bot Service

The Azure Bot Service is a cognitive service offered to build AI capabilities, focusing on conversation-based experiences. Bots are a common feature found on many B2B- and B2C-based websites. The Bot Framework and the Bot Service are complete offerings that allow developers to build, test, deploy, and manage intelligent bots in a single location. Developers can utilize the Bot Framework to create bots using a modular and extensive SDK and tools, templates, and related AI services. The features included in the framework also handle questions and answers, natural language, and speech. Bot interactions also support conversations that provide access to services external to Azure through a conversational interface. A user can also interface with a social channel, including Facebook, Slack, or Microsoft Teams. A bot service, which is modeled in Figure 4-43, operates as follows:

1. A typical model will receive a request or reason based on the input it receives. It will then perform a task based on the action.

2. The bot will then ask the user for information or access one or more services on behalf of the user.

3. Once the requested activities occur, the bot will perform the necessary recognition services based on the user's input to complete the necessary interpretation.

4. The bot concludes that it will generate a response, which is then sent to the user, and the bot tells the user the state of its activity.

5. Depending on the outcome and the configured channel, users interact with the bot using three models: text, audio, or video.

Figure 4-43
Bot Service
operating model

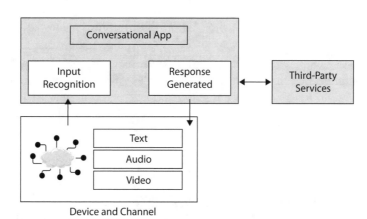

As shown in Figure 4-44, configuring a bot works much like a modern web application on the Internet with an API. The main difference is a template is used to configure the message stack and you must select a core technology.

A simple bot can receive a message and echo it back to a user with very little code if necessary. Once the Bot Service is fully configured and ready to be set up, a developer can plan, build, test, publish, connect, and evaluate all Azure Portal features.

Figure 4-44
Configuring a
bot service

Serverless Computing

Some developers and system administrators may want to bypass the need to manage infrastructure. If the objective for an organization is to build a custom application without handling infrastructure overhead, serverless computing is a viable option to consider. With the serverless application, Azure can provide all the infrastructure on behalf of the organization. All the organization is responsible for is the development effort, while Microsoft is responsible for provisioning, scaling, and managing the infrastructure to run the application code.

Serverless computing does not mean that no underlying operating system and hardware are being deployed. Just the opposite. It simply means that the technical and administrative burden is not the responsibility of the development team. The onus is on the hosting provider, so the developer can focus on the organization, allowing for product optimization. Two ways to deploy serverless capabilities in Microsoft Azure is using Azure Functions and Azure Logic Apps. The next three sections cover these areas in depth.

Azure Functions

The Azure Functions service allows a user to host a single method or function using several popular programming languages in the Azure cloud environment. A function is an event that is triggered by a computing activity. The event extends across one or more Azure applications using programmatic code such as C#, Python, JavaScript, Java, or PowerShell. What usually happens is an event will be triggered by request. The request then queues an action. The action will then result in a response. The function only triggers one event at a time.

As your applications scale, so does Azure Functions. You are not charged for the use of a function unless it is triggered. Functions are appropriate when demand is unpredictable. Applications such as IoT solutions may benefit from Azure Functions, given the unpredictability of event data. Another example might be the use of a trigger built into a business application for querying message data.

Azure functions are stateless. When a function is stateless, no knowledge or previous interaction request handles any event's information. That's ideal when you need an application to restart each time it responds to an event for performance purity and storage purposes.

 EXAM TIP You might be asked when you should use Azure Functions. You use Azure Functions if you are concerned with the code that runs a service, not the infrastructure that runs the code.

Logic Apps

Unlike Azure Functions, Logic Apps are serverless low-code applications hosted as part of the Azure Cloud Services. Logic Apps allows users to automate and orchestrate discrete tasks, business processes, and workflows. You use Logic Apps for more complex use cases such as integrating apps, data, systems, and services across an enterprise, where orchestration is evident.

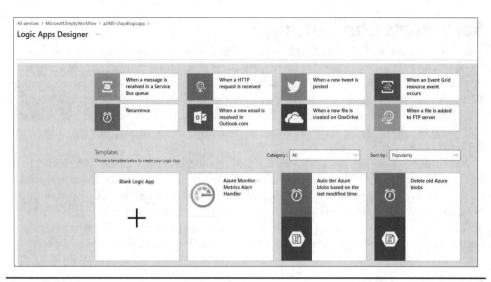

Figure 4-45 Azure Logic Apps creation interface

To design a logic app, you interact with a web-based interface. Once the design is complete, you can then execute the logic that triggers Azure services without requiring an administrator to write code. The user experience is consistent with Power Automate, a way to create and share automated workflows using Microsoft 365 (Figure 4-45). Developing an app requires linking a trigger to actions with connectors. The process for linking begins when a trigger, an event such as a timer that executes, sends a message to a queue. Once the message is received, the action is required to take the next step to execute the step in the task, business process, or workflow. The cycle can iterate many times, presuming the programming language used allows for looping logic or decision support. Microsoft offers over 200 connectors to create enterprise integrations. Only when there are no actions or connectors to support the logic is it necessary to apply custom code.

Azure Functions or Azure Logic Apps

Both Azure Functions and Azure Logic Apps are serverless. While Azure Functions provides serverless compute services, Logic Apps is more appropriate for serverless orchestration. The pricing is different between the two services. For Azure Functions, you pay based on the number of executions and runs. Logic Apps is billed based on the number of executions and your connection type. To decide which option is best, use these criteria to determine the appropriate fit:

- **Performing orchestration across APIs** Azure Logic Apps
- **Executing custom algorithms or code to support parsing** Azure Functions
- **Integrating with existing automated tasks built in to other programming languages** Azure Logic Apps
- **Requires visual workflow or writing code** Depends on the workflow and business process complexity

DevOps Solutions

The Microsoft Azure platform includes a collection of SaaS-based DevOps tools to help organizations throughout application planning, development, delivery, and operations. Each business area is distinct with its offerings. As you will see, there are many products that one can utilize within each of the DevOps solution pillars.

Planning offers teams the ability to manage work across all of Azure. You can see project visibility across most products, assuming you have the appropriate security credentials. Feature highlights include project management support to define and track work using Kanban boards, backlogs, dashboards, and reporting outputs. All these activities can be completed using Azure Boards. Teams can manage development efforts with transparency and support scheduling using GitHub. Combining the power of visual business intelligence is also possible if you are licensed to use Power BI.

Developing applications in Azure can be completed using numerous Microsoft-based solutions. You have the choice to work with Visual Studio or Visual Studio Code by Microsoft for coding development. Then, you can collaborate with a team of developers using GitHub once that code is ready to be shared. For those that need to automate testing and require continuous integration with Azure, you can utilize Azure Pipelines. Within the environment, all these activities may require workflow orchestration. That's why you may want to consider utilizing GitHub Actions. To bring all these assets together quickly so that you can create a repeatable business operation, you would use Azure DevTest Lab.

Deployment of applications depends on business need and approach. Should your organization require automatic deployment with full control to continuous delivery for customers, you would utilize Kubernetes on Azure. When your environment requires creating multiple cloud environments using a template-based design, you utilize Azure Resource Management in conjunction with Azure Pipelines for continuous delivery pipelines to any of these environments. There are, of course, third-party solutions, such as Jenkins, that can be utilized to support some of these pipeline configurations.

Operations ensures that your implementations work as they should. Whether you are looking to get alerts, gain insights from log data and telemetry, or ensure the health of your system resources, you can utilize all of your environments with Azure Monitor. If security and compliance are a concern, Azure Security Center can limit your threat exposure and remediate vulnerabilities.

In this section, you will learn what is necessary for the AZ-900 exam. While there are many more DevOps solutions in the Azure portfolio, Microsoft only requires you to know four main solutions: Azure DevOps, GitHub, GitHub Actions, and Azure DevTest Labs.

Azure DevOps

As a developer, managing a project can be a daunting task. Supporting a team in terms of planning work, collaborating on code development and deployment, and supporting the build-out of an application can be even more challenging. That's why Microsoft built Azure DevOps to help teams create a culture of collaboration engrain processes among teams. Developers, project managers, and contributors can cohesively come

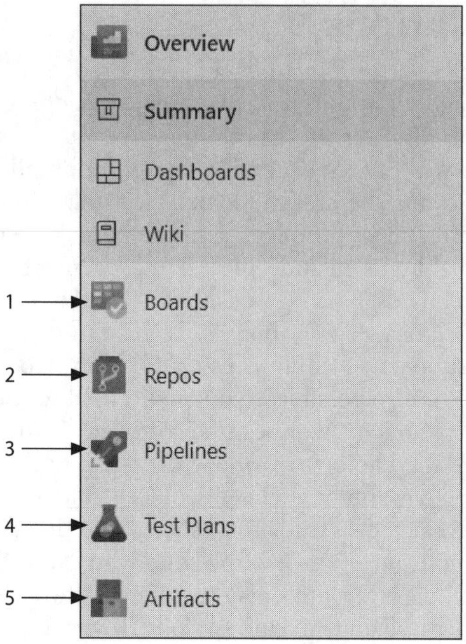

Figure 4-46
Azure DevOps
navigation

together to work on software development efforts. Given that projects in Azure are cloud-based, organizations can build products faster than using traditional development methodologies.

With Azure DevOps, you have two options: you can work in the cloud using Azure DevOps Services or on-premises using Azure DevOps Server. Azure DevOps provides a complete suite of features that one can access through a web browser or an IDE client. Each of these services can be utilized as a standalone service based on your business's need. As seen in Figure 4-46, numerous options make up Azure DevOps. Each major feature has a number associated with it. These features are described in Table 4-12.

Item	Feature	Description
1	Boards	A suite of agile project management tools to help plan and track work, code defects, and issues using Scrum and Kanban methodologies.
2	Repos	Offers either Git repositories or Team Foundation Version Control (TFVC) through Visual Studio for source control of your source code.
3	Pipelines	Allows for build and release services to support continuous integration and delivery of applications.
4	Test Plans	A mix of tools to help test applications. Offers both manual and exploratory testing options. Also supports continuous testing.
5	Artifacts	Allows a team to share packages ranging from Maven, npm, NuGet, etc. Availability is for both public and private sources. Can integrate packages in Azure Pipelines.

Table 4-12 DevOps Tools Overview

Azure Boards

Suppose you are familiar with issue and project management tools intended for agile development by vendors such as Atlassian (Jira), Monday.com, Wrike, Smartsheet, Asana, Basecamp, or Trello. In that case, it will come as no surprise to you that Microsoft has adopted some of the best features from its Microsoft Project platform and integrated them into Azure DevOps for scrum development. When you are using Azure Boards, you can create Kanban boards, story items, features, backlogs, sprints, and queries for a project.

Azure Boards offers a complete collection of tools to help manage list-based items. Each of the tools within the offering supports a filtered set of work items. The following capabilities are defined within the Azure Boards offering and are illustrated in Figure 4-47:

- **Boards** A board presents a complete view of all work items using cards. The cards can be organized using a drag-and-drop model. Think of placing cards on a whiteboard full of Post-it notes. Like the Scrum and Kanban practices, you can visualize the flow of activities for a team.

- **Work Items** When you are given a task, you will likely want to look at things quickly. In Azure Board terms, it is called a Work Item. You can pivot or filter to find these items based on several criteria. The search and filtering capabilities built in are the equivalent of a drill-down search.

- **Backlogs** If you need to review items in a list format, the backlog design in Boards is the best option to review all of your project issues. A product backlog presents your project plan and the repository of all information assets needed to track your team's activities. A portfolio backlog also enables you to group and organize a backlog into a hierarchy, like an organizational chart, so that you can prioritize work.

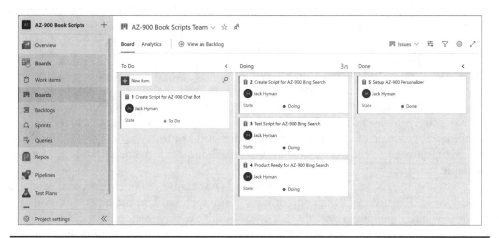

Figure 4-47   Azure DevOps Boards

- **Sprints**   If you have a backlog of items and your team requires a filtered view of these items for an iterated work path, also referred to as a sprint, you would use this feature within Azure Boards. From the backlog menu, you can assign work based on iterations. Using the drag-and-drop editor, you can manipulate tasks as you or your team sees fit. Once you are satisfied with the task order, you can view the work as a separate backlog. This tool is best utilized for those wanting to follow scrum practices.

- **Queries**   When looking to review the filtered list of work items based on criteria you define within the query editor, you would use the Queries capability in Azure Boards. Features such as finding a group of work items, listing work items for the purposes of sharing, and creating status or trend charts are all available options.

Azure Repos

It does not matter if you have a small or large development project; you and your team must control the project source code. Version control tools are an essential ingredient to manage these types of projects. Within the Azure portfolio, Azure Repos is the tool to help you manage all your source code centrally.

A version control system offers an organization the ability to help manage a codebase, small or large, over time. As you or your team edit the code, it is easy to tell the system how to control it. Whether you want it to take a snapshot, which is a copy at the moment in time, or a complete backup of your files, the system can safely and securely manage your source code. In addition, the version control system can recall any portion of the code.

There are numerous benefits to using a version control system, whether you are a single developer or a team. Whether you need to fix bugs or develop a new feature, a version control system allows you to record every development instance. You can review and roll back any version of code you have available with ease. Two repository instances can be utilized, either *Git*, a distributed version control solution, or the *Team Foundation Version Control (TFVC),* a centralized version control solution. Git is more commonly used today, given it is cloud-based, while TFVC is bound to a server and IDE-based.

Azure Pipelines

There may come a time when you want to build and test your code projects automatically. Suppose you wanted to make those projects available to others, especially when that code is developed in one language and you want to ensure it works cross-platform. In that case, you should make sure your code is available as needed. Azure Pipelines combines the power of continuous integration and continuous delivery (CI/CD) to ensure that any time code is deployed, it is tested and built to specification and made available to others.

It is best to use Azure Pipelines when you and your team need to ensure consistent and quality code. Regardless of the code delivery format, the code must be readily available to users. Azure Pipelines provides a quick, easy, and safe way to automate the delivery of projects and the code for users to access. Users may consider using Azure Pipelines because it works with virtually all languages and platforms. You can also deploy it to different types of targets at the same time. Azure Pipelines can be built on Windows, Linux, or macOS systems, while also integrating with GitHub. Since there is tight integration with GitHub, integration with Azure native and open source projects is also possible.

The Three Cs

Continuous integration (CI), continuous delivery (CD), and continuous testing (CT) are often talked about interchangeably. These topics are distinct in their own way. Make sure you know the difference.

- **Continuous Integration**   This is used by developers to automate the merging and testing of code. Implementing CI helps catch bugs early in the development cycle so that it is less expensive to fix errors later.

- **Continuous Delivery**   This is a process to help build, test, and deploy code to one or more production environments. When you deploy and test in multiple environments, the focus is on code quality, whereas in CI systems, you are producing the deployable artifacts for the infrastructure and apps.

- **Continuous Testing**   Either on-premises or in the cloud, developers choose to use automated build–deploy–test workflows. They can choose technologies and frameworks that test the changes on an as-needed basis due to scalability considerations.

Azure Test Plans

Quality control and testing is a vital component of any software system. With Azure, there are several options that a developer can choose from. Under the umbrella of manual testing, the developer can test their solution in four different ways: planned, conducting user acceptance testing, exploratory testing, or soliciting user feedback. Each method is unique because manual testing provides developers a dedicated approach to testing while also ensuring quality control. To use Azure Test Plans, a developer must have either an Enterprise, Test Professional, or MSDN Platform Account. The benefits of each method include the following:

- **Planned manual testing**   Organize tests into test plans and test suites. You must assign designated testers and test leads.

- **User acceptance testing**   Testing is carried out by user acceptance testers to verify the value of delivery to meet the customer requirements. A secondary purpose is to ensure the reuse of test artifacts created by an engineering team.

- **Exploratory testing**   Testing is carried out by various stakeholders that are part of a development, including developers, testers, user experience (UX) team members, or product stakeholders. Each member may be responsible for one or more facets of a software system without using the test plans or test suites themselves.

- **Stakeholder feedback**   Stakeholders outside the organization carry out testing. Users may include sales, marketing, finance, and operations.

Azure Artifacts

Azure Artifacts is an extension of the Azure DevOps Services and Server. While it comes preinstalled with Azure DevOps Services, Azure DevOps Server 2019 and 2020, and Team Foundation, Server 2017 and 2018 still require installation before they can be used. You can create and share several packages, including Maven, npm, and NuGet, via a package feed from a public or private source with a team of any size. Also, these packages can be fully integrated using package management through CI/CD pipelines.

 TIP   Azure Artifacts is now the new home of the Packages Page under the Build and Release Page group. It replaces the previous UX navigation of the Azure DevOps Services and Team Foundation Server (TFS).

GitHub

In the previous section, we discussed Azure DevOps as a way for developers to collaborate. Another popular tool that is used by developers globally is GitHub. Interestingly, Microsoft acquired GitHub in 2018 to connect with the open source developer community. GitHub's core web portal repository is an open source system called Git. Linus Torvalds, who also developed the Linux kernel and by default the operating system, also was responsible for the founding of Git in 2005. Torvalds created Git as a fast and efficient way for teams to collaborate on open source software development. Fast forward three years to 2008. A team of ambitious developers came together and created a hosting platform called GitHub, a streamlined Git repository and catalog for source code. What no one realized at the time was this open source project would become the world's largest code repository. There are 55+ million developers, 3+ million organizations, 100+ million repositories, and 70 percent+ of the Fortune 50 companies using GitHub. To sign up for a free account and explore the environment, go to https://github.com.

Developers seldom make modifications to a GitHub repository. Instead, they will update the repository locally. Once they update their code locally, those revisions will be posted to the repository globally. Posted revisions to a repository are referred to as forking. If you have tested your changes to the source code and they are ready to be deployed back into the source repository, you suggest that you merge the code back into the source repository.

 TIP   Develops often prefer GitHub over Azure DevOps because of the variety of source control features for code repositories. While GitHub is a great solution for developers to edit their source code using just about any editor, a bit more than that needs to be done. GitHub may not solve every technical solution. You must consider testing, building, and automation requirements.

Developers use GitHub for more than just storing code repositories. They often test their applications by building Docker images and pushing code instances for enterprise platforms. For enterprises, repetitive tasks can introduce potential risks. That is why developer organizations opt for automated workflows so that each time a new version of their software is compiled, they can be assured the product is up to date and properly compiled.

GitHub Actions

Automated workflows are implemented using *GitHub Actions*. With GitHub Actions, users can create event-driven workflows within the GitHub environment. Developers can complete certain actions like pushing code to change a GitHub repository automatically. Events are managed by the developer. The developer will define their own workflows using a text file that is scripted in YAML. A developer can also select one of the preconfigured options available from the GitHub Actions environment, available in the GitHub Marketplace. To get started using the GitHub Marketplace, and specifically with GitHub Actions, open one of the repositories shown in Figure 4-48.

1. Click the Actions tab at the top of the page. There are some recommended actions based on the current open repository.

2. Next, you can select one of the actions currently available.

3. Finally, follow the steps to set up this workflow action.

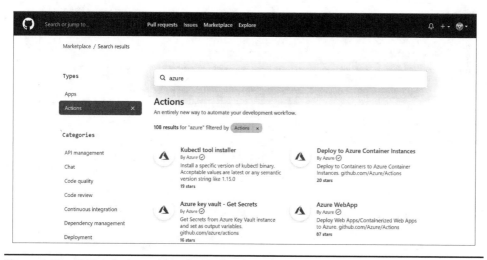

Figure 4-48   GitHub Actions within the Marketplace

Azure DevTest Labs

Azure DevTest Labs helps you automate the management process of building, setting up, and taking down a virtual machine (VM) environment that might contain one or more configurations of your project. When a developer tests their products across various environmental conditions, they can fully appreciate the state of their project build and the operating system it resides on. Azure DevTest is not limited to virtual machine environments alone. If you deploy a resource in Azure, including an ARM template, it can be provisioned and tested using DevTest Labs. Bear in mind, though, that some pre-provisioning is required. You must consider a lab environment that already has the properly configured tools in place, thereby supporting quality assurance.

To create a DevTest Lab, follow these instructions:

1. Go to All Services, then All, then DevOps.

2. Select DevTest Lab.

3. Click the New button in the Navigation menu.

4. A new page appears, allowing you to create a new DevTest Lab (Figure 4-49).

Figure 4-49   Configure a new DevTest Lab environment

5. Follow these steps to complete the configuration:

- Select the subscription and resource group and provide a lab name and location where you would like to have the DevTest Lab hosted.

- Indicate if the lab environment will be public or not (toggle on or off).

- Should you decide to complete advanced configurations, move to the tabs to the right. The tabs include Auto-Shutdown, Networking, and Tags.

- If you are ready to complete the setup process, click Review + Create on the bottom left.

Once a DevTest Lab environment is created, you will need to add a resource such as a VM or web app so that a developer can test the solution inside the environment. To add a resource to a DevTest Lab, follow these steps:

1. Click the Add button on the Navigation menu (Figure 4-50).

2. A list will appear with the possible options that one can test in the Azure DevTest Lab.

3. Select the solution that is appropriate for your testing use case. In this case, the selection is Web App (Figure 4-51).

4. Enter an environment name for the DevTest Lab and click Add.

You can complete a similar set of actions for a virtual machine environment, another common use case for Azure DevTest Lab, following these same steps.

Figure 4-50   Adding resources to a DevTest Lab

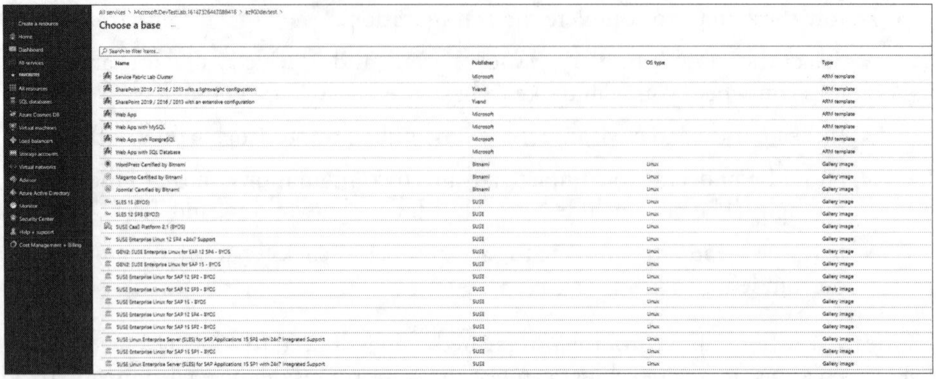

Figure 4-51   Select the DevTest Lab base

Chapter Review

Chapter 4 covered a broad range of core Azure Cloud Services. Among the services and solutions discussed are the latest technologies within the Microsoft Azure portfolio that appear on the exam. By no means are these all the technologies available in the Azure Cloud, nor is this the extent of what you as a cloud developer, system administrator, or end user need to know to consider yourself an expert. For the exam, you are expected to learn key concepts and, in some instances, how to configure the environments where appropriate. Here is a listing of each technical domain and the respective technical solutions discussed throughout the chapter to summarize each of the main areas discussed and associated technologies:

Management Tools

- **Azure Portal**   Web-based user experience to conduct all Azure Cloud activities, including managing cloud services.
- **Azure PowerShell**   Azure's equivalent to the Windows PowerShell module that allows users to manage resources using the PowerShell framework.
- **Azure CLI**   Web-based command-line tool that is cross-platform compatible and allows for scripting in multiple languages.
- **Azure Cloud Shell**   Web-based tool that allows for Bash- or PowerShell-based command-line access from almost any device.
- **Azure Mobile App**   Another support tool to help manage cloud resources and monitor Azure environments using an Apple iOS or Google Android device.
- **Azure Advisor**   An automated consultant that provides recommendations in five areas: reliability, security, cost, performance, and operational excellence.
- **Azure Resource Management Templates**   JSON files used to create and modify Azure resources using Azure Resource Manager.

- **Azure Monitor**   Aggregates metrics across Azure based on custom-created reports to help identify issues. Offers alerts, notifications, and drill-down custom reporting features.
- **Azure Service Health**   Provides incident-related guidance that may affect resources in your Azure environment.

IoT Solutions

- **IoT Hub**   Allows users to manage devices and route messages to and from IoT-enabled devices.
- **IoT Central**   Helps users monitor their IoT devices.
- **Azure Sphere**   Secures IoT devices.

Data Analytics Solutions

- **Azure Synapse Analytics**   Formerly SQL Data Warehouse; allows users to store big datasets and handle data analysis in clusters.
- **HDInsight**   A clustered Hadoop product for processing big datasets.
- **Azure Databricks**   Helps model data from data warehouses for effective machine learning modeling.

AI and Machine Learning Solutions

- **Azure Machine Learning**   A cloud-based solution to create and train machine learning models.
- **Cognitive Services**   A collection of APIs to create advanced machine learning solutions.
- **Azure Bot Services**   Built on the Azure AppService and utilizes machine learning; an easy way to build AI-driven collaboration.

Serverless Computing Services

- **Azure Functions**   Intended for executing serverless compute components.
- **Azure Logic Apps**   Intended for use when applications require advanced connectors, triggers, and actions that require serverless orchestration.

DevOps Solutions

- **Azure DevOps**   A way to plan, develop, deliver, and ensure that operations are properly managed whether you work independently or with a team.
- **GitHub**   Intended for source code management across teams.
- **GitHub Actions**   Works alongside GitHub to add event-driven workflows to GitHub.
- **Azure DevTest Labs**   Solutions that allow for access to ready-made virtual machines, configured based on a predefined specification. You need to create an initial configuration, which then can be propagated for use many times.

Questions

1. Which of the following management tools is a command-line interface that is browser-based and machine- and OS-independent?

   A. Azure CLI

   B. Azure Cloud Shell

   C. Azure Portal

   D. Azure PowerShell

2. Select the response that best fits the questions:

	True	False
Azure Cloud Advisor can automatically correct issues it discovers without assigned user permission.	○	○
Azure Cloud Advisor provides visibility into Azure-wide outages.	○	○
Azure Cloud Advisor updates can be postponed up to 90 calendar days.	○	○

   A. True, True, True

   B. True, False, True

   C. False, False, True

   D. False, False, False

3. Review the following scenario and replace the word you believe is inaccurate with one of the following choices.

   Azure CLI incorporates both Bash and PowerShell using the browser-based experience.

   A. Azure Cloud Shell

   B. ARM Templates

   C. Azure PowerShell

   D. The statement is accurate.

4. Review the following scenario and replace the word you believe is inaccurate with one of the following choices.

Azure Portal allows for either the use of the Home page or custom dashboards as a way for users to interact with cloud resources throughout the platform.

   A. Azure Monitor

   B. Azure IoT Central

   C. Azure Machine Learning

   D. The statement is accurate.

5. If a user cannot run PowerShell as an Admin or Superuser, which command line should they execute?

   A. `Install-Module -Name Az -AllowClobber -Scope CurrentUser`

   B. `Install-Module -Name Az -AllowClobber -Scope Superuser`

   C. `Install-Module -Name Az -AllowClobber -Scope Administrator`

   D. `Install-Module -Name Az -AllowClobber -Scope None`

6. Which of the following is not a capability that one can complete with the Azure Mobile App?

   A. Monitor the health and status of Azure resources

   B. Diagnose and fix issues using the Azure Portal or one of the command-line interfaces

   C. Run command-line operations to manage Azure-specific resources

   D. Create machine learning models

7. The most efficient way to distribute Azure Resource Management (ARM) templates is using which tool?

   A. Azure Cloud Shell

   B. Azure Resource Groups

   C. Azure Resource Manager

   D. Azure PowerShell

8. Your organization is experiencing an outage on all its virtual machine instances. Where should you check first to determine the cause of this issue?

   A. Azure Status page

   B. Azure Resource Health page

   C. Azure Service Health page

   D. Azure Advisor

9. Select the correct pairing of definitions based on the options presented. Place the items found in the right column in the correct order.

Secures IoT-based devices	Azure IoT Hub
A SaaS-based platform for monitoring IoT devices	Azure Sphere
Manage devices and route messages to and from IoT-enabled devices	Azure IoT Central

   A. Azure IoT Sphere, Azure IoT Hub, Azure IoT Central

   B. Azure IoT Hub, Azure IoT Hub, Azure IoT Central

   C. Azure Sphere, Azure IoT Central, Azure IoT Hub

   D. Azure IoT Central, Azure IoT Hub, Azure IoT Central

10. Under what circumstances would you configure your Synapse Analytics environment to be always available?

   A. Synapse Analytics must always be available regardless of circumstances

   B. During unpredictable, burst-based workloads

   C. To ensure reserved processing power and optimized savings

   D. During predictable batch jobs

11. Which of the following solutions is used to help model data from sources such as data warehouses and data lakes to train machine learning models?

   A. Azure Databricks

   B. HDInsight

   C. Azure Synapse Analytics

   D. Cognitive Services

12. Which of the following solutions is like a Hadoop cluster for processing big data?

   A. Azure Databricks

   B. HDInsight

   C. Azure Synapse Analytics

   D. Cognitive Services

13. Review the following scenario and replace the word you believe is inaccurate with one of the following choices.

Azure Functions are intended for use when applications require advanced connectors, triggers, and actions delivered using serverless orchestration.

A. Cognitive Services

B. Azure Logic Apps

C. Azure Bots

D. The answer is accurate.

14. Review the following scenario and replace the word you believe is inaccurate with one of the following choices.

Microsoft DevOps is a Software as a Service cloud solution for managing the build, deployment, delivery, and operational activities in Azure.

A. Infrastructure as a Service

B. Platform as a Service

C. Hybrid computing

D. The answer is accurate.

15. Select the response that best fits the questions:

	True	False
Azure DevOps is available as both a cloud and noncloud offering.	◯	◯
Azure Pipelines is used to help plan and track work, code defects, and issues using Kanban methodologies.	◯	◯
GitHub is a centralized DevOps tool to manage source code for a project.	◯	◯

A. False, False, True

B. True, False, False

C. False, False, False

D. True, False, True

Answers

1. **B.** Azure Cloud Shell is a web-based management tool accessible from virtually any device. Users can utilize the command-line interface in either Bash or Power Shell mode.

2. **C.** False. You need to authorize any changes before Cloud Advisor can update where automation is offered.

    False. Azure Monitor, not Azure Advisor, offers visibility into system-wide outages.

    True. Azure allows you to postpone updates up to 90 days.

3. **A.** A user can access both PowerShell and Bash command-line tools from Cloud Shell only.

4. **D.** Only this option offers users two ways to expose all features in Microsoft Azure.

5. **A.** Setting the scope for the current user as Administrator or Superuser is not supported. In this case, you still need to set the scope.

6. **D.** You can only review the state of Machine Learning services; you cannot create any using the Azure mobile app at this time.

7. **C.** Azure Resource Manager is a container to hold templates.

8. **A.** The best practice is to check on global system performance first before focusing on individual resources and services.

9. **C.** Azure Sphere secures IoT Devices.

10. **B.** Unpredictable, burst-based workloads is the only condition that meets all the criteria described in the question.

11. **A.** Azure Databricks is the correct response, since the solution helps model data from data warehouses and data lakes to train machine learning models.

12. **B.** HDInsight is a clustered Hadoop product for the processing of big data.

13. **B.** The statement is inaccurate, as Azure Logic Apps is intended for serverless orchestration.

14. **D.** DevOps is a collection of a cloud-based web applications that connect to each Azure IaaS or PaaS source.

15. **B.** True. Azure DevOps is available as a cloud service offering, called Azure DevOps Services, or an on-premises offering, called Azure DevOps Server.

    False. Azure Boards, not Pipelines, is used to help plan and track work, code defects, and issues using Kanban methodologies.

    False. GitHub is used as the repository for the code, but Azure Reports handles centralized code control within Azure DevOps.

General Security and Network Security

In this chapter, you will learn to
- Describe core security concepts in Azure.
- Identify core and network security technologies available in Azure.
- Configure specific security solutions to protect your environment.

So far, you've read about the importance of security in Microsoft Azure in theory. Securing cloud infrastructure is among the most important responsibilities for a cloud professional. Within the Azure platform, there are many security features and functions you need to familiarize yourself with. Since organizations are not just moving a document or an application to the cloud, but their entire business, far more operational controls must be put in place to ensure data is safe from those who should not have access.

Azure can address the security requirements that an organization might have by applying several solutions available in its portfolio. You'll learn about the core and network security offerings available in the Azure platform.

Core Security Features

Think back to every major technology event over the past several decades. What is the one thread all IT professionals worry about more than anything else? If you said security, you are correct. Unlike other technical disciplines, security is not something that requires simple wiring and configuration, and you are done. Quite the opposite. The configuration aspect is just a small part of the process. Knowing what features can help you mitigate the risks in the Azure platform is what you'll learn about in the next few sections.

Azure Security Center

One of the IT industry's biggest challenges is that there is simply not enough security talent available to address all facets of information security vulnerability. Some organizations may need five to ten people to monitor systems if processes were manual. And let's be honest here, there was a point when manual system management was commonplace.

Now, however, organizations can use a unified infrastructure security management system that offers a strengthened security posture for data centers and provides advanced threat protection across cloud workloads. In other words, no longer does the organization need many resources to complete the work that one person can now accomplish.

One of the biggest challenges that any organization may face is keeping up with the most up-to-date security requirements. Can you imagine keeping up with hundreds, if not thousands, of regulatory and compliance control requirement modifications that impact your security posture? That's why it is important to keep your resources safe by building tightly integrated solutions with your cloud hosting provider and its security offerings.

When moving to the cloud, you need to make sure your workloads are secure. That means ensuring those responsibilities from the data center are now repositioned to handle new activities whether you are still managing infrastructure (IaaS) or only responsible for applications (PaaS). Even if your organization is fully embracing software as a service, an organization must still consider underlying security requirements. That's why Azure Security Center is so instrumental in cloud management and orchestration. Azure Security Center offers users the tools necessary to harden networks, secure services, and ensure security regulatory compliance in implementing a well-defined security posture.

Azure Security Center offers users two service tiers: a free tier and one that utilizes the Azure Defender Service. Table 5-1 describes the two-tier pricing approach.

To review all the features in Azure Security Center, go to the navigation plane. Select Security Center. When you click on the menu options, Security Center, a screen like the one in Figure 5-1 appears. You will notice a Secure Score, Regulatory Compliance Pane, Azure Defender Pane, and Azure Firewall Pane. You should be aware of several other navigation items on the left side, including Security Alerts, Recommendations, and Inventory. If you have the Firewall Service and Defender Service enabled, you will see analytics appear in the Azure Security Center. Otherwise, the only two features available are those offered under the Free tier. Each of the features mentioned has a distinct role in supporting the security posture of an organization.

Pricing Tier	Description
Free	The free tier only offers continuous assessment and security recommendations of the Azure environments within a subscription.
Azure Defender	The paid tier offers all features offered in the Free tier plus adaptive application control and network hardening, regulatory compliance dashboards, threat protection management for any Azure virtual machine environment, protection for all non-Azure servers when connected, threat protection for PaaS applications and services, and Microsoft Defender for Endpoint support. On average, per server protection is $15.00. Some services are charged per gigabyte.

Table 5-1 Two-Tier Azure Security Center Pricing Model

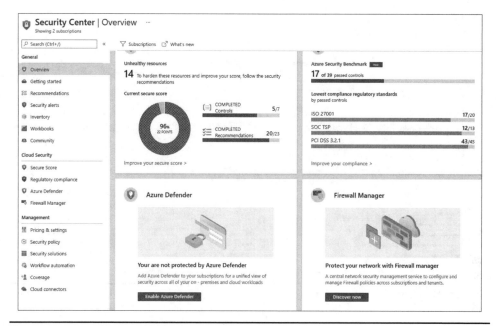

Figure 5-1   Azure Security Center Free tier view

Secure Score

Secure Score evaluates all the resources across your subscriptions. A score is derived from providing a user a state of security based on predefined and custom rules set in the Azure subscription. There is a maximum score of 100 percent. A score is not an average, though. Instead, it weighs the posture of resources across subscriptions. Based on weighting, usage, importance, and criticality, a score is produced. Figure 5-2 illustrates an example of a Secure Score.

Figure 5-2
Secure Score

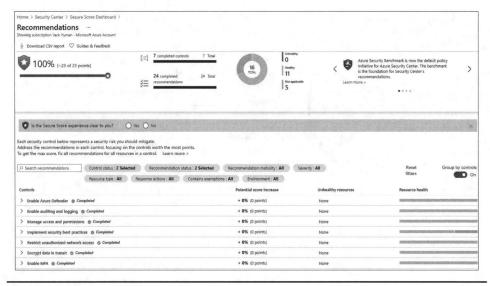

Figure 5-3   Recommendations details

Recommendations

Suppose a user clicks on the Secure Score Card. In that case, the user has an opportunity to further evaluate the issues that might prevent the subscription instance from earning a higher Secure Score. First, you need to select the subscription on the Recommendations Overview page. As seen in Figure 5-3, you'll see a drill-down of all subscription recommendations on the secondary page. In this case, all recommendations have been completed.

Regulatory Compliance

The Azure Security Center Dashboard's regulatory compliance card provides an overview to the user on how compliant the environments are against key international regulatory measures. The most prevalent are ISO-27001, PCI DSS 3.2.1, and SOC TSP. Considering the three international standards and combining them with Microsoft-specific measures, there is also an Azure Regulatory Compliance Score. The score combines 11 domain areas: network security, identity management, privileged access, data protection, asset management, logging and threat detection, incident repose, posture and vulnerability management, endpoint security, backup and record, and governance and strategy.

The challenge for most organizations is identifying which assessment to perform. Azure Security Center streamlines the process by providing guidance using a variety of indicator types. The Azure Security Center assessments analyze the risk factors in the environment against industry and Microsoft practices. As you make changes in

Azure Security Center, your Regulatory Compliance Score changes. The refresh is not instantaneous as Security Center updates on average every 24–36 hours. The same thing is true with Azure Secure Score.

Azure Defender

Advice is sometimes simply not enough. To act upon that advice proactively is every organization's main objective, as any adverse data event can be quite costly. However, security vulnerabilities are unpredictable. You need a technical solution that can act on your behalf to thwart malicious activity. Proactive support is possible when an organization enables Azure Defender within the Azure Security Center. Azure Defender is an extended detection and response (XDR) solution for threat protection. Azure Defender provides XDR for not only Azure but also hybrid cloud environments. Remember, Azure Defender is a premium service for those wanting to use Azure Security Center. When considering your organization's need, Microsoft guides you in stating what services you are charged for in every instance of Defender utilized. Each of the following services requires a separate Azure Defender instance:

- App Services
- Storage
- SQL
- Kubernetes
- Container Registries
- Key Vaults
- Resource Manager
- DNS
- Third-Party Servers

 EXAM TIP   Microsoft often moves reports to other areas of Azure, which may confuse users. It is projected that all reports in Defender are slowly migrating to the Threat Protection Status Report section of Azure as of Summer 2021. Make sure you watch out for the location and name change on the exam.

To protect third-party systems in your environment, you can implement Azure Arc and then enable Azure Defender. While Azure Arc is a free service, enabling Azure Defender on those third-party systems results in a charge for each instance that Arc is installed.

Arc works by being installed on any non-Azure resources. This can include virtual machines, Kubernetes pods, or Kubernetes clusters, as an example. Once the service is installed, the machine registers with Azure Defender, which means services are now ready for use.

Security Alerts

Azure Security Center is responsible for creating various alerts. Security alerts, though, are among the most important because it helps diagnose issues on resources deployed either on-premises or in the cloud, hybrid or otherwise. A security alert triggers based on a detection event. Alerts are only enabled when you subscribe to Azure Defender. Again, alerts are based on each resource monitored under a pay-for plan.

There are specific differences between a security alert and a security incident. Whereas an alert is a notification that Security Center generates as soon as there is a threat detected on a resource, a security incident is a collection of related alerts that bring together a list of all the alerts and classify them using a combination of signal levels and descriptors to quickly help you understand the breadth of the attack. An incident addresses the attack path and the resources affected. An alert merely tells you that you need to quickly review the issue as there may be a mission-critical issue. With Azure Security Center, both Security Alerts and Security Incident data are accessible to users with an Azure Defender Subscription purchase. Figure 5-4 represents an example output from Azure Security Center from a series of previous Security Alerts.

Figure 5-4   List of previous Security Alerts

Total Resources	Unhealthy Resources	Unmonitored Resources	Unregistered subscriptions
19	14	0	0

Resource name ↑↓	Resource type ↑↓	Subscription ↑↓	Agent monitoring ↑↓	Azure Defender ↑↓	Recommendat... ↑↓
Visual Studio Enterprise Subscription – MPN	Subscription	Visual Studio Enterprise Subscr...		On	···
cowebsitepublic-mysqldbserver	Azure Database for MySQL ser...	Jack Hyman - Microsoft Azure ...			···
az900devtest8520	Key vaults	Jack Hyman - Microsoft Azure ...		Off	···
az900mlspace9025830096	Storage accounts	Jack Hyman - Microsoft Azure ...		Off	···
az900iothub12165430952	Storage accounts	Jack Hyman - Microsoft Azure ...		Off	···
aaz900devtest245	Storage accounts	Jack Hyman - Microsoft Azure ...		Off	···
az900mlspace2363066784	Key vaults	Jack Hyman - Microsoft Azure ...		Off	···
az900iothub17845723063	Key vaults	Jack Hyman - Microsoft Azure ...		Off	···
dbstoragervvqtaas6mwiw	Storage accounts	Jack Hyman - Microsoft Azure ...		Off	···
cs71003bffda65707cf	Storage accounts	Jack Hyman - Microsoft Azure ...		Off	···
az900container	Container registries	Jack Hyman - Microsoft Azure ...		Off	···
companywebsitekv	Key vaults	Jack Hyman - Microsoft Azure ...		Off	···

Figure 5-5   Inventory in Azure Security Center

Resource Hygiene and Inventory

Sometimes it is difficult to keep track of every resource within a subscription. The central location that you can find information on all resources is housed in Azure Security Center under Inventory. With *Inventory*, you can see all resources and the state of health for each resource versus across a subscription. A user can take a more proactive approach in correcting specific issues for each resource than dealing with the issues on a per-incident basis. For example, in Figure 5-5, you'll notice that there are 19 resources. Of those resources, 14 require corrective action to improve the health of the cloud resource. The darker the bar is on the right side, the more urgent and likely significant technical issues are with the resource.

Clicking the resource presents a detailed view of the specific fixes required to bring the resource to complete health. You should be aware that some are suggestions that can be fixed easily by clicking a single button called Quick Fix, while others require a bit more time and configuration. When you are trying to analyze health and reliability, this is commonly referred to as *Resource Hygiene*.

Supposed you were to go to a doctor; would it be an emergency if your visit was to simply get your height and weight checked? Likely not. If you were sick and needed medicine, your medical care urgency increases exponentially. Depending on the severity of the illness, the recommendation scale changes, as does the overall health status. The same practice holds true for managing the health of your Azure Resources, which is referred to as Resource Hygiene. You manage resources based on their current health state. The state is determined by the severity of issues and the number of issues combined. A detailed set of recommendations are provided in Figure 5-6.

Figure 5-6   Resource Hygiene recommendations

Azure Key Vault

Most applications have some form of sensitive data. An example might be how an application connects to another system or how an application that uses a database that may have a connection string that is encrypted with a username and password. If both examples exposed the credentials to end users, a security risk is obvious.

Azure Key Vault provides a safe method to hide credentials such as secrets, keys, and certificates centrally. If you have an item stored in Azure Key Vault, you can apply a security policy that calls out the user or application that requires the specified credential. Azure Key Vault encrypts all the encryption keys, which means Microsoft will never know what your data is made of, including your encrypted keys and files.

To create a Key Vault, follow these steps:

1. Select All Services from the Navigation plane.

2. Select Security.

3. Locate Key Vaults.

4. Select Key Vaults.

5. Click the New Button on this page.

6. You will now be able to create a new Key Vault. On this page, you are asked to enter a few items.

- **Subscription** Select subscription appropriate to where resources are located.
- **Resource Group** Select resource group where there is billable mapping.
- **Key Vault Name** Name.
- **Region** Location for storing encrypted data.
- **Pricing Tier** Select either Standard or Premium.
- **Days to Retain Deleted Vault** Select from 7 to 90 days.
- **Purge Protection** Enable or disable purge protection. If enforced, there is a mandatory retention period for any deleted vaults and vault objects.

You might be curious about a few configurations that may also come up as questions on the exam. The only difference between the Standard tier and the Premium tier is how keys are stored in the pricing tier. With Premium, keys are stored in a Hardware Security Module (HSM). The HSM is a separate component designed specifically to separate the content from its origination location, storage container, and how it processes cryptographic data.

TIP If Federal Information Processing Standards (FIPS) 140-2 are mandated within your organization, the use of the Premium Key Vault, which allows for HSM, is nonnegotiable.

Azure Key Vault allows users to import keys, secrets, and certifications from third-party sources. It is also possible to generate all the above within Azure Key Vault natively. You will need to configure each of the scenarios based on the critical need. To create either a Key, Secret, or Certificate, go to the left side navigation of the Azure Key Vault, select the appropriate link (Figure 5-7), and select the link of choice.

Let's assume you want to generate a self-signed certificate. You would go about completing this process following these steps:

1. Click Certificate.

2. Next, click the Generate/Import button.

3. The screen in Figure 5-8 appears. You will be asked to enter the following data:

- Method of Certificate Creation.
- Certificate Name.

Figure 5-7
Azure Key Vault
navigation

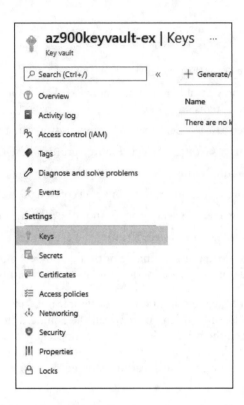

4. Type of Certificate Authority: Either managed by a certificate authority or not. Determines many of the other options.

- **Subject** Provide a unique name for the certificate.
- **DNS Name** Website name (i.e., www.az900exam.com).
- **Validity Period in Months** Number of months the certificate should be valid before requiring renewal.
- **Content-Type** Select either PKS #12 or PEM.
- **Lifetime Action Types** Gives you the option how to renew the certificate via a dropdown.
- **Percentage Lifetime** Select a number between 0 and 100 percent where you want the certificate renewed.
- **Advanced Policy Configuration** Additional configurations as noted in Figure 5-9.

Once complete, press Create. If all credentials pass, a new certificate is then created. The certificate is generated containing a 4,096-bit key. Similar use case creation scenarios can be completed for keys as well as secrets.

Create a certificate ...

Method of Certificate Creation
Generate

Certificate Name * ⓘ
az900certificate01

Type of Certificate Authority (CA) ⓘ
Self-signed certificate

Subject * ⓘ
cn=chapter05

DNS Names ⓘ
1 DNS name

Validity Period (in months)
12

Content Type
PKCS #12   PEM

Lifetime Action Type
Automatically renew at a given percentage lifetime

Percentage Lifetime

Advanced Policy Configuration
Not configured

Figure 5-8   Creating a certificate

Figure 5-9
Advanced Policy
Configuration

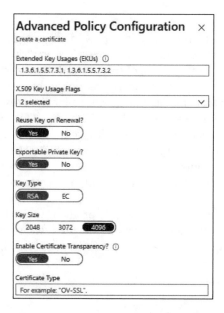

Advanced Policy Configuration ×
Create a certificate

Extended Key Usages (EKUs) ⓘ
1.3.6.1.5.5.7.3.1, 1.3.6.1.5.5.7.3.2

X.509 Key Usage Flags
2 selected   ∨

Reuse Key on Renewal?
Yes   No

Exportable Private Key?
Yes   No

Key Type
RSA   EC

Key Size
2048   3072   4096

Enable Certificate Transparency? ⓘ
Yes   No

Certificate Type
For example: "OV-SSL".

Azure Key Vault is often used to store encryption keys for Azure VMs. For example, Security Center will make recommendations to create a set of encrypted VM disks if you create a virtual machine instance. This is not done automatically. A virtual machine disk is stored as a virtual host disk file. When the host operating system runs the virtual machine, it must access the security key to decrypt the virtual host disk and run it. Azure Key Vault acts as the agent to orchestrate such communications for encryption and decryption.

If you decide to use Azure Key Vault to store disk encryption keys, access policies must be configured to allow the Azure Key Vault to handle disk encryption. You can set this up by going to Access Policies and ensuring that Azure Disk Encryption for Volume Encryption is enabled. Alternate ways to enable disk encryption include PowerShell, CLI, Cloud Shell, and an ARM template.

 TIP Ensure that when enabling encryption in Azure Key Vault, all your assets are assigned to the correct subscription and region, or else creating certificates, keys, and secrets is not possible.

Azure Sentinel

It's no secret that company's love to buy lots of security tools. Many organizations buy several of the same types of security tools when it is completely unnecessary. The two most common investment areas are SOAR (security, operation, automation, and response) and SIEM (security information and event management) systems. Securing resources and data can be tough. Knowing what to monitor properly is even more difficult. That's why many organizations continually make investments in these two technology classes to solve difficult business problems. Microsoft realized the business challenge across the industry and combined the two technology types into a single solution called Azure Sentinel.

 TIP It's important you know the difference between SOAR and SIEM solutions. SOAR, which stands for security orchestration, automation, and response, is a suite of software solutions and tools that allow organizations to streamline security operations in three key areas. Those areas are threat and vulnerability management, incident response, and security operations. On the other hand, SIEM, which stands for security information and event management, is when software products and services evaluate security information management and security event management in real time. An organization is able to evaluate security alerts generated by applications and network hardware through a centralized application environment.

Azure Sentinel is not an Azure-only product. Quite the contrary. It can provide security analytics reporting and analysis for on-premises, third-party cloud hosting providers, and Microsoft Azure. It just so happens to operate in Microsoft Azure natively.

Using Azure Sentinel, like other Azure Security products, requires the creation of a workspace. Once the workspace is created, you will need to enable at least one Azure Log Analytics instance for capturing all data. Capturing log data is mandatory for using a SIEM, specifically when analyzing User Behavior Analytics security features with Azure Sentinel.

When you want to create a new workspace (Figure 5-10), you can create a Log Analytics Workspace as a prerequisite. Fill in the following fields:

- **Subscription**   Select Subscription that will require billing.
- **Resource Group**   Billable Group where logs are stored.
- **Instance Name**   Name for Log Analytics Workspace.
- **Instance Region**   What geographic region will logs be stored.

Once you have created at least one Log Analytics Workspace, press Add at the bottom of the Create Azure Sentinel page. You are then required to Connect to data sources or Create Security Alerts.

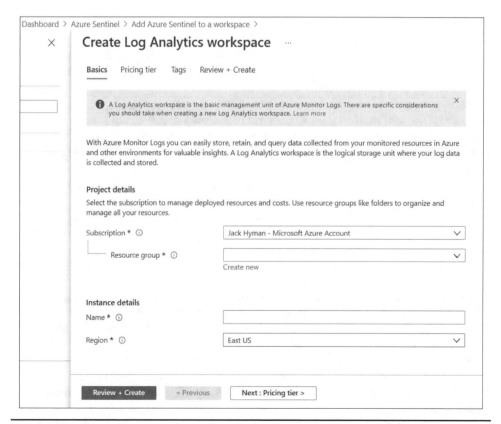

Figure 5-10   Azure Sentinel Create Log Analytics Workspace

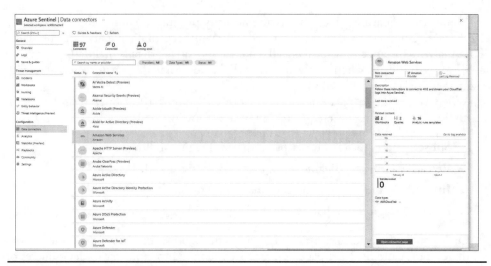

Figure 5-11   Amazon Web Services connector configuration for Azure Sentinel

Once your Azure Sentinel Instance is fully deployed, select Data Connectors. You'll see a selection of Microsoft-specific and third-party connectors. To connect to a third-party connector, highlight the connector and complete the requirements on the right side. In the example in Figure 5-11, an Amazon Web Service data connector is being configured for Azure Sentinel.

Each connector has a prerequisite and next steps process to configure the respective connector. You will need to follow those instructions so that the connector works properly with Azure Sentinel. Some connectors will have license requirements; others will not. The instructions guide you in the configuration so that you do not need to make incorrect assumptions.

Azure Sentinel sits above the SIEM, which can help monitor speed and scale across many systems once configured using current and previous analytics data. Once a data connector is configured, the log data must be stored in a collection. In this case, you want to map it to an Azure Monitor Workbook. The Azure Monitor Workbook allows for data across one or more connectors to be easily consumable inside Azure Sentinel.

The data collection is then stored for past and present to look for patterns of suspicious activity. If unusual activity is detected, a security professional in the organization delegated with notification rights is notified of the threat. Sentinel also includes a library of pre-built attack patterns and threats. These queries are provided for user querying so that the system can run autonomously against your resources. These built-in rules can be found under Hunting (Figure 5-12).

Should a problem be detected, Azure Sentinel can respond using a Playbook. *Playbooks* are workflows that tell a system how to handle a situation upon an alert triggering. Instead of waiting for manual intervention, the Playbook can automatically respond on behalf of a system administrator or the organization if the process to rectify the process is well documented. Playbooks make use of Logic Apps to execute workflow activities.

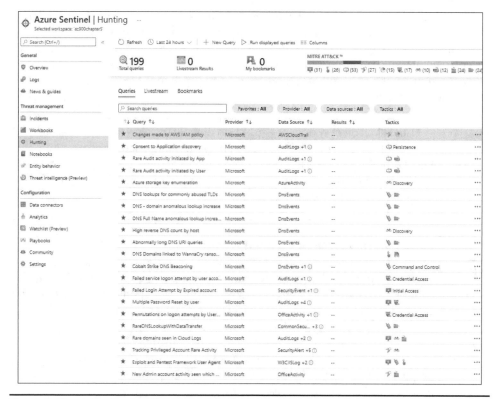

Figure 5-12   Azure Sentinel Hunting pre-built rules

Azure Dedicated Hosts

As an organization moves its operations to the cloud, it's not uncommon that a requirement comes up from time to time for a dedicated host instance to replace the infrastructure supporting the on-premises servers. Whether it is Azure or another cloud service provider, a host computer is a physical computer with an operating system. The virtual machine resides on that computer instance. With Azure, if you create a virtual machine, those virtual machines are dedicated to you. The host system has virtual machine instances running on it that may be used by other organizations and customers, not just you and your organization for its specific needs.

Azure Dedicated Hosts are instances where a dedicated virtual machine environment resides on a shared host computer that can support many people. If you work in an industry that requires rigid compliance and regulatory controls, shared management is often not permitted. You'll need a dedicated solution to host those virtual machine instances so that no system can interrupt the services of your operation once you transition to the cloud. A great analogy is this: a shared VM is an apartment, whereas a dedicated host is a single home where only a single person lives. That person has a mission-critical responsibility that requires a unique environment, not differentiation.

With Azure Dedicated Hosts, the virtual machine stands on its own, independently, allowing you to run no other solution except the specific host instance. Having an Azure Dedicated Host is a great way to secure your data, ensure system integrity, and maintain strict system isolation. The cost for ensuring the system is compliant and meets the rigor of such rigidity is the trade-off. You do pay more for an Azure Dedicated Host, but the security assurances are worth it.

 EXAM TIP You may not see a question directly utilizing the words *Azure Dedicated Hosts*. Instead, a question may mention a dedicated host in conjunction with a discussion of IaaS or PaaS architecture implementation. Watch out for the subtle integration of words that can make a world of difference in answering a question.

When to Consider Azure Dedicated Hosts

Azure is a public cloud first and foremost. Most organizations find it acceptable to run a virtual machine in a shared environment. When there is a need for dedicated hosting requirements, but you still want to support a public, not private or hybrid infrastructure, you best option is to consider Azure Dedicated Hosts.

Microsoft Azure Dedicated Host allows an organization to run their virtual machines on a dedicated host, not shared with other customers. Usually, organizations share tenants with virtual environments. With Azure Dedicated Host, you are provisioned with your own hardware but can still support public cloud requirements for other mission-critical needs.

Azure Defense Strategies in Depth

Defense in Depth is a global concept. So far, we've talked much about how to diagnose security based on compliance, regulatory, and threat protection measures in place using the Azure platform. But let's now take it a step further as we haven't addressed the underlying strategy that employs different layers of security.

Cloud security is like a castle. Each entry point, wall, window, exit, and hallway is an analogy to a different security concept. In the past, security references were exclusive to perimeter security, signature-based anti-virus solutions, and perhaps some hardware solutions. Fast forward to the requirements for the cloud. The needs are far more advanced, require more than just a few applications, and address a broad void. *Defense in Depth* takes the form of the castle that houses your data. If your castle didn't have any locks on it, any individual could simply go to a door, open it, and grab some data. If you add defensive layers, there are moats, which are protective casings that help create a set of checks and balances for those coming in and out of the castle.

The Azure Firewall, as discussed earlier, acts as the perimeter defense. Perimeter defense is the outside defense for the entire castle. If the intruder attempts to attack, the firewall prevents the attack from occurring if there is no permission granted at the door. Think of the proverbial huge wall one must climb to get onto the property.

Each wall of the castle forms another security layer. There are checkpoints. If you want to enter a checkpoint, you must maintain certain authentication and authorization credentials. Otherwise, the system will prevent entry. Hence, you are experiencing the use of solutions such as Endpoint Protection, available with Azure Defender.

Every so often, a home needs repair. So do castles. When a system needs a patch, these patches prevent exploits either at the operating systems level or application level. Using Recommendations, Security Alerts, and Security Incidents allows you to prevent many unnecessary attacks by getting ahead of the issue. If there is a need for a deeper dive into the operating system for vulnerabilities, one might use vulnerability scanning to review these issues. You can see where the issues are, where to focus, and prioritizing the Azure Security Center issues. If there were needs to ensure specific systems had unique security locks on them, perhaps you could use Azure Key Vault mechanisms.

Finally, the agent at the tower is represented by the SIEM solution. In this case, that is Azure Sentinel. The person who is at the top of the castle watchtower can see everyone. That individual has visibility into what everyone is always doing. How do they do this, though? They monitor the activity by evaluating current and historical data for risk behavior. Using User Behavior Analytics helps capture the actor whether they are doing the activity intentionally or unintentionally through activity and log data.

In summary, *Defense in Depth* means that security is not just a single application anymore. It requires the inclusion of many fronts coming together to address the enemy, as it is often difficult to circumvent cybersecurity attacks ahead of the curve.

Network Security Groups (NSG)

Network Security Groups (NSG) filter network traffic to and from Azure resources. Those resources are found in a virtual network. Network security groups contain security rules that control inbound traffic. The traffic is either allowed or denied based on the rules set forth by the Azure resources. Based on the Azure rule, you must specify the parameters, including the source, destination, port, and protocol. The security enforced contains as little as zero rules or as many as desired based on the needs of the Azure subscription. Some properties must be tied to the Azure subscription. Those properties are listed in Table 5-2.

Property	Explanation
Name	Unique network security group name
Priority	A number between 100 and 4,096 where rules are processed in the order based on the number
Source or destination	Individual IP address, classless inter-domain routing (CIDR) block (10.0.0.0/28, for example), service tag, or application security group.
Protocol	TCP, UDP, ICMP, etc.
Direction	Inbound/Outbound, Ingress/Egress
Port range	Individual or range of ports available. Possible ranges may include 80 or 10000–10005.
Action	Allow or Deny

Table 5-2 Network Security Group (NSG) Properties

When evaluating network security groups, rules are evaluated by using a priority process. The five-tuple information order of source, source port, destination, destination port, and protocol that allows or denies the traffic are responsible for handling security. Security rules do not allow for creating two rules with the same priority and direction.

Here is a hypothetical flow of traffic among subnets based on Figure 5-13.

- Subnet 1 receives data from a virtual network. The data comes from a virtual network that runs Azure resources, including an Azure Firewall.

- In Subnet 2, a communication request is received. Eventually, a request between Subnet 1 and Subnet 2 occurs whereby the handshake is recognized.

- Once the handshake is formalized in Subnet 2, communication commences in Subnet 3 with additional resources. In this case, it is the data tier to retrieve the data.

Ensuring the environment is secure means that no communication should occur between Subnet 1 to Subnet 3 and vice versa. Only Subnet 2 can act as the agent of communication for transport. That means only Subnet 1 should communicate with the other virtual network that runs an Azure Firewall. That could be outside the subnet. That's why you would use a NSG rule to enforce policies such as managing the protective measures or the so-called moats.

NSG can be associated with a subnet or with a network interface attached virtual machine. You can only have a single NSG association; however, there can be up to 1,000 rules per single NSG applied, allowing many added tasks.

NSG interference is often a concern among cloud professionals. Each rule must have an established priority between 100 and 4,096. A rule that is indicative of a lower priority is given preference over higher priority. That means any network traffic is applied against the rule using the lowest priority number. In file and rank order, if traffic matches a rule, the traffic is applied and is then processed.

On the other hand, when traffic does not meet the criteria, the lowest priority rule is considered. The process flow continues repetitiously until a match is made or no match is made. Azure allows a traffic range up to 65,535, which should be ample to avoid any form of error.

Figure 5-13
Multi-tier
application
example

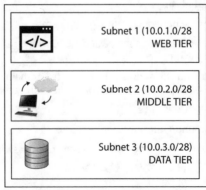

Azure Virtual Network (10.0.0.0/28)

Dashboard >

Network security groups ✩ ⋯

+ Add   ☰☰ Edit columns   ◯ Refresh   ⇄ Try preview   ♡ Feedback | ⊘ Assign tags

Subscriptions: 2 of 3 selected – Don't see a subscription? Open Directory + Subscription settings

Filter by name...	2 subscriptions ∨	All resource groups ∨

2 items

☐	Name ↑↓	Resource group ↑↓	Location ↑↓
☐ 🛡	az900vminstance-nsg	CompanyWebsite	East US
☐ 🛡	workers-sg	databricks-rg-az900-databricks-3euvmjdyshzxw	East US

Figure 5-14   Adding a new NSG

You can create a new NSG by searching for Network Security Group on the top bar on the Azure Portal. Upon pressing enter, you'll be prompted to Add a New Network Security Group if one does not already exist. The interface to add a new NSG is appears in Figure 5-14. Once a new NSG is created, a user can customize the inbound and outbound traffic for the specified NSG. In the case of Figure 5-15, a list of all traffic options is listed. The ability to customize Inbound and Outbound rules is formidable from the left side navigation under settings. A user would either click Inbound Security Rules or Outbound Security Rules along with the Add Button. An example of customizing an Inbound rule is visible in Figure 5-16.

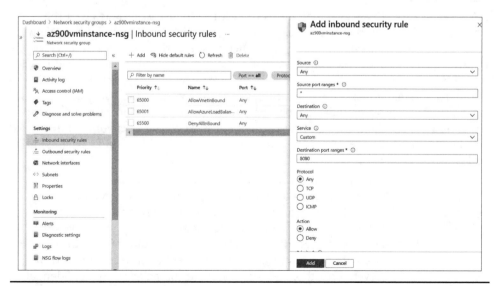

Figure 5-15   All NSG Inbound and Outbound Security rules

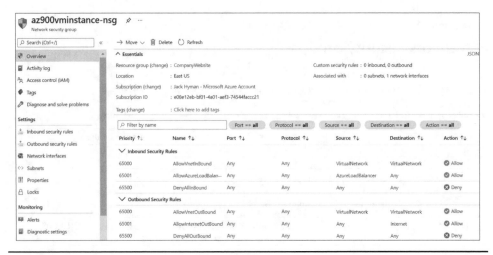

Figure 5-16 NSG—customizing an Inbound Security rule

The last feature you should be aware of when reviewing NSG is the use of service tags. The service tag is an identifier utilized by Microsoft to help systems better identify characteristics of a network that are essential for communication on a network or subnetwork. The service tag is called upon by a rule to manage the traffic flow. Often, the tag is treated as an allow or deny tag. To use a service tag, a user must call the tag from the Source menu in the Inbound or Outbound Security Rules page. Once that is complete and activated, a user can begin to disseminate traffic to and from the NSG as desired.

Azure Firewall

Network security is now as important as protecting cloud-based assets given the transactional activity on virtual networks. If your organization uses Azure Virtual Network resources, Azure Firewall—a cloud-based network security service—should also be implemented for your organization. A typical use case for using Azure Firewall is when organizations have a virtual machine that end users regularly interact with within the Azure networking context. Implementing just-in-time virtual machine access (JIT) for Azure Firewall is often considered a best practice in this circumstance. By implementing an Azure Firewall, there is a significant reduction in exposure to network volume-based attacks. You only provide controlled access to VMs when needed, using assigned NSG and Azure Firewall rules.

EXAM TIP Remember that an Azure Firewall uses a static public IP address to address virtual network resources. The use of a static public IP allows outside firewalls to identify traffic originating from your virtual network. Since a firewall is a security device that supports both software and hardware, you apply rules to your environment to protect your network. Rules prevent unauthorized parties from acquiring access to confidential data on your computer.

By creating an Azure Firewall, you establish policies that help determine the ports to be protected, how long the ports should remain open, and determine a list of IP addresses that can be accessed. These are all capabilities that help your organization stay in control while ensuring users can do what they need to request access. All requests are logged and tracked in an activity log. These activity logs are helpful whether they be used just for Azure Firewall or for other security products such as Azure Sentinel, which we discuss in another section. Logs support easy monitoring and audit access. Finally, Azure Security Center exposes Azure Firewall activities such as approved requests, configured VMs using the Firewall, and address connectivity details to your Azure Firewall destination network address translation (DNAT).

Up Close: Azure Firewall Rules

Three types of firewall rules can operate in the Azure environment: NAT Rules, Network Rules, and Application Rules.

- **NAT Rules**   Rules used to forward traffic from a firewall to another device on a network.
- **Network Rules**   Rules that enable traffic on a specific IP address range or port to communicate based on parameters you specify.
- **Application Rules**   Rules based on application-specific parameters that communicate across the enterprise, within the network. These also target specific domains.

In addition to the firewall rules, there are unique threat intelligence features in the Azure Firewall that protect known IP addresses and domains from being the victims of attacks. This data is collected and managed as part of the Microsoft Threat Intelligence Feed.

Azure DDoS Protection

A distributed denial of service (DDoS) attack is one of the most common yet, costly attacks that can impact any business operation. When organizations consider the threat to moving IT infrastructure resources to the cloud, one area that often raises concern is a DDoS attack. A DDoS attack can disturb operations entirely from network connectivity, making access to systems unavailable to end users. Attacks can be widespread or highly targeted at a specific endpoint on the Internet.

When you sign up for an Azure subscription, you are protected by Azure's core infrastructure DDoS Basic Protection services for free. Microsoft's network and global scale are vast, so you can be assured that the defense against common network infrastructure for always-on traffic monitoring and real-time mitigation is second to none. You are not responsible for any configuration or system changes. Similar to PaaS services, DDoS Basic is part of the core infrastructure requirement with no end-user intervention.

Why then would an organization be willing to pay a premium for DDoS support then? It comes down to requiring advanced mitigation features, automatic tuning, logging, alerting, and telemetry. These features are simply not included in DDoS Basic. You pay a sizable monthly fee for premium services to ensure your infrastructure is always secure by getting these add-on security benefits:

- Native platform integration
- 365/24/7 monitoring
- Adaptive Tuning
- Multi-layered protection with a Web Application Firewall (WAF)
- Attack Analytics at scale
- Real-time metrics and alerts
- Cost containment

DDoS Protection at the Standard tier monitors traffic at all times. It uses a combination of machine learning to better understand your traffic over time so that it can quickly handle any event based on your network activity's profile. When you upgrade to DDoS Standard, you also have the option to integrate your logs from the SIEM system so that the aggregation of data from a large number of sources provides a complete view of your data for analysis and a state of safety for all systems supported.

Chapter Review

As you wrap up Chapter 5, a few themes should resonate with you about securing your Azure cloud environment. Whether you are migrating to Azure or are already familiar with the platform and its capabilities, security is central to ensuring operational continuity. Organizations may have resources on-premises, hybrid, or entirely in the cloud. To maintain a well-defined security posture, Microsoft has developed a series of solutions to solve common security concerns. For example, Azure Security Center is an all-in-one security analysis solution for Azure and on-premises resources. It combines the capabilities of policy and compliance, resource security hygiene, and threat protection under a single umbrella. Azure Security Center measures success using a Secure Score scoring system to help the cloud professional better evaluate risk.

Additionally, integrated into Security Center are premium services such as Azure Defender and Azure Firewall. Azure Defender provides extended security alerts and advanced threat protection for resources such as virtual machines, SQL databases, containers, and web applications. Azure Firewall is meant to protect malicious compromising network activity.

Core features go beyond Security Center alert management and defense. Cloud environments have a variety of requirements when it comes to handling secrets, keys, and certificates. Azure Key Vault handles those functions. Should there be a need to maintain encrypted data in a hardware device, a premium offering utilizing a hardware security module (HSM) is available, making Azure Key Vault FIPS 140-2 compliant.

Keeping up with malicious activity is constantly a business challenge. Even when an organization has the most sophisticated tools, it is likely to struggle because of its tools not communicating with one another, especially those between the SIEM and SOAR platforms. That's why Microsoft created Microsoft Azure Sentinel, a scalable, cloud-native security information event management (SIEM) and security orchestration automated response (SOAR) solution. Azure Sentinel provides users intelligent security analytics and a threat intelligence platform for the enterprise. The single-point security solution offers security alert detection, threat visibility, proactive hunting, and threat response.

The very last concept in the core security section covers Azure Dedicated Hosts and Defense in Depth. There may be times where your organization requires dedicated infrastructure for its resources, specifically its virtual machine environments. That's why Microsoft has created Azure Dedicated Hosts for those virtual environments to have their own infrastructure without any interruption. Finally, with the discussion of all these tools, it becomes evident that security plays an integral role in cloud operations.

Cloud security should be treated like a castle in that each component has its own unique operational entity and responsibility. Think of castles as little moats. When working to bring all the moats together, cloud security offers an organization a defensive strategy that requires aligned response across all business operations, which leads to the final section of the book: network security.

Allowing anyone into the so-called castle would be a major problem. That's why you need to implement Network Security Groups (NSGs). An NSG is a rule that allows you to filter traffic on a network to a specific source to control traffic input and output. Not all traffic is equal, though. You will want to prioritize the traffic, using a range from 100 through 4,096. A lower priority number takes precedence over a higher number.

Similarly, if your organization wants to ensure that there are outsiders that can get into the castle, you will implement a firewall to fend off malicious network traffic. The reason why firewalls are put in place ties back to defense. One attack type, a DDoS (distributed denial of service), can create havoc with a net effect being complete shutdown or significant operational degradation. Microsoft offers two levels of DDoS protection, Basic and Standard. Basic is included as part of the Microsoft Azure cloud service offering and is limited to general security alerts and system-wide corrective error corrections. When you are looking to fix resource-specific threats and maintain 365/24/7 protection, migrating to the Standard plan is necessary.

Questions

1. Which of the following is not a type of Azure Firewall rule?

A. NAT rules

B. Network rules

C. Application rules

D. DDoS rule

2. When managing NSG traffic, what is the available traffic range allowed at the uppermost limit?

   A. 1,000

   B. 4,096

   C. 65,535

   D. There is not bound range.

3. Match the correct definition from the left column to the right column.

A combined SOAR and SIEM security incident solution	Azure Dedicated Host
Filters network traffic to and from Azure resources	Network Service Group
Dedicated virtual machine environment that resides on a shared host computer that can support many people	Azure Sentinel

   A. Azure Sentinel, Azure Dedicated Host, Network Security Groups

   B. Azure Sentinel, Network Security Groups, Azure Dedicated Host

   C. Azure Dedicated Host, Azure Sentinel, Network Security Group

   D. Network Security Group, Azure Sentinel, Azure Dedicated Host

4. The only way to ensure FIPS 140-2–compliant security for keys, certificates, or secrets using Azure Key Vault is to:

   A. Create an encrypted key.

   B. Create an encrypted certificate.

   C. Create an encrypted secret.

   D. Utilize a Hardware Security Module.

5. Fill in the following statement with the correct response.

   _____ enables you to protect your Azure resources from denial of service (DoS) attacks with always-on monitoring and automatic network attack mitigation.

   A. Azure Firewall

   B. Azure Security Center

   C. Azure DDoS Standard

   D. Azure Defender

6. Which of the following is not true about Secure Score?

   A. Secure Score is based on weighting, usage, importance, geographic location, and criticality.

   B. Secure Score evaluates all the resources across your subscriptions.

   C. There is a maximum score of 100 percent.

   D. A score is not an average as it weights the posture of resources across subscriptions.

7. Select the regulatory and compliance measure that does not appear as part of the Secure Center dashboard.

   A. ISO-27001

   B. ISO-9001

   C. PCI DSS 3.2.1

   D. SOC TSP

8. Determine if the answer is True or False in the following three statements:

	True	False
Security Alerts and Incidents Management are available to only those who pay for a Premium License of Azure Defender.	◯	◯
Azure Defender costs $15.00 per month, per resource.	◯	◯
You can actively manage all resources in a subscriptive through Inventory.	◯	◯

   A. True, False, False

   B. True, False, True

   C. False, False, True

   D. False, True, False

9. Resource Hygiene quality is determined by two factors. What are they?

   A. The severity of issues and recency of the issue

   B. The severity of issues and number of resources in a subscription

   C. The severity of issues and the number of issues

   D. The severity of issues only.

10. Complete the following statement:

    Network security groups have a priority between _____. Rules with _____ numbers are given greater attention.

    A. 100 to 4,096, lower priority

    B. 1,000 to 4,096, lower priority

    C. 100 to 4,096, higher priority

    D. 1,000 to 4,069, lower priority

11. Which of the following Microsoft network security products utilize IP addresses and domains data to protect victims of attacks? The data collected becomes part of the Microsoft Threat Intelligence Feed.

    A. Azure DDoS Basic

    B. Azure Security Center

    C. Azure Firewall

    D. Azure Dedicated Hosts

12. Defense in Depth is analogous to what type of building?

    A. House

    B. Castle

    C. Apartment building

    D. Boat

Answers

1. **D.** DDoS is not a type of rule. It is a type of attack.

2. **C.** 65,535 is the uppermost limit for traffic when managing NSG groups.

3. **B.** Azure Sentinel is defined as a combined SOAR and SIEM security incident solution. Network Security Groups are defined as a way to filter network traffic to and from Azure resources. Azure Dedicated Hosts are dedicated virtual machine environment that resides on a shared host computer that can support many people.

4. **D.** You can create an encrypted certificate, key, or secret, and it will still not be FIPS 140-2 compliant. The only way to meet compliance is when any of the above are placed on separate hardware using the Hardware Security Module.

5. **C.** DDoS Standard is the only service offering that offers 365/24/7 monitoring for attacks with always-on monitoring and automatic network attack mitigation.

6. **A.** The reason why this statement is inaccurate is because of one element, geographic location. Geography has no influence on Secure Score.

7. **B.** While ISO-9001 may somehow be evaluated by an organization as part of their quality management systems process, which is what ISO-9001:2015 measures, this is not one of the regulatory and compliance measures within the scope of Azure's evaluation.

8. **A.** True. Only those who pay for premium services receive alerts, notifications, and incident data proactively.

   False. The price per VM resource might be $15.00 per month. Other resources, though vary greatly.

   False. Inventory can be reviewed for an entire subscription, but active maintenance in a single location is impossible.

9. **C.** Both the number of resources and recency contribute to the number of issues.

10. **A.** The range is bound from 100 to 4,096, and lower ranking order gets preference.

11. **C.** Azure Firewall includes all of the features described. Azure Firewall is a service that can be accessed from Azure Secure Center, but it does not directly integrate such features.

12. **B.** Defense in Depth is analogous to a castle. As stated earlier in the chapter, if your castle didn't have any locks on it, any individual could simply go to a door, open it, and grab some data. If you add defensive layers, though, there are moats to act as protective casings that help create a set of checks and balances for those coming in and out of the castle.

Identity, Governance, Privacy, and Compliance

In this chapter, you will learn to
- Describe Core Identity Services
- Address Azure Governance Features
- Identify Azure Policy and Compliance Resources

In Chapter 5, you learned about the key tools that Microsoft Azure includes for security across its portfolio. Throughout the chapter, there were several instances where policy, compliance, and governance came up as an underlying theme. This chapter addresses those very topics in greater depth, reviewing both the conceptual and technology perspectives.

Authentication and Authorization

How many times a day are you asked to log in to your e-mail and supply a username and password for that account? Or perhaps when you've logged into the Azure Portal, you are asked for not only your username and password but a secondary form of identification such as a six-digit code that is generated from your mobile device. When you click the Submit button to validate these credentials, you are authenticating your identity. *Authentication* is the process of validating that you are who you claim to be. With Microsoft Azure, the identity platform uses the OpenID Connect Protocol for handling authentication.

Each time you authenticate, the application must be granted the authority to commit to an action. The authorization process specifies what access you are allowed and what you can do with the data. Microsoft uses OAuth 2.0 for handling authorization.

Authentication and authorization are not limited to websites or enterprise applications. In fact, when you log into Azure, you are being authenticated. Every time you access a new Azure resource, the application requires authorization to complete the actions that you are looking to take. Based on privileges, you may or may not be able to complete specific activities. For example, you may create a new resource but not access the billing information if the administrator does not grant you those permissions. Authorization is what handles granting you those permissions or lack thereof in Azure. The service that handles the authentication and authorization activity in Azure is Azure Active Directory. As you learn in the next section, Azure Active Directory has far more capabilities than just authentication and authorization of application and resource credentials.

Azure Active Directory

Azure Active Directory is the cloud-based identity service in Azure that supports authentication and authorization. Azure enables user access to Azure resources as well as third-party resources through associations. The resource can be with another cloud resource or even on-premises using the same set of user credentials found in Azure Active Directory.

Like in traditional Active Directory, Azure Active Directory stores a user's identities; a user consists of a username, password, location, and properties relevant to their location. Depending on the number of applications and assignments, a user may have one or more roles in the directory assigned. For example, you may have an administrator and super-user role, depending on the application. The user ID and password are used to support the user authentication. When calling the user ID, the role is then found for authorization to perform an action based on activities allowed in Azure AD.

To manage your Azure account, Microsoft automatically creates an Azure Active Directory account for you upon creating an Azure subscription. The account is intended to control your subscription and resources. There are premium account options available beyond the basic account created, though. To access the Azure Active Directory account configured for you upon sign up, follow these steps:

1. In the search bar, type **Active Directory:**.

2. Upon clicking ENTER, the Azure Active Directory screen will appear. Figure 6-1 is an example of what you may expect to see.

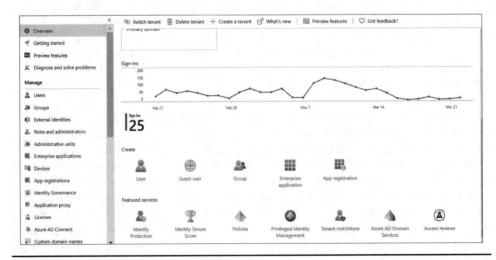

Figure 6-1   Azure Active Directory overview

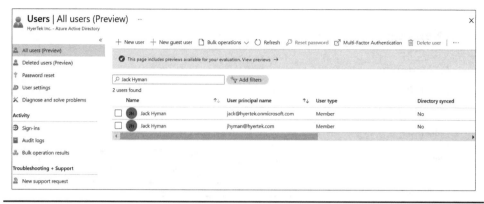

Figure 6-2 Searching for users in Azure Active Directory

To search for all the users in the directory with a specific name, enter the user's name in the search user box (where Jack Hyman is) and press ENTER. You will find that there are two entries in this case in the example presented (Figure 6-2).

If you are installing new Microsoft-based applications and a new user is being provisioned, an account will also be created against your Azure Active Directory account. Should you want to add a new user manually, click the New User button. A form will appear that allows you to enter the credentials for a new user account. Figure 6-3 illustrates the form that allows you to add the new user manually.

Sometimes, you may want to add a guest user to your Azure Active Directory. These are users from outside the organization who may need access to resources or applications. The feature called Azure Active Directory B2B (business to business) allows for collaboration for users who need to connect from outside the organization to access specific resources. These users are referred to as guest users. To add a guest user, go to the new guest user button. This will allow you to create a new user account on behalf of the guest or invite the user to create their own credentials to connect to the applications (Figure 6-4). When a guest is invited, there is a caveat. The user's e-mail address must be associated with a Microsoft account. If the user does not already have a Microsoft account, they will need to create an account. Upon connecting the account, the user, depending on how the account was configured by the Azure Active Directory Administrator, may connect to hundreds of applications and perhaps even have administrative access to specific cloud functions within Azure.

 EXAM TIP   Like Azure AD B2B, allowing users to get guest access to your Azure AD as a business, Azure AD B2C (business to consumer) allows users to access the Azure AD application by signing in using social accounts. These features are consistent with Consumer Identity Access Management platforms products.

Dashboard > Users >

New user ...
HyerTek Inc.

♡ Got feedback?

Help me decide

Identity

User name * ⓘ   [az900   ✓] @ [jackhyman.com ∨] 🗐
                                      The domain name I need isn't shown here

Name * ⓘ   [Book Author   ✓]

First name   [Book   ✓]

Last name   [Author   ✓]

Password

                               ⦿ Auto-generate password
                               ◯ Let me create the password

Initial password   [••••••••]

                               ☐ Show Password

[Create]

Figure 6-3   Add a new Azure Active Directory account.

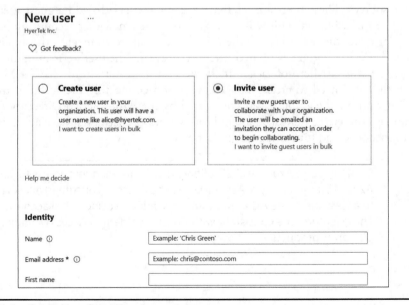

New user ...
HyerTek Inc.

♡ Got feedback?

◯ **Create user**
Create a new user in your organization. This user will have a user name like alice@hyertek.com.
I want to create users in bulk

⦿ **Invite user**
Invite a new guest user to collaborate with your organization. The user will be emailed an invitation they can accept in order to begin collaborating.
I want to invite guest users in bulk

Help me decide

Identity

Name ⓘ   [Example: 'Chris Green']

Email address * ⓘ   [Example: chris@contoso.com]

First name   [ ]

Figure 6-4   Create New Guest User Account screen

Revoking access is just as important as being able to add user access. Should a user no longer require access to an account, whether they are an organization or guest user, you want to be able to revoke access promptly. If access is provided using single sign-on, credentials can be removed in the Azure Portal easily. Once disconnected, the user cannot access the account again as they will not authenticate against the master account password.

One final note about Azure Active Directory. Up to this point, we have mentioned all the features that are available with the free version of Azure Active Directory, embedded within Azure Portal. There are premium versions of Azure Active Directory to support Microsoft 365 applications and more advanced security configurations such as those requiring multi-factor authentication. To compare the difference between the free version and the premium versions, go to https://azure.microsoft.com/en-us/pricing/details/active-directory/.

Conditional Access, Multi-Factor Authentication (MFA), and Single Sign-On (SSO)

Not all users have the same level of access when using large enterprise systems or websites. Can you imagine every single user on the Internet having access to your bank account? That would be quite a security violation. Only a very limited number of users should have access to such precious data. That's why organizations put specific security controls to protect data in place, whether intended for the enterprise or personal consumption. This section will introduce you to three approaches: conditional access, multi-factor authentication, and single sign-on access.

Conditional Access

Using the Azure Active Directory Premium 1 or 2, you will use a feature called Conditional Access. You need to create policies that must be applied against a user account. The policies must have assignments and access controls that require configurations to access resources. Assignments define what policies and how they are applied. Policies can be applied to any combination of users, groups, or roles in an Azure Active Directory account, even against guest user accounts. In fact, policies can be applied to just about any Microsoft enterprise application.

When configuring assignment conditions, including defining the platform, you want to specify the location, even by IP address. Access controls also decide the conditional access policies that should be enforced. Block access is by far the most restrictive access control. You can use access controls to require that a user use specific devices to meet criteria. Other control types that might be considered include multi-factor authentication. To create a conditional policy, follow these steps:

1. Enter **Azure AD Conditional Access** in the Azure Portal search bar.

2. Upon clicking ENTER, click on the New Policy button.

3. On the next page, select the conditions based on your current environment to create a policy appropriate for your needs (Figure 6-5).

4. Once all conditions meet your needs, click Create.

Figure 6-5
Configuring
Conditional
Access

Dashboard > Conditional Access >

New ...

Conditional access policy

Control user access based on conditional access policy to bring signals together, to make decisions, and enforce organizational policies. Learn more

Name *

Example: 'Device compliance app policy'

Assignments

Users and groups ⓘ

0 users and groups selected

Cloud apps or actions ⓘ

No cloud apps or actions selected

Conditions ⓘ

0 conditions selected

Access controls

Enable policy

Report-only   On   Off

Create

Multi-Factor Authentication

Another feature only available with the Azure Active Directory Premium versions is multi-factor authentication (MFA). Standard login and password are par for the course with Azure Active Directory. That requires nothing more than authentication and authorization of credentials, assuming there are a username and password in place. Unfortunately, a username and password are sometimes not enough. Hackers are notorious for breaking into accounts if a username or password is not sophisticated enough. Perhaps account credentials may even be compromised through a cyberattack. That's where multi-factor authentication solves several problems. Multi-factor authentication supplies an extra layer of security by adding onto credentials that you already know, such as your username and password. Examples of add-on credentials include a phone number or the use of an SMS on a mobile device. More extensive MFA might include facial recognition, fingerprints, or voice recognition.

Figure 6-6
Multi-Factor
Authentication
button

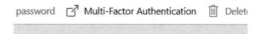

password ⟐ Multi-Factor Authentication 🗑 Delete

For every level of authentication added, you increase the security and verification process significantly. Three verification methods result in 3FA, while two verifications result in 2FA. Azure multi-factor authentication offers two-factor authentication by default.

To enable multi-factor authentication in Azure Active Directory, follow these steps:

1. Go to the Users Link in Azure Active Directory.

2. Select the users you would like to assign MFA to by clicking the checkboxes to the left of the names.

3. Click the button that says Multi-Factor Authentication (Figure 6-6).

4. You may be asked to log in to the MFA settings page.

5. Again, select all the accounts you would like to assign MFA to.

6. Each account is confirmed and then added to the list for enablement.

7. Once you are ready, click Enable (Figure 6-7).

8. A pop-up appears warning you that you are about to enable MFA. Follow the prompts to confirm you, in fact, want to confirm each account. Click Enable Multi-Factor Auth when ready (Figure 6-8).

TIP   Once multi-factor authentication is enabled, make sure the user is aware that there is a second step to authenticate. They may need to authenticate using their e-mail or perhaps their mobile device.

Figure 6-7
Enable
multi-factor
authentication

MULTI-FACTOR AUTH STATUS	
Disabled	**2 selected**
Enabled	
Disabled	
Disabled	quick steps
Enforced	Enable
Enforced	Manage user settings
Disabled	

Figure 6-8
Pop-up to
confirm
multi-factor
authentication

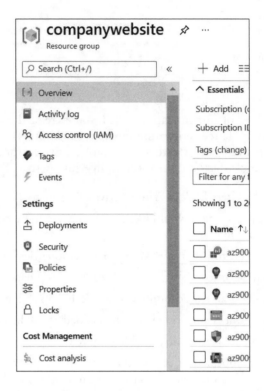

Single Sign-On

How many times have you had to repeatedly type the same username and password for applications even though it is the same exact set of credentials? It becomes a frustration for sure. That's why organizations often look to single sign-on (SSO) to cut down the number of repeated sign-in attempts so that a user does not have to log in and enter user credentials many times. SSO offers many benefits, including convenience and additional security assurances.

When working with SSO, the device must connect to Azure AD. Once the device connects to Azure AD, the user can connect to Azure resources across the enterprise, whether for Microsoft solutions or other enterprise applications that can connect using SSO. If the resource is on-premises, the resource requires Azure AD Connect to support the configuration between the on-premises resources and Azure.

SSO can handle two sign-in methodologies: password hash synchronization and pass-through authentication. Password hash synchronization can copy a user's password to a hashed format via Azure AD. Since passwords are hashed, passwords are unable to be retrieved automatically. When users submit credentials, algorithms that generate hash will compare the passwords in Azure AD. If the credentials match, the user is authenticated. Otherwise, the user is rejected.

Pass-through authentication allows for passing user login credentials in Azure AD for any on-premises pass-through authentication agent. If an agent sends the authentication to the on-premises Active Directory instance. Once authenticated, Azure AD Connect can use the pass-thru of credentials so that Azure AD can authenticate with Azure AD and the user resources.

Azure Governance Features

Enterprise organizations that place their resources in the Cloud often have the same exact problems that brought them to the Cloud in the first place, unless, of course, they put some structure in put in place. Cloud sprawl results in many different Azure services, and you'll need to have control over those resources. Ensuring that the proper security and fine-grained access controls are in place helps manage resources depending on the security and permissions. Whether for cost or resource management, putting controls in place can help ensure your Azure cloud resources are secure. In this section, you learn about the technology offerings that Microsoft has developed to automate governance in Azure, including Role-Based Access Control, Resource Locks, Resource Tags, Azure Policy, Azure Blueprints, and the Cloud Adoption Framework for Azure.

Role-Based Access Control (RBAC)

It's not uncommon to have several IT personnel managing your Azure cloud environment. A good security practice is to grant only those users who need access the rights they need to perform the jobs. The users should only have access to those resources based on their assigned roles. Managing individual access requirements and then updating each of those requirements can be cumbersome. Azure allows you to control access through *Azure Role-Based Access Control (Azure RBAC).*

With RBAC, four key elements must be addressed:

- **Security Principle** The security principal is an identity. An identity can be anything from a user, a group, an application, or a special entity called a managed identity. Managed identities are how you authorize Azure services when you need to access resources.

- **Role** Sometimes referred to as a role definition, a security principle interacts with an Azure resource.

- **Scope** The scope helps define the level for which a role is applied. It enforces the level of control, especially when it is concerned about the security principle.

- **Role Assignment** A role assignment is mapped to a security principle through a given scope. The definition of access for the security principle is defined by a role assignment.

There are also three principles built-in roles. The roles are the owner, contributor, and reader. The roles have a strong correlation with scope. Other roles are specific to certain types of Azure resources.

RBAC is applied to a scope. A Scope is when you have a resource or set of resources that require a specific set of access controls. Example scopes might include a subscription, a resource group, a management group, or a resource. Granting access to a parent scope means that these permissions are inheritable to all children's scopes. For example, when you assign an owner role to a user at the management group scope, the owner can manage all items in a subscription assigned to the management group. Similarly, if the reader role is assigned to a group at the subscription scope, the role can view every resource and resource group in the confines of the subscription. Unlike the reader role, a contributor can manage resources within a specific resource group; however, they cannot manage other resource groups inside a subscription.

There are many use cases when RBAC should be used. The most significant use cases as it pertains to handling IaaS and PaaS in Azure include:

- Allowing a user to manage a virtual machine in a subscription and another user to manage a virtual network.
- When a database administrator group manages SQL databases across an entire subscription.
- If an application requires access to resources within a resource group.

When you are looking to give a user access to a resource using RBAC, you must open the resource that requires access in the Azure portal. To do this, follow these steps:

1. Click Access Control (IAM) in the portal to configure RBAC (Figure 6-9).
2. Click Add in the Add a Role Assignment box. This allows you to add a role.

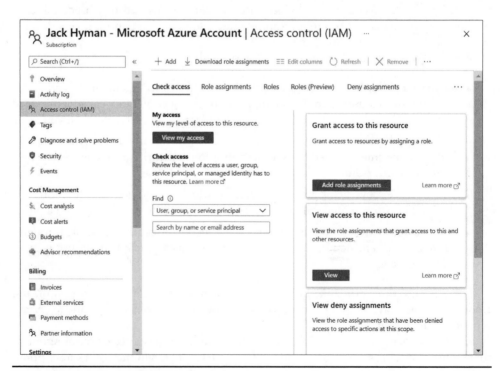

Figure 6-9   Role-Based Access interface

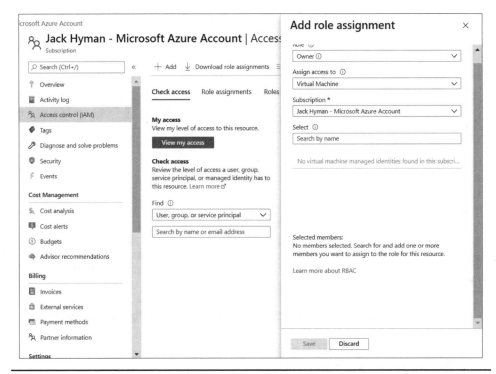

Figure 6-10   Configuring Role-Based Access for a resource or user

3. You will be shown a list of users and object types in the Azure Active Directory based on the assigned access level (Figure 6-10).

4. Any object type that allows for an assignment is presented in the list.

5. Click Save once you've selected the resource, resource group, or object of choice. The item will be added to the list with role-based access.

Resource Locks

Have you ever deleted or accidentally made a change to a system only to regret it later on? This all-too-common problem happens in the loud as well. That's why Microsoft offers a feature called resource locks, a way to prevent resources from accidentally being deleted or changed. It does not matter even when Azure has Role-Based Access Controls in place; individuals with the proper access controls to delete a file may be able to do so. A great analogy to a resource lock is a flashlight system or stop sign to warn a user that the resource should not be deleted.

Resource locks can be managed using Azure Portal, PowerShell, Azure Cloud Shell, Azure CLI, or an Azure Resource Manager template. To manage a specific resource and place a lock on that resource, use the steps on the following page.

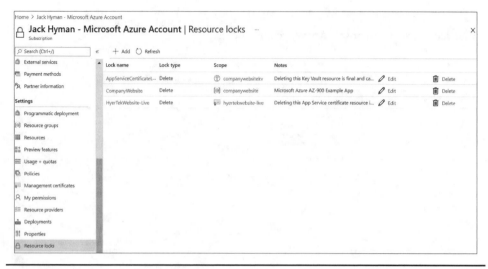

Figure 6-11 Resource lock access

To add, modify, view, or delete a lock in the Azure Portal, follow these steps:

1. Go to the Settings section of a resource.

2. Click the Lock Link (Figure 6-11).

3. A new form appears which lists all the current locks available (Figure 6-12).

4. Click Add. You will be asked to add the name of the app, select the type of lock, and describe the app.

5. Upon completing the entry of all fields, click OK.

6. The lock is added to the list if there are existing locks in place. If this is the first time creating a lock, you'll need to create the name of the lock first. Then, you'll be able to add the lock to the list afterwards.

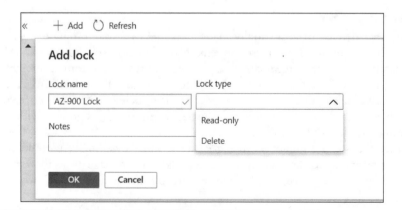

Figure 6-12 Resource lock options

When applying a lock to a subscription, resource group, or resource, you have two choices: CanNotDelete or ReadOnly. CanNotDelete means authorized people can still read and modify resources, but they will not delete the resource unless they remove the lock. ReadOnly means that a person can read a resource, but they cannot delete or change a resource. The ReadOnly lock is like restricting all authorized users to permission granted under the conditions of a Reader in RBAC.

TIP Just because a resource is locked does not mean the process is permanent. You can still make changes by following a two-step process. You must first remove a lock. Then, after removing a lock, you must apply an action to grant permission to any action to perform the required need. The extra step ensures that you know that the lock is being undone since resource locks apply no matter the RBAC permissions.

Resource Tags

Keeping your cloud organized is increasingly important as your data footprint grows. Two reasons this is important is to control costs and processes. One choice is to organize related resources in their own subscription. You can use resource groups to manage these related resources. Another method is to use resource tags. A resource tag supplies information or metadata about the resource when trying to classify and codify resource management, cost management, optimization, operations management, security, governance and regulatory compliance, workloads such as virtual machines, and automated solutions.

Tags can be added, modified, or deleted through each data entry method, including the Azure Portal, PowerShell, Azure CLI, Azure Resource Manager template, or Rest API. You can also add tags by using Azure Policy by applying tags to resource groups to ensure that a resource can inherit tags to parent resource groups.

TIP Azure resource tags consist of a specific structure. At a minimum, they consist of a name and a value. You may be able to assign one or more tags to an Azure resource.

Azure Policy

It's one thing to create orderly systems and implement locks to prevent the deletion of resources. However, you need to enforce organizational standards to assess compliance at scale. That's why Microsoft developed Azure Policy to provide an aggregated view of policy issues using a dashboard view of actions. You can evaluate the overall state of an environment with the ability to see at a granular basis how resources are behaving. Azure Policy helps bring any resource into compliance through bulk automated remediation capabilities. Common uses include using governance for consistency, regulatory compliance security, costs, and management.

With Azure Policy, the policy definitions are already pre-crafted on your behalf for common use cases. As they are built into the environment. Azure Policy data and objects are encrypted at rest. Azure Policy evaluates each resource by comparing the properties of a given resource against the respective business rules. Business rules, known as policy definitions, are written in JSON format. Business rules are often grouped together to form policy initiatives, commonly referred to as a policySet. As soon as a business rule is crafted, a policy definition is assigned to a scope that Azure supports, including a management group, subscription, resource group, or individual resources. Regardless of the assignment, these apply to all resources that apply to a Resource Manager's scope.

To evaluate resources using Azure Policy, a lifecycle process is often put in place. A resource is created, updated, or deleted against a policy assignment under one of three conditions:

- A policy is often initiated against an assigned scope.
- A policy that is already assigned may be updated.
- During a compliance evaluation cycle, activity may occur over 24 hours.

When resources are found to be noncompliant, resources may respond in one of three ways:

- Denying the resource change to the policy
- Logging the changes to the resources
- Deploying related changes to the resources that maintain corrective actions

Azure Policy makes these business responses possible by setting the policy rule portion of a policy definition.

Azure Blueprints

Everyone knows what it takes to build a commercial office building or a home, an architectural blueprint. The engineer and architect sketch a project design to depict exactly what parameters are required. With Azure Blueprints, a cloud architect does the exact same thing: they create a repeatable asset for Azure resources to implement and adhere to organizational patterns, standards, and requirements.

Azure Blueprints help development teams create new environments to ensure that their environments meet compliance using built-in components, including storage, databases, networking, and security. When brought together, these assets can speed up the delivery process. Azure Blueprints can orchestrate resource templates and artifacts with assignments, ARM templates, resources, and resource groups.

Unlike Azure Policy and ARM Templates, Azure Blueprints are stored in a globally distributed Azure Cosmos database. Blueprint objects are replicated across multiple Azure regions, which is not the case with Azure Policy or ARM Templates unless they are configured to do so. Replication offers low latency, high availability, and consistency for all objects. Other ways Azure Blueprints are different from ARM Templates and Azure Policy are described in Table 6-1.

Azure Blueprints	Azure ARM Template	Azure Policy
Azure Blueprints packages the artifact types together. They allow you to compose versions of those packages, including continuous integration and continuous delivery (CI/CD) pipeline options in a single container. Packages have sets of resource groups, Azure Policies, role assignments, and ARM Template deployments.	Azure ARM Templates are intended for environment setup exclusively. Unlike an Azure Blueprint stored in an Azure Cosmos database. ARM templates are documents that do not exist natively in Azure. They are stored either locally or in source control. Templates are used for deployments for one or more Azure resources. Once a template is deployed, no active connection remains. An ARM Template can be a part of an Azure Blueprint.	Whereas Azure Blueprints are package or container having specific sets of standards, patterns, and requirements with Azure services, Azure policies are often included as artifacts in the Azure Blueprints definition. It is nothing more than a standard.

Table 6-1   Comparing Azure Blueprint vs. ARM Template and Azure Policy

Cloud Adoption Framework for Azure

By now, you probably recognize that a cloud transformation is not simple. It takes a considerable amount of effort. There are many piece parts involved in planning, organizing, and building a highly scalable architecture. To learn how to make a move, you need more than just a little bit of guidance and best practices. There is a bit of guidance about architecture, resource management, governance, and policies that you must adhere to.

The breadth of the Microsoft platform is significant. The knowledge is spread out across the Azure platform and across many product organizations. In fact, within product organizations, there are countless numbers of customer use cases and anecdotal pieces of advice that can be used to help build Azure. To share the knowledge with customers, Microsoft has developed a Cloud Adoption Framework for Azure. Consider the Framework a single point location for bringing together all the best resources from Microsoft employees, partners, customers, and even third-party integration experiences. The website is organized into a well-defined framework so that you can review and download each asset rapidly.

The framework contains resources for those wanting to build a complete Azure environment. Features of the Cloud Adoption Framework for Azure include:

- Strategy
- Planning
- Readying
- Migration
- Innovation
- Governance
- Management
- Organization

To access the Cloud Adoption Framework, go to https://docs.microsoft.com/en-us/azure/cloud-adoption-framework/.

 EXAM TIP If you are looking for a one-stop shop for all documentation beyond this book for your exam, the Cloud Adoption Framework for Azure is a great launchpad to gather those resources.

An Overview of Security, Privacy, and Trust

In business, security, privacy, and compliance are paramount to forging trust in any two-way relationship. Microsoft believes that trust is an important ingredient in their relationship with their customers, and therefore provides relevant information to ensure customers feel confident in doing business with them.

Microsoft offers details on how they keep your most precious assets, data, and resources secure by ensuring data is not accessible from those who should not have authorized access. Users need to be sure that when Microsoft becomes their cloud provider, the data you put in their cloud is secure. Microsoft is committed to ensuring that should an incident occur, they inform their customers of such activity.

When you move to the cloud, you are handing off responsibility for regulatory compliance to your cloud provider, including data protection standards. You may not be responsible for many aspects of the infrastructure; you must have faith that your provider is prudent in its upkeep of state, federal, and international requirements. Remember, compliance is a shared responsibility no matter how you want to look at it because your business is still the data owner. Microsoft simply administers the infrastructure for the regulatory controls.

Understanding and adhering to regulations, such as the European Union General Data Protection Regulation (GDPR) and California Consumer Privacy Act (CCPA), has become a common concern in B2B businesses since 2016. For example, if personal (customer) data is exchanged by a business in the course of, say, exporting goods from California to the EU, both policies are automatically triggered. Not following the policies may result in steep fines. To ensure that the organizations implementing cloud compute capabilities abide by the regulations, organizations are strongly encouraged to follow ISO 27001. Government organizations are persuaded to follow the National Institute of Standards and Technology (NIST) SP-800 53 protocols for government data. When it comes to cybersecurity and privacy, the rules fall under NIST 800-171. As the Department of Defense and some civilian agencies move forward streamlining cloud and cybersecurity policy, more formal instruction will be provided as part of the Cybersecurity Maturity Model Certification (CMMC) framework, which includes both NIST SP 800-171 and SP 800-172.

The body of documents that Microsoft supplies its customers to support security, privacy, compliance, and trust include the Microsoft Privacy Statement, Online Service Terms, and Data Protection Amendment. Other source documents can also be found in the Trust Center.

Microsoft Privacy Statement

If there is anything that Microsoft wants to impress upon its customers, it is that privacy a top priority. Microsoft outlines how it handles privacy across all its product lines, including Azure, and the purpose of its policy programs in detail. The Azure privacy statements incorporated with the Microsoft Privacy Statement address services, websites, apps, software, servers, devices, and cloud solutions. To learn how Microsoft protects a customer's privacy, go to https://privacy.microsoft.com/en-us/privacystatement.

Online Services Terms (OST) and Data Protection Addendum (DPA)

Every time you purchase a new Microsoft product or service, you must agree to service terms. This includes when you signed up for Azure. These service terms are found in Microsoft documents commonly referred to as Online Service Terms (OST). The OST explain what you can and cannot use a service for in Azure. The documentation provides guidance on what is considered legal and illegal based on the country of jurisdiction.

Part of the OST includes data regulations, referred to as the Data Protection Addendum (DPA). The DPA outlines the processing and security terms for all Microsoft services. These documents can be found at https://www.microsoft.com/en-us/licensing/product-licensing/products.

Trust Center

Whether you are using Microsoft Azure or another Microsoft-based cloud application, there is a centralized location online called Trust Center where you can find all the security, privacy, and compliance information. Trust Center is accessible by going to https://www.microsoft.com/en-us/trust-center/.

Trust Center offers Azure users' information on security solutions—specifically how Microsoft applies security practices such as privacy and data management within the cloud. While it does not go into every single product offered in the Azure environment, it offers best practices through checklists, whitepapers, and documentation to help users stay compliant.

Azure Compliance Documentation

There are thousands of regulatory and compliance measures a company must follow when they are doing business internationally. Microsoft has made it easy for businesses to use Azure by compiling all the documentation in a single location. If there are compliance and regulatory measure that must be adhered to for a given geographic region, Azure compliance documentation exists to support you on each regulatory effort. You can access the global compliance documentation library at https://docs.microsoft.com/en-us/azure/compliance/.

Azure Sovereign Regions

When you think of Azure Cloud, you probably have thought about Azure and its public-facing access exclusively. This is the most common cloud use for personal and enterprise use. Did you know that there are four different hosted Azure clouds? There is the Azure Public Cloud, which we've discussed at length. Then there is the U.S. government, Germany, and China clouds as well. The Microsoft Azure Cloud consists of 60+ regions across all cloud instances worldwide, and it keeps on growing.

Since each cloud is separate, it has its own endpoints, which means it has its own Azure Portal site and URL. The Azure Portal URL addresses for the respective clouds include:

- **Azure Public Cloud**   https://portal.azure.com
- **Azure U.S. Government Cloud**   https://portal.azure.us
- **Azure German Cloud**   https://portal.microsoftazure.de
- **Azure China Cloud**   https://portal.azure.cn

Azure Public Cloud

Most users only have access to the Azure Public Cloud. Whether you create an account with Microsoft, most users only have access to the Azure Public Cloud. When you create a new Azure subscription after a trial, you either set up a pay-as-you-go or enterprise agreement account through an Enterprise Agreement (EA). There are rare conditions that allow you to gain access to a subscription under the U.S. government, Germany, or China Azure clouds.

Azure U.S. Government Cloud

The U.S. government has a dedicated cloud available for their exclusive use just for their needs. To gain access, an authorized Cloud Service Provider that conducts business with the U.S federal government and is a Microsoft Partner must act as the sales and solution expert. The U.S. government Azure Cloud consists of many Azure regions such as the U.S. DOD, U.S. Gov, and U.S. Secret. Each of these regions is FedRamp (Federal Risk and Authorization Management Program) compliant. FedRamp is a type of security assessment and authorization for cloud products and services used by U.S. federal agencies. All data centers are located in the United States exclusively. Depending on the U.S. government agency entity, the GovCloud type provisioning will vary. With the Azure U.S. Government Cloud, not all Private and Public Preview features become available simultaneously as those in the Public Cloud. That's because there is a bit more rigor that ensures the system and service quality meet the federal government's security requirements.

Azure German Cloud

As a result of the EU GDPR regulations, a sovereign cloud was set up in Germany that consists of two regions. The purpose of the cloud is for those in the EU, particularly in Germany, with data sovereignty requirements mandated by German law to ensure that their data workloads stay resident in the country. Only those that customers in Germany can access the Azure German Cloud. They cannot provide resources outside the sovereign region. While there is also an Azure Public Cloud in Germany, the purpose of the sovereign cloud is for strict data compliance exclusively.

Azure China Cloud

Azure's China Cloud consists of four Azure Regions. For those within China with data sovereignty requirements as mandated by Chinese law that mandate data must stay within the confines of the country, the cloud is intended to support those data and workloads exclusively. Like the U.S. government and Germany clouds, the Azure China Cloud is only available to a limited customer base based on specific use cases.

Chapter Review

The chapter addressed topics on identity, compliance, and governance. First, the chapter discusses the technologies Microsoft offers in Azure to ensure identity, compliance, and governance can be delivered to users. That includes a significant discussion on Azure Active Directory, Authentication, and Authorization. While Azure AD is critical to identity management, more granular controls are necessary to ensure identity and compliance in the cloud. Microsoft Azure suggests using conditional access, multi-factor authentication, and single sign-on to further protect users and their identities as cloud compute resources are just as susceptible to security vulnerabilities on-premises platforms.

Governance plays a critical role in protecting cloud computing infrastructure as well. Users who look to control application interactions manage resources based on role-based access controls (RBAC). Ways to handle governance through automation include Azure Policy, Resource Locks, Resource Tags, and Azure Blueprints. Azure Policy allows one to define rules that can be applied to Azure resources when created and managed. Resource Locks prevent changes to resources, including resource deletion. Tags allow for better organization of resources in the Azure Portal. Azure Blueprints allow for the automation of configurations and resources in a repeatable template for future deployments. Within the template, you can include Azure Policy, Resource Tags, and ARM Templates. A final guiding solution is the Cloud Adoption Framework for Azure. The framework brings together best practices and information from Microsoft, including its employees, partners, and customers, to create a world-class cloud platform.

When you decide to use Microsoft Azure as your Cloud Service Provider, there are many agreements that you also jointly commit to as a customer and partner. Those include the Microsoft Privacy Statement, Online Service Terms, Data Protection Addendum, and Azure Compliance Documentation. Additionally, Trust Center contains Microsoft's security and compliance approach across all of its solutions, including Azure Cloud.

The chapter ends with a discussion on Azure Sovereign Regions. Microsoft is not just isolated from its Public Cloud infrastructure. It also includes a Government Cloud, Germany Cloud, and China Cloud. These regions are set up to intentionally isolate data due to government regulatory mandates under various conditions.

Questions

1. Which of the following is not a sovereign region?

   A. Azure Public Cloud

   B. Azure Government Cloud

   C. Azure Germany Cloud

   D. Azure China Cloud

2. Azure Blueprint may contain which of the following governance assets? (Select all that apply.)

   A. Resource Locks

   B. Azure Policy

   C. Tags

   D. All the above

3. Which Microsoft document repository centrally houses all the security, privacy, and compliance information about Azure?

   A. Azure Blueprints

   B. Trust Center

   C. Cloud Adoption Framework

   D. Azure Sovereign Regions

4. Complete the following statement by selecting the correct term.

   _____are documents that do not exist natively in Azure. They are stored either locally or in source control. Templates are used for deployments for one or more Azure resources.

   A. Azure Policy

   B. Resource Tags

   C. ARM Templates

   D. Azure Blueprints

5. Which of the following are not best practices as part of Azure Policy processes?

   A. A policy is often initiated against an assigned scope.

   B. A policy may delete unnecessary resources every 24 hours.

   C. A policy that is already assigned may be updated.

   D. During a compliance evaluation cycle, activity may occur over 24 hours.

6. The Microsoft Privacy Statement incorporates all of the business terms except:

   A. services

   B. websites

   C. apps

   D. consulting agreement terms

7. Which of the following supplies information or metadata about a resource when trying to classify and codify resource management, cost management, optimization, operations management, security, governance and regulatory compliance, workloads such as virtual machines, and automated solutions?

   A. Resource Lock

   B. Resource Tag

   C. Azure Policy

   D. Azure Blueprints

8. Complete the following statement.

   _____ is when you want to ensure users should and should not access resources in Azure.

   A. Authentication

   B. Conditional access

   C. Role-based access

   D. Authorization

9. What is the purpose of single sign-on?

   A. To prevent users from removing resources.

   B. To allow users to access resources across many applications without having to re-enter credentials several times.

   C. To define rules that apply to Azure resources that can be replicated in a template.

   D. To act as an identity service in Azure.

10. This type of authenticating requires a secondary device such as an e-mail, SMS message, or voice-based call to generate a random number for authentication.

    A. Role-based access control

    B. Azure Active Directory

    C. Multi-factor authentication

    D. Resource Lock

11. Which tool allows for collaboration for users who need to connect from outside an organization to access specific resources, specifically guest enterprise users?

    A. Azure Active Directory B2B

    B. Azure Active Directory B2C

    C. Azure Active Directory B2G

    D. None of the above

12. Complete the following statement:

_____ and _____ provide information on how a Microsoft Azure customer may use services and how data will be shared in the platform.

  A. Microsoft Privacy Statement, Online Service Terms (OST)

  B. Online Service Terms (OST), Microsoft Privacy Statement

  C. Online Service Terms (OST), Data Protection Addendum (DPA)

  D. The Microsoft Privacy Statement, Data Protection Addendum (DPA)

Answers

1. A. Azure Public Cloud is the only cloud listed that is not part of an Azure Sovereign Region.

2. D. An Azure Blueprints are a repeatable CD/CI deployable asset containing all of the asset types.

3. B. Trust Center handles all the security, privacy, and compliance information for Microsoft Azure.

4. C. ARM Templates are document based, not Azure Blueprints. With Azure Blueprints, they are stored in Azure Cosmos D.

5. B. Deleting unnecessary resources every 24 hours is the only process that is not the best fit, although it could happen.

6. D. Microsoft Professional Services are not covered under any Privacy Statement. All other selections are amply covered under the Privacy Statement.

7. B. Resource Tags are organization mechanisms.

8. D. Authorization is when you want to ensure users should and should not access resources in Azure.

9. B. Single sign-on is best defined as allowing users to access resources across many applications without re-entering credentials several times.

10. C. Multi-factor authentication is two-factor authentication that requires you to enter a secondary form of identification in addition to a username and password.

11. A. Azure Active Directory B2B is meant for enterprise businesses, while B2C is for consumers.

12. C. This is the only condition that meets both criteria based on the two document types referenced in the statement.

Cost Management and Service-Level Agreements

In this chapter, you will learn to
- Describe factors that contribute to the cost of delivering Azure cloud
- Use calculators to realize the cost of ownership and pricing of Azure productivity
- Plan Azure solutions for cost optimization
- Identify the principles of the Azure service-level agreement
- Discuss the Azure service lifecycle

This last chapter of the text is filled with best practices on sizing, scaling, pricing cloud solutions, and service commitments for the Azure platform. Microsoft places a fair amount of emphasis on these areas throughout the exam, although the section may not seem as important as the technologies. Guess again! When you are planning your technical implementation, you need to understand the Azure Services lifecycle. Why? Because it can make a significant difference in both your budgeting and architectural planning. Besides, when organizations require specific service-level guarantees, they assume rules are standardized in the service-level agreement. SLA standardization does not necessarily equate to service-level standardization. In fact, combing solutions or depending on multiple environment types to manage a product does not yield standard service-level agreement terms. And you will learn why that is the case in this chapter. These are just some of the gotchas that you will need to pay close attention to as you prepare for your AZ-900 exam.

Planning and Managing Costs

If you have come this far in the text, you've likely sampled some of the exercises and tested out use cases along the way. You've been asked to even commit to pricing each time a service was provisioned. The service pricing could be presented anywhere from a cost per hour to perhaps a monthly cost in some instances. While some products are free within Azure, there is still an underlying infrastructure cost associated with implementing cloud resources. Storage, and in some instances, bandwidth, results in a charge.

Infrastructure pricing varies under a few other circumstances: geography, redundancy of system instances, and system implementation features. Keeping geography bound to a single region will yield cost savings. But what happens when you are a multinational corporation? Undoubtedly, your goal is to ensure high availability so that no location experiences system degradation. That's where the business analyst and cloud professional must consider the features they intend to implement while also addressing system use patterns and the cost associated with those implementation. In this next section, we address two factors that heavily influence Azure pricing: infrastructure utilization and cost optimization strategies.

Pricing Factors That Affect Cost

Pricing varies based on a variety of factors. Two factors drive cost more than anything: subscription type and geographic attributes. Additionally, the type of resources you utilize and your commitment to using that resource over time, which ties back to the subscription type, can affect your pricing.

Subscription Type

Depending on the type of Azure subscription you or your organization pay for, Microsoft may provide you an allowance. For example, an Azure trial subscription offers user-specific products and services for free for 12 months. During the first 30 days, you are also given an allowance ($200 for commercial, $100 for education accounts). With that allowance, a user gets access to around 25 product types that are always free based on your regionality. As soon as you have exceeded your allowance spend on the free trial, a user is charged on their credit card or alternate payment method under the pay-as-you-go model where an invoice is sent monthly for services utilized, based on usage. Under the pay-as-you-go model, a user can then commit to a long-term contract from one to three years, reducing the price of many resources as several third-party service offerings. If you do not commit to a long-term reservation, you are charged the full rate. In some instances, you are locking down a resource for a flat rate, while other times, prices stay variable but heavily discounted. Those clients that are under an Enterprise License Agreement (ELA) have specific terms tied to their Azure agreement. These are negotiated between the organization and Microsoft based on a committed contract length. In some instances, organizations are given uncapped usage to certain resources, while other times, pricing may be heavily discounted. The most important thing to know here is that subscriptions do influence pricing, so make sure you understand what you will be paying for based on your term commitment.

Resource Type

Each item you provision a resource in your Azure subscription, the resource is added to a Resource Group. Some services might be free, but they still need storage. Other times, you may require optimized CPU capacity or memory capacity, which is considered a type of customization. Another example might be your storage choice. Some people prefer block blob storage, while others must use table storage. The two storage types vary in price depending on some conditions, whether based on purchased quantity, IOPS performance, or geographic region. Referencing the earlier section related to subscriptions, resource types are heavily influenced by usage commitments. On the pay-as-go model, you are paying the full price. If you commit to a three-year term, you may receive a discount as great as 72 percent, depending on the resource type.

Services and Metered Usage

Usage meters in Azure are no different than the gas gauge in your car or the utility meters in your home. Take, for example, your electricity. Every month you start at 0kwh. Some days you decide to keep your computer on and others you turn it off. The power consumption from the computer creates a variable condition in your electricity bill.

On the other hand, a refrigerator will always be on. That is a constant charge that one should expect to contribute to an invoice at the end of each month. Usage in cloud computing follows that exact same model. A virtual machine is always on and running unless you turn it off to reduce spend, which could be the case for a development or test environment. That is not the case with production. Variations in usage will occur on many meter counts when it comes to a virtual machine. Factors might include CPU time and utilization, IP Address access, network traffic variability (ingress and egress), and disk operations.

As you know, capabilities such as Azure Functions will only create a transaction when an event is triggered. You may not have a single event cause an Azure Function to run for three months, and then, suddenly, several hundred triggers occur in a matter of days. The fluctuation of usage will result in a variation to the billing statement. Don't forget that where you are in the world and where the resource is being used also play a significant part in pricing. Cloud compute costs within the bounds of a region are far less than going outside that region. For example, a user in Boston requests a resource from the East U.S. Data Center. That is one price. That same user requests a resource from one of the data centers in Brazil South. The cost will be exponentially higher for resource consumption from the Brazil South data center due to network traffic expenses. The important takeaway from this section about usage is that features used, the amount consumed, and geography all influence usage variability.

Azure Marketplace

Azure Marketplace products and services are sometimes free. Other times, the service provider charges a fee to use the service for custom features. Microsoft also includes third-party vendor products in the Marketplace where you can BYOL (bring your own license). In some instances, you don't pay for the license through Microsoft. On other occasions, Microsoft acts as the broker for the vendor issuing the license through Azure Marketplace.

Be careful and watch the pricing metrics on each page—they are displayed clearly. It's already been well established that a service might be free, but you still need to pay for the infrastructure that supports the service. Imagine being charged for a web template when there are at least six variations of the same template for free in Azure Marketplace. This is not uncommon. Look at WordPress pricing variability as an example (Figure 7-1).

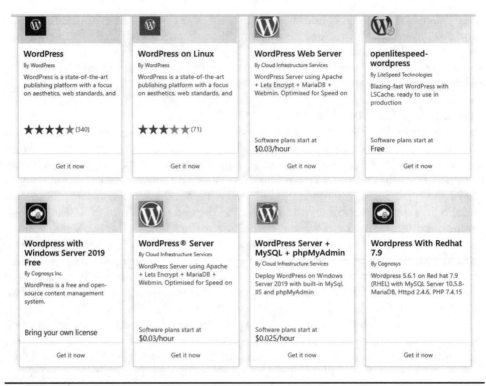

Figure 7-1 Azure Marketplace pricing availability

Locations

When provisioning a resource in Azure, a user must select the Azure region where the resources will be hosted. If all your customers are based in North America, it makes no sense to host your data in a region outside the country (or continent), depending on geographic circumstances. Let's assume all your customers are fairly geographic limited to the East United States. Should you select the West U.S. 2 or stick with one of the data centers available on the East Coast. For the purposes of performance and price, select one of the East U.S. options. Should you need redundancy, the best option is to pick a data center within the region complementary in services and price. In this case, it could be any of the data centers in the Central U.S. region (North or South). Your goal is to pick a region where the pricing is at par and cloud resource availability does not differentiate, which will cause a spike in spending.

EXAM TIP You may be wondering why the geographic region, specifically regions and Availability Zones, contribute heavily to Azure price differentiation. Often it is the cost of redundancy, but some costs are tied purely to geopolitical and regulatory matters. Because geographic regions influence network traffic flow, ingress and egress network activity influences pricing as well.

Table 7-1
Billing Zones in
Microsoft Azure

Zone	Country/Continent
Zone 1	United States, Europe, Canada, UK, France
Zone 2	Asia Pacific, Japan, Australia, India, Korea
Zone 3	Brazil
DE1	Germany

Network Traffic

Bandwidth and billing zones influence pricing. Bandwidth movement within an Azure Data center varies depending on the direction of traffic. Inbound data transfers, also referred to as *ingress*, are free. Outbound data transfers, also referred to as *egress*, vary depending on the data transfer zone. If the transfer occurs within the same zone, the pricing differential is marginal. Outside the bounds of the zone, pricing can be significantly higher.

Remember, a zone is a geographical grouping of Azure regions for the purposes of billing. Table 7-1 illustrates the different billing zones within Azure.

Factors That Can Reduce Costs

For the exam, you are expected to know four specific factors that can reduce Azure costs. Those factors are reserved instances, reserved capacity, hybrid use benefits, and spot pricing. Microsoft wants to impress upon you that with long-term commitments and a shift to the cloud, your ability to attain greater discounts increases. There are, of course, caveats in how much discounting is provided. This section covers the critical requirements that Microsoft wants you to know and added considerations to reduce spending and optimize performance.

 EXAM TIP It is not uncommon to find questions on the AZ-900 that ask for the "best fit" or the "most right" answer. Several questions may have to do with ways to perfect the Azure environment while reducing costs. This entire section should amply prepare you to answer questions concerning the major contributors to cost reduction, not just long-term commitments.

Utilize Built-In Monitoring Solutions

If you are not using resources in Azure, why pay for them? You want to match your utilization targets to optimize the systems in place for performance and cost. Azure Advisor, as you learned previously, can help you target the proper size environment. If there are also dormant or underutilized resources, Advisor can prompt you to remove such resources. These recommendations are based on usage patterns and performance metrics, which can help reduce your spending.

Spending Limits

When users are provided free trials and credits with Azure, they may want to limit their usage to not go over their monthly budget. For example, when you sign up for Azure, you are given a $200.00 credit to be used the first month of service. If you want to avoid going over the monthly allowance, you should set up a spending limit and budget alert to prevent accidental overages. With spending limits, you can simply use the notification features to keep track of your monthly spending. Alternately, if you've spent your allowance, a limit can be configured to shut down all deployed resources in production until the next cycle begins. There are plenty of other configuration options, including deletion of resources too. If there is a desire to upgrade services at any point, a user can increase their spending options under a pay-as-you-go subscription.

Quotas, or limits of the number of resources that are deployed in a subscription, are another method to limit spending. If you want to limit the number of resources a user or even an organization can provision, quotas should be enforced. Limiting resource creation helps reduce erroneous performance concerns. You also free yourself from worrying about unnecessary charges to an Azure subscription account.

Reserved Instances

Microsoft loves predictability. They reward customers for committing to long-term cloud purchases. Of all the cloud resources, Virtual Machine Instances are among the most consumed. Should your organization realize that it requires the use of a Virtual Machine Instance long term, committing to a Reserved Instance (RI) can result in significant cost savings. Reserved Instances are virtual machines reserved on Microsoft's IaaS cloud for exclusive use for either one or three years. RIs should be used when there are known workloads and capacity is predictable. Microsoft supplies a discount rate of up to 72 percent for a three-year term. If combined with other savings mechanisms such as Hybrid Benefits, the cost savings could be as high as 82 percent. Recognize that not all products are available for Reserved Instance Reservations across all geographies. Also, not all product configurations are discounted under the reservations model.

While the terms are flexible to swap reservation instance commitments during your contract, there are some limits to allowable refunds should a contract need to be broken. One last point is that to get discounted pricing Microsoft expects the vendor to pay for the services up-front. Under an Enterprise Agreement, terms and conditions may apply for future invoicing under specific conditions using Azure Monetary Commitments, a type of prepaid price lock-in.

Reserved Capacity

Specific to database resources, Microsoft recognizes that organizations are also shifting their database workloads to the cloud. That's why they've created another reservation type called *Reserved Capacity*. With Reserved Capacity, you commit to a one- or three-year term for a specific database platform and a fixed volume of usage during the period. What you are paying for is the compute costs for the given period. To figure out the capacity price, you must know the Azure region, deployment type, performance tier, and term.

Unlike reserved instances, you do not need to assign the reservation to a specific resource such as a database. Instead, the reservation matches existing deployments running the type of resource capacity. The deployed resource automatically gets the applied benefit. You are committing to a fixed price for a specific volume of usage covering a specific length of time. By buying capacity, you eliminate the need to receive pay-as-you-go invoices. Something to keep in mind is that you are paying for the compute capacity only. Software, networking, and storage charges are separate.

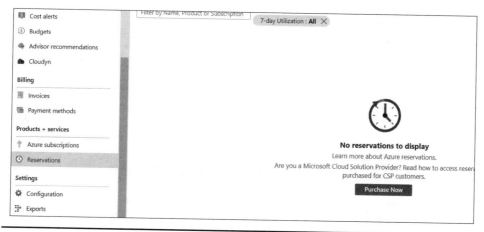

Figure 7-2   Setting up a reservation

To set up a reservation:

1. Locate Cost Management and Billing in the navigation.
2. Under Products, select Reservations.
3. Click the Purchase Now button in the center of the screen (Figure 7-2).
4. Select the resource type you would like to configure a reservation for, as seen in Figure 7-3.
5. Select option that fits yours need. In this case, a VM has been selected. A discount of 62 percent for a three-year term applies.

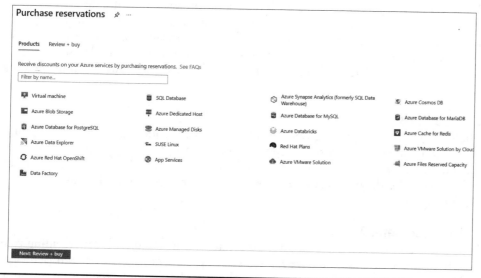

Figure 7-3   Select resource requiring reservation

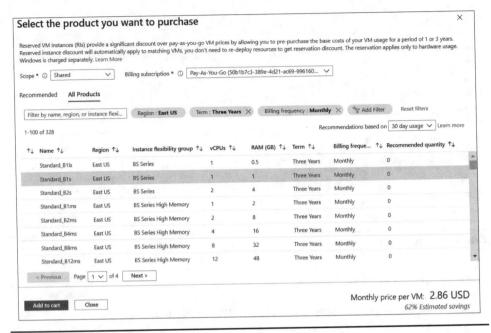

Figure 7-4   Selecting resource and adding to cart

6. Click Add to Cart on the bottom of the screen (Figure 7-4).

7. Once you've selected all the items you want to commit to for a reservation, follow the prompts to review and buy.

Location

Some regions cost less than others. Pick the region closest to the subscription's location, and the resources are then likely to offer the best pricing. Do not pick a region halfway across the world because it looks cheaper. It won't be, because you must pay for outgoing networking capacity. Bandwidth plays a part in the pricing equation, so keep connectivity cost in the back of your mind to select the best geography for implementing an Azure subscription.

Cost Savings

Microsoft creates new pricing options and subscription offerings from time to time, especially in storage and virtualization configuration options. Again, evaluating your spending every so often against what is available can potentially reduce your monthly invoice. Look for the plan that offers maximum performance while offering the greatest cost-savings benefits.

Hybrid Use Benefits

Unless you use SaaS- or PaaS-based infrastructure, you are responsible for providing your own licensing. One way to reduce Azure expenses includes selecting the most efficient and affordable operating system for your application. For example, there is no reason to get a pricey Windows Enterprise Server license if you can utilize an open source freemium license for an application. A second option is to repurpose software licenses on Azure if you and your organization are entitled to Azure Hybrid Benefits under a software assurance agreement.

Resource Management

Resizing resources, deleting underutilizing resources, and deallocating resources are three ways to drastically reduce Azure spend. Here's why:

- **Resizing Resources** If the resource is consuming too much capacity for items (such as storage, CPU utilization, memory) relative to the needed footprint, resizing can help reduce unnecessary expenses.

- **Deleting Resources** If a resource is not used, erase it. Until it is erased, there is almost always a charge associated with a resource. By deleting resources, the subscription is kept clean, you prevent your environment from unnecessary cyberattacks, and save money at the same time.

- **Deallocating Resources** When resources require active usage, it makes sense to have them powered on. What happens, though, when those resources are not being utilized for days, weeks, or months? Does it make sense to pay for something not being used? Absolutely not. That's why deallocating resources from active consumption can save an organization a significant amount of money. Shutting down virtual machines when they are idle for a certain period is an example of deallocating resources. Should your organization want to configure such features automatically, consider enabling *autoscaling* during the setup of resources such as virtual machines.

Spot Pricing

There may be times where you would like to deploy more infrastructure, knowing that the need is temporary. Example workloads that fall into this category include batch processing, dev/test environments, and large workloads. When Microsoft has excess capacity, it is willing to reduce the price of its infrastructure for virtual machine deployments. The Azure Cloud user benefits from is a reduced rate so long as they agree to the terms utilizing spot instances. Azure provisions the VM for the user so long as there is ample capacity. If the data centers capacity drops below Microsoft's designed threshold, the Spot Instance is evicted. For these resources, an organization is not given a commitment for uptime, which means no service-level agreement is put in place. Furthermore, no guarantees exist for high availability.

 TIP Azure Spot Instances provide significant cost savings but also come with some risks. Do not invest in building workloads against spot instances. Should Microsoft need to evict your spot instance, it can do so within 30 seconds. If you know important items are being created on a spot instance, make sure to set up a frequent backup routine.

Migrating from IaaS to PaaS

When an organization usually moves from on-premises to the cloud, the infrastructure starts with an IaaS only or hybrid cloud approach. It's a more natural way to transition resources without causing significant disruption. However, the always-on nature of virtualization means an invoice that keeps on tallying charges, even when operations are idle. Those applications that can be migrated one step further into a platform-based solution could reduce costs significantly on several fronts. Whether it is the cost of keeping the environment, the application licensing cost, or the reduction in charges since utilization is only charged against a resource when used, PaaS is a more efficient cloud computing method.

Use Case: IaaS vs. PaaS Savings

An organization migrates several servers running SQL Server on a virtual machine to Azure from their on-premises data center. The configuration still requires a cloud administrator to manage the operating system, database provisioning and license, security, and necessary compliance requirements. The virtual machine always stays on unless, of course, it is scheduled to shut down during certain hours. The invoice keeps accruing charges, and the organization sees no cost savings for labor. What is being described is a migration from on-premises to IaaS, as the only thing Microsoft must supply is the bare infrastructure.

By migrating from IaaS to PaaS, an organization can rid itself of the Azure SQL Database's underlying infrastructure requirements. The Azure SQL Database runs in the cloud. You only pay for what you consume, not a separate licensing fee in addition to the infrastructure to house the database. Furthermore, suppose any of the applications are homegrown and can be migrated to a PaaS-based setting. In that case, the expense associated with managing the hosting environment goes down as there is no cost associated with software updates, patch management, and worrying about storage optimization. All activities are done using on-demand provisioning. If the organization decides to reserve capacity or instances, this too adds to the cost savings. Remember though, reservations are associated with CapEx, not OpEx, given the organization is making a long-term financial commitment, not a one-time-only purchase.

Pricing Calculator and Total Cost of Ownership Calculator

As part of any planning discussion that you might have about Azure, you'll want to know two key metrics. The first metric has to do with the cost of implementing Azure and the various products offered. A second measure is your overall cost savings compared to keeping your solution on-premises, whether it is a large data center or the server under your desk. Microsoft offers two calculators to help you better estimate the product cost and total cost of ownership in Azure.

Pricing Calculator

As seen in Figure 7-5, the Azure Pricing calculator helps you estimate the expenses based on the products required to run your infrastructure. You can calculate pricing for any Generally Available service with the calculator. When using the calculator, you must first select the required products as part of your infrastructure. Once you've selected all the products, you will want to configure each product against specific needs. For example, in Figure 7-6, a virtual machine is being custom configured. As you make configuration changes, the pricing and allowable added product options also dynamically change.

If you intend to buy a resource against a reservation, you also have the opportunity to identify potential cost savings as part of the pricing calculator. Should you want to learn more about a product, including servicing license agreement terms, you should click on the information icon to the right of the product to retrieve product details and documentation.

Another possibility to consider as you are pricing options are support plans. Support pricing can significantly increase the cost of services. You should evaluate your business need before selecting a plan, as not all products require the same level of support.

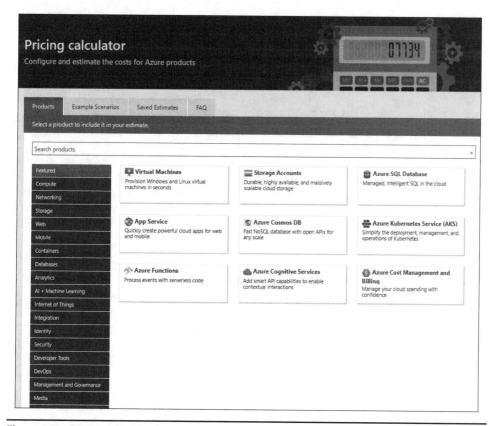

Figure 7-5   Pricing calculator homepage

Figure 7-6 Pricing calculator estimate for a virtual machine

Should you have an Enterprise Agreement, Microsoft Online Services Agreement, or Customer Agreement in place already, you can configure these options as part of the calculated price. Finally, all price estimates can be saved and shared with others. To save an estimate, you will need to establish an Azure account so that you can refer back to the quote at a later time.

Total Cost of Ownership Calculator

By now, you should already know the thesis that Microsoft and all other cloud vendors tell customers about migrating from on-premises to the cloud. There are enormous cost savings over time that can be recognized by taking a cloud-first approach. That's the Total Cost of Ownership (TCO) calculator's entire point: recognizing the actual cost savings over time.

The first step in proving the estimated cost savings is entering information about your existing infrastructure, including internal operating expenses. You need to configure the TCO calculator to your specific workload. Just about any possible configuration can be added to the TCO calculator from storage, operating system, databases, and even labor to support the existing workloads. Once you finish entering all the as-is assumptions, press Next. The next page will present an account of assumptions Microsoft has made on your behalf based on the data provided. The result estimates the total cost savings over time when using Azure under like-kind cloud-ready conditions. The first half of the page presents a visual depiction of cost savings across a variety of scenarios. (Figure 7-7). You'll see a more granular assumption at the bottom of the page comparing on-premises versus cloud expenses that the TCO calculator uses to derive the cost savings (Figure 7-8). Like the pricing calculator, this report can be downloaded and shared with others.

TIP   To access the Pricing calculator, go to https://azure.microsoft.com/en-us/pricing/calculator/. The Total Cost of Ownership calculator can be reached at https://azure.microsoft.com/en-us/pricing/tco/calculator/.

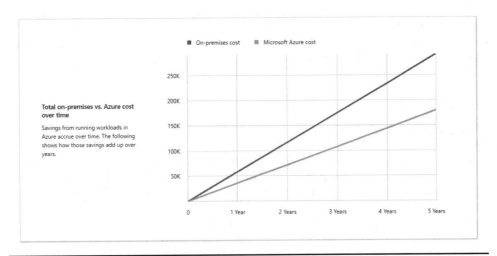

Figure 7-7   TCO calculator cost savings

Cost over 5 year(s)   Cost over 5 year(s)

On-premises cost breakdown summary		Azure cost breakdown summary	
Category	Cost	Category	Cost
Compute	$184,823.35	Compute	$61,169.76
Hardware	$88,578.00	Data Center	$0.00
Software	$21,301.75	Networking	$270.00
Electricity	$10,971.60	Storage	$116,302.81
Database	$63,972.00	IT Labor	$1,937.50
Data Center	$41,417.35		
Networking	$38,363.93		
Storage	$22,932.00		
IT Labor	$3,875.00		
Total	$291,412.00	Total	$179,680.00

Estimated on-premises cost (5 year(s))	Estimated Azure cost (5 year(s))
⌄ Compute cost	Azure compute cost
⌄ Data center cost	Azure data center cost
⌄ Networking cost	Azure networking cost
⌄ Storage cost	Azure storage cost
⌄ IT labor cost	Azure IT labor cost

Figure 7-8   TCO detailed report

Azure Cost Management

Azure Cost Management is a free tool in Azure that helps customers analyze their expenses at a granular level. Cost Management offers several options to help analyze and control spending. You can also review forecasted expenses and access invoices from the Cost Management toolset. The key tools that you should become acclimated with include:

- Cost Analysis
- Cost Alerts
- Budgets

Cost analysis helps one understand the cost of running Azure at a given point in time or using many filters to aggregate costs so that you can identify spending trends. A user can see accumulated costs during a billing cycle. Cost analysis also offers the ability to estimate costs expectations against a budget. Figure 7-9 provides an example of a cost analysis against a budget of $125 for a given month.

Budgets are helpful if you are looking to control cloud spending and better understand operational costs in using cloud compute resources. If configured to trigger against thresholds and spending lits, budgets can prevent you or your organization from overspending. Budgets can be configured to send cost alerts when spending thresholds exceed the configured amount. A *cost alert* is nothing more than a notification informing one or more users that a budget condition should be evaluated based on a

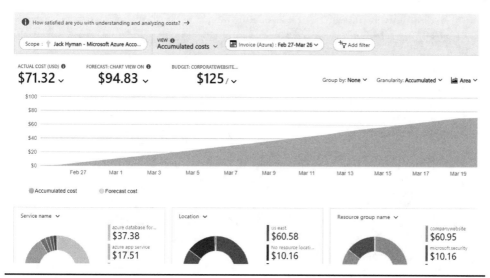

Figure 7-9 Cost analysis example

configured rule in Azure Cost Management. Budgets and Cost Alerts integrate many of the same features. Figure 7-10 illustrates the details needed to configure a Budget. If you look at the bottom of the figure, you'll notice a forecasted amount. Figure 7-11 illustrates how Azure determined the forecasted amount using past spend and current resource expenses to project a budget. Once the initial configuration for a budget is set, configuring a cost alert is the last requirement, as illustrated in Figure 7-12.

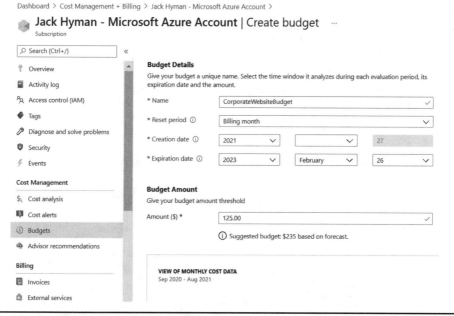

Figure 7-10 Configuring a budget in Azure Cost Management

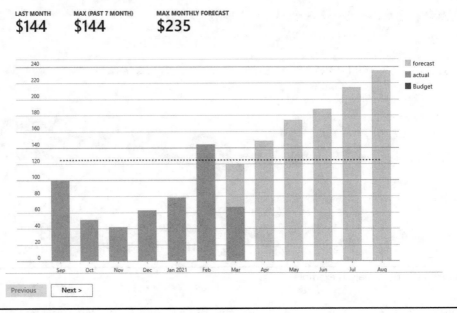

Figure 7-11   Reviewing a projected budget forecast

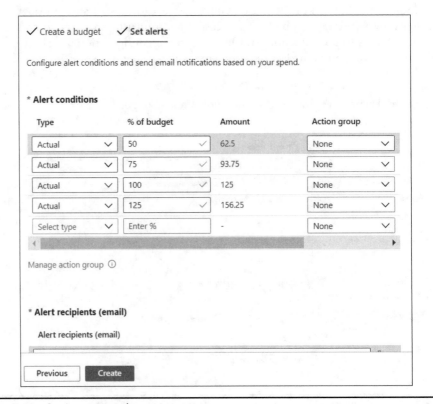

Figure 7-12   Setting up cost alerts

Azure Service-Level Agreement

Whether you are using Microsoft Azure for personal reasons or working for a multinational organization, you expect a certain level of service from Microsoft in return for the services they provide. When you obtain services for Azure cloud, Microsoft provides its customers with a formal agreement that states the performance standards that one should expect should they utilize the service. The formal agreement is referred to as a service-level agreement (SLA). Microsoft generally commits to a 99.0 percent uptime or greater on all cloud resources when the capability is in production and the resource is generally available (GA).

A typical SLA will have the following elements:

- Introduction/product expectations
- General conditions to meet the SLA for a product
- Specific terms, including uptime conditions

Each service offering has its own SLA. You do not need to get an Azure subscription to review any Microsoft SLA's terms and conditions. Although each product has a distinct area where one can access an SLA, anyone can review the terms for each Microsoft product on the Microsoft Azure website https://azure.microsoft.com/en-us/support/legal/sla/.

SLA Percentages, Downtime, and Credits

In every SLA, there is a committed uptime for services. Generally, the commitment is from 99 percent to 99.99 percent. On rare occasions, though, an SLA will commit to 99.99 percent or 99.999 percent. That extra tenth of a percentage point is significant as it significantly reduces the allowable downtime per week, month, and year. Table 7-2 provides a review of percent uptime commitments versus the allowable downtime threshold.

Let's assume for a moment that a resource has a 99.9 percent SLA guarantee. Each month, there is a planned outage for up to 10 minutes. Based on the SLA terms, Microsoft service standards are considered acceptable as the commitment is to not have degraded services for more than 21.6 minutes per month. However, should there be a systemic outage that brings the Azure environment down within the selected region for greater than 21.6 minutes each month, Microsoft will issue a *service credit* to the customer.

SLA Percentage	Downtime Per Week	Downtime Per Month	Downtime Per Year
99	1.68 hours	7.2 hours	3.65 days
99.9	10.1 minutes	43.2 minutes	8.76 hours
99.95	5 minutes	21.6 minutes	4.38 hours
99.99	1.01 minutes	4.32 minutes	52.56 minutes
99.999	6 second	25.9 seconds	5.26 minutes

Table 7-2 SLA Guarantees vs. Downtime

Table 7-3	Monthly Uptime Percentage	Service Credit Percentage
SLA Uptime vs. Service Credit Percentage	<99.99	10
	<99	25
	<95	100

According to the claim approval process, service credits are the percentage of how much you've paid during a given period credited back to you. In the case where the SLA agrees to 99.9 percent, and during a given month, there is a 30-minute outage, Microsoft will have to reimburse you for those 9.4 minutes of downtime, which translates into a percentage of an organization's monthly spend. Table 7-3 illustrates the uptime versus service credit compensation breakdown based on the terms of an SLA.

EXAM TIP Watch out for the type of resource you are being asked to evaluate. Free resources are not covered under the terms of an SLA. Also, should you need to file a claim, most resources allow for a period of up to two months to request a credit from Microsoft for service issues. Otherwise, Microsoft is under no obligation to provide a service credit.

Calculating Composite SLA Terms

Not all products and services offered under Azure have the same SLA terms. When you decide to provision several resources for a Resource Group under a single subscription, the highest SLA commitment is no longer applicable. What needs to be figured out is a composite of SLA terms or the combination of SLA agreement percentages to determine a reasonable downtime. Take a single Azure virtual machine with a 99.9 percent SLA and an Azure SQL Database with a 99.99 percent. The formula to use would be $0.999 \times 0.9999 = 99.78$ percent. The composite SLA term is 99.78 percent. While the Azure SQL Database service has a reduced SLA time, the VM commitment stays at 99.9 percent.

EXAM TIP Remember that a composite SLA is an aggregate of all SLA terms. Should a resource have a lower SLA term, those conditions still are intact. For example, should an aggregate of App Service at 99.95 percent and Azure SQL Database be 99.99, the composite SLA is 99.94 percent, assuming both products are work together. Standalone, though, the SLA commitments stand firm.

Service Lifecycle in Azure

The good old days of software development have evolved where development is no longer isolated to a few users until a product is released to the general public. Instead, vendors such as Microsoft make available products and services fairly early on in the development process to gauge end-user feedback, collect and define unrecognized requirements to the internal team, and enhance the product's interoperability. In Azure Cloud, this process is called the *service lifecycle*. The service lifecycle defines how Azure service becomes available to the public.

Development always starts internally at Microsoft. The product team identifies the requirements for the specific product and then begins building the product in iterations. Following an initial development period internally, a product will be released for early feedback to select end users. The first stage of the lifecycle is called the *Private Preview*. Customers are invited to try the service for a limited period. These are users who provide active feedback to Microsoft to help the development team shape the future of the product. Private Previews are services offered as is. Microsoft will not commit to any SLA for these products. General customer support is not offered, only direct feedback and interaction with the product development team. Before implementing an entire technical strategy around a private preview, you need to think twice. Not all private preview products end up becoming a public preview or generally available. Microsoft will seldom charge a customer for a preview, especially when internal feedback is provided to development.

Once the development team feels they have ample feedback and the product is mature enough for a broader audience, a product moves from the Private Preview to a Public Preview. The *Public Preview* gives all Microsoft users, not just a select few, access to a new product and its features. With Public Previews, Microsoft has no product commitments; hence, no SLA terms are put in place. Additionally, products at this stage are generally free to the public. Again, suppose Microsoft gets enough feedback that shows a product or service does not meet General Availability's quality standards, Microsoft will likely discontinue the product with little notice. Therefore, actively implementing a preview product into production is strongly discouraged.

A product that reaches *General Availability (GA)* is available as a consumable, often billable product on Azure. Unlike in Public and Private Preview, where customer support does not provide assistance, the support team is now obligated to provide support so long as there are terms and conditions in an SLA. If a product is still free, Microsoft is technically not required to offer support, although they often depend on your inquiry and the purchased support tier. GA products and services can be actively integrated into workloads for public consumption.

Chapter Review

In Chapter 7, you've had an opportunity to learn about contributing factors that influence pricing in Microsoft Azure, as well as ways to reduce your expenses. Factors that influence the price of services include subscription type, resource type, services, metered usage, selection of options from the Azure Marketplace, location of Azure deployment, and network traffic. Some of the same factors contributing to price fluctuation in Azure can also influence cost reduction when using Azure. Factors that can reduce cost are the use of built-in monitoring solutions to ensure cost overruns do not occur, setting spending limits, prepurchasing instances and compute capacity, geographic location of resources, continuing to ensure the best cost savings are applied to a subscription, resizing of resources to assure unnecessary spend is accounted for, deleting unused resources, deallocating resources when not in use, committing to spot pricing for non-production workloads versus paying full price, and migrating from IaaS to PaaS exclusively. The combination of all these cost-saving factors can optimize your Azure spending considerably.

Getting an estimate on the cost of products and services can be a bit overwhelming at times. Microsoft has centralized resource pricing into a single calculator, the Pricing calculator, to better understand the potential cost for an Azure cloud deployment. A user selects the products to be incorporated into the infrastructure. Once complete, the user configures each product selected to better estimate pricing. Price estimates can be shared with others or saved for later.

To better acclimate potential customers with the benefits of using Azure, Microsoft offers the Total Cost of Ownership calculator. A user enters their as-is infrastructure along with working assumptions such as labor and utility spend. When the user completes their input, they can see how Microsoft benchmarks their environment against a potential Azure configuration, with cost savings benchmarks provided to the user for several years out.

Once a user commits to using Microsoft Azure, they will likely want to track their spending. Azure Cost Management is a centralized tool to help users access their invoices, the current state of their cloud spend in real-time, review cost projects for cloud usage, and configure budgets to ensure spending is in line with expectations.

When committing to use Azure Cloud, or any cloud service provider, for that matter, understanding the vendor's service commitments can be crucial. This is especially true for mission-critical businesses. At the end of this chapter, you became familiar with the purpose of the service-level agreement (SLA) and how Azure calculates its commitment to service with customers using several factors, including the percentage of uptime, downtime limits, credits for excess downtime, and composite SLA terms.

The last section of the chapter covers the Azure service lifecycle. There are three stages: Private Preview, Public Preview, and Generally Available. Private Preview is intended for the development and testing of a future Azure product. Limited users gain access to the feature. The lifecycle phase is used to flesh out product deficiencies and requirements. Once a product is mature enough, it moves to a Public Preview. All Azure users gain access to the product. The product is still a work in progress, so there is no guarantee it will become a real product Microsoft intends to offer as part of Azure. Therefore, any long-term planning should not actively integrate beta products until they have reached GA status.

No SLA guarantees are placed on both Private and Public Preview products. Most Private and Public Preview products are free to use until they are released for general availability. Once a product reaches GA, Microsoft Support provides customer support. Often, these products become billable products. Assuming the product is billable, GA products offer SLA terms.

Questions

1. Which of the following service lifecycle states offer products and services SLA support?

   A. Private Preview

   B. Public Preview

   C. General Availability

   D. All of the above

2. Correct the following statement, should it be needed.

Public Preview is limited to select Azure users who can beta-test a product during development, as they are given access by Microsoft. Such users must actively provide feedback to Product Development.

  A. Private Preview

  B. General Availability

  C. Service Lifecycle

  D. The current term is correct.

3. Correct the following statement, should it be needed.

The *Total Cost of Ownership Calculator* can help Azure users estimate their current charges accumulated when using Azure for a given month.

  A. Pricing Calculator

  B. Cost Alerts

  C. Cost Analysis

  D. The current term is correct.

4. This question requires you to evaluate the use case. Select the condition that makes the following statements correct.

You have an application made up of an Azure web app with a service-level agreement (SLA) of 99.95 percent and an Azure Cosmos DB with an SLA of 99.99 percent. The composite SLA for the application is the product of both SLAs, which equals 99.94 percent.

  A. No change is necessary.

  B. 99.95 percent

  C. 99.99 percent

  D. 0.04 percent

5. Select True or False for each of the following statements.

	True	False
Azure pay-as-you-go pricing is an example of a CapEx expense.	◯	◯
Azure Reserved Capacity is an example of a CapEx expense.	◯	◯
Azure Reserved Instances are an example of a CapEx expense.	◯	◯

  A. False, True, True

  B. False, False, False

  C. True, True, True

  D. True, False, True

6. Service-level agreements typically include all the following, except:

A. Product expectations

B. General conditions to meet the SLA for a product

C. Specific terms, including uptime conditions

D. Product pricing

7. Select all the options that are applicable from the drop-down menu.

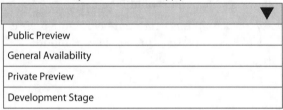

Azure services are available to all users during what stage
of the service lifecycle. Select all that apply.

▼
Public Preview
General Availability
Private Preview
Development Stage

A. Public Preview

B. General Availability

C. Private Preview

D. Development Stage

8. Select True or False for each of the following statements.

	True	False
Transferring a VM from Azure to an on-premises network results in additional data transfer charges.	○	○
Transferring a VM to Azure from an on-premises network results in additional data transfer charges.	○	○
The cost of services is different across Azure regions.	○	○

A. True, True, True

B. True, False, True

C. True, False, False

D. False, True, False

9. Correct the following statement, should it be needed.

You can use *Azure Cost Management* to send e-mail alerts when the current billing period's cost reaches 50 percent of the given monthly budget.

    A. Budget Alerts

    B. Azure Recommendations

    C. Health Checks

    D. The statement is accurate.

10. Which of the following conditions can heavily influence the pricing of a product or service in Azure Marketplace?

    A. Service provider

    B. Licensing requirements

    C. Storage requirements

    D. All of the the above

11. Which of the following is a guarantee for Azure SQL Server?

    A. Location

    B. Uptime

    C. Capacity

    D. Memory and compute performance

12. Match the terms found on the right with the definition found on the left.

Estimate the cost savings possible by migrating infrastructure from a data center to Microsoft.	Pricing calculator
Save money by committing to one-year or three-year plans for Azure products.	Total Cost of Ownership calculator
Estimate your cloud costs for new deployment or variations of your existing workloads.	Azure reservations

    A. Total Cost of Ownership calculator, Pricing calculator, Azure reservations

    B. Pricing calculator, Total Cost of Ownership calculator, Azure reservations

    C. Pricing calculator, Azure reservations, Total Cost of Ownership calculator

    D. Total Cost of Ownership calculator, Azure reservations, Pricing calculator

Answers

1. **C.** Since Private and Public Preview do not require Microsoft to provide an SLA since it is still in beta and cannot guarantee 100 percent working conditions, only General Availability is accurate.

2. **A.** Private Previews are limited to select Microsoft users who beta-test a product during development.

3. **C.** Cost analysis provides near real-time estimates of current costs and forecasted costs based on a user's accumulated Azure usage.

4. **A.** The formula $0.9999 \times 0.9995 = 0.999405$. That translates to 99.94 percent. A composite SLA does not take the lowest or highest SLA value and accept those terms.

5. **A.** True. A pay-as-you-go plan charges a customer every month for services utilized, hence OpEx.

   True, True. Both Azure Reserved Instances and Azure Reserved Capacity allow you to buy capacity in advance.

6. **D.** All features are inclusive of an SLA except for explicit product pricing.

7. **A, B.** Both options allow all users to access services via Azure Portal. Only General Availability provides guaranteed service-level commitments.

8. **B.** The key to the last two questions is the words from and to.

   True. From Azure too Data Center means egress (outgoing) traffic.

   False. To Azure from Data Center means ingress (inbound).

   True. Outbound traffic results in an added charge, whereas ingress does not. Cost does vary from region to region.

9. **A.** Budget Alerts is a feature within Azure Cost Management that is the most appropriate response to the question.

10. **B, C.** Service providers are irrelevant. The pricing of the product posted by the service provider can make a difference, but not the provider themselves.

11. **B.** The only guarantee listed that applies to Azure SQL Server is uptime.

12. **D.** The Total Cost of Ownership calculator estimates the cost savings possible by migrating infrastructure from a data center to Microsoft. Azure reservations save a user money by committing to one-year or three-year plans for Azure products. The Pricing calculator estimates your cloud costs for the new deployment or variations of your existing workloads.

Objective Map

Exam AZ-900

Objective	Chapter
Describe Cloud Concepts	
Identify the benefits and considerations of using cloud services	
• Identify the benefits of cloud computing, such as high availability, scalability, elasticity, agility, and disaster recovery	1
• Identify the differences between capital expenditure (CapEx) and operational expenditure (OpEx)	1
• Describe the consumption-based model	1
Describe the differences between categories of cloud services	
• Describe the shared responsibility model	1
• Describe Infrastructure-as-a-Service (IaaS)	1
• Describe Platform-as-a-Service (PaaS)	1
• Describe serverless computing	1
• Describe Software-as-a-Service (SaaS)	1
• Identify a service type based on a use case	1
Describe the differences between types of cloud computing	
• Define cloud computing	1
• Describe public cloud	1
• Describe private cloud	1
• Describe hybrid cloud	1
• Compare and contrast the three types of cloud computing	1

Objective	Chapter
Describe general security and network security features	
Describe Azure security features	
• Describe basic features of Azure Security Center, including policy compliance, security alerts, secure score, and resource hygiene	5
• Describe the functionality and usage of Key Vault	5
• Describe the functionality and usage of Azure Sentinel	5
• Describe the functionality and usage of Azure Dedicated Hosts	5
Describe Azure network security	
• Describe the concept of defense in depth	5
• Describe the functionality and usage of Network Security Groups (NSG)	5
• Describe the functionality and usage of Azure Firewall	5
• Describe the functionality and usage of Azure DDoS protection	5
Describe identity, governance, privacy, and compliance features	
Describe core Azure identity services	
• Explain the difference between authentication and authorization	6
• Define Azure Active Directory	6
• Describe the functionality and usage of Azure Active Directory	6
Describe Azure governance features	
• Describe the functionality and usage of role-based access control (RBAC)	6
• Describe the functionality and usage of resource locks	6
• Describe the functionality and usage of tags	6
• Describe the functionality and usage of Azure Policy	6
• Describe the functionality and usage of Azure Blueprints	6
• Describe the Cloud Adoption Framework for Azure	6
Describe privacy and compliance resources	
• Describe the Microsoft core tenets of security, privacy, and compliance	6
• Describe the purpose of the Microsoft Privacy Statement, Online Services Terms (OST), and Data Protection Amendment (DPA)	6
• Describe the purpose of the Trust Center	6
• Describe the purpose of the Azure compliance documentation	6
• Describe the purpose of Azure Sovereign Regions (Azure Government Cloud services and Azure China Cloud services)	6

About the Online Content

This book comes complete with TotalTester Online customizable practice exam software with more than 80 practice exam questions and ten simulated performance-based questions.

System Requirements

The current and previous major versions of the following desktop browsers are recommended and supported: Chrome, Microsoft Edge, Firefox, and Safari. These browsers update frequently, and sometimes an update may cause compatibility issues with the TotalTester Online or other content hosted on the Training Hub. If you run into a problem using one of these browsers, please try using another until the problem is resolved.

Your Total Seminars Training Hub Account

To get access to the online content, you will need to create an account on the Total Seminars Training Hub. Registration is free, and you will be able to track all your online content using your account. You may also opt in if you wish to receive marketing information from McGraw Hill or Total Seminars, but this is not required for you to gain access to the online content.

Privacy Notice

McGraw Hill values your privacy. Please be sure to read the Privacy Notice available during registration to see how the information you have provided will be used. You may view our Corporate Customer Privacy Policy by visiting the McGraw Hill Privacy Center. Visit the **mheducation.com** site and click **Privacy** at the bottom of the page.

Single User License Terms and Conditions

Online access to the digital content included with this book is governed by the McGraw Hill License Agreement outlined next. By using this digital content you agree to the terms of that license.

Access   To register and activate your Total Seminars Training Hub account, simply follow these easy steps.

1. Go to this URL: **hub.totalsem.com/mheclaim**

2. To register and create a new Training Hub account, enter your e-mail address, name, and password on the **Register** tab. No further personal information (such as credit card number) is required to create an account.

   If you already have a Total Seminars Training Hub account, enter your e-mail address and password on the **Log in** tab.

3. Enter your Product Key: **74q4-xgzj-0v04**

4. Click to accept the user license terms.

5. For new users, click the **Register and Claim** button to create your account. For existing users, click the **Log in and Claim** button.

   You will be taken to the Training Hub and have access to the content for this book.

Duration of License   Access to your online content through the Total Seminars Training Hub will expire one year from the date the publisher declares the book out of print.

Your purchase of this McGraw Hill product, including its access code, through a retail store is subject to the refund policy of that store.

The Content is a copyrighted work of McGraw Hill, and McGraw Hill reserves all rights in and to the Content. The Work is © 2022 by McGraw Hill.

Restrictions on Transfer   The user is receiving only a limited right to use the Content for the user's own internal and personal use, dependent on purchase and continued ownership of this book. The user may not reproduce, forward, modify, create derivative works based upon, transmit, distribute, disseminate, sell, publish, or sublicense the Content or in any way commingle the Content with other third-party content without McGraw Hill's consent.

Limited Warranty   The McGraw Hill Content is provided on an "as is" basis. Neither McGraw Hill nor its licensors make any guarantees or warranties of any kind, either express or implied, including, but not limited to, implied warranties of merchantability or fitness for a particular purpose or use as to any McGraw Hill Content or the information therein or any warranties as to the accuracy, completeness, correctness, or results to be obtained from, accessing or using the McGraw Hill Content, or any material referenced in such Content or any information entered into licensee's product by users or other persons and/or any material available on or that can be accessed through the licensee's product (including via any hyperlink or otherwise) or as to non-infringement of third-party rights. Any warranties of any kind, whether express or implied, are disclaimed. Any material or data obtained through use of the McGraw Hill Content is at your own discretion and risk and user understands that it will be solely responsible for any resulting damage to its computer system or loss of data.

Neither McGraw Hill nor its licensors shall be liable to any subscriber or to any user or anyone else for any inaccuracy, delay, interruption in service, error or omission, regardless of cause, or for any damage resulting therefrom.

In no event will McGraw Hill or its licensors be liable for any indirect, special or consequential damages, including but not limited to, lost time, lost money, lost profits or good will, whether in contract, tort, strict liability or otherwise, and whether or not such damages are foreseen or unforeseen with respect to any use of the McGraw Hill Content.

TotalTester Online

TotalTester Online provides you with a simulation of the Microsoft Azure Fundamentals AZ-900 exam. Exams can be taken in Practice Mode or Exam Mode. Practice Mode provides an assistance window with hints, references to the book, explanations of the correct and incorrect answers, and the option to check your answer as you take the test. Exam Mode provides a simulation of the actual exam. The number of questions, the types of questions, and the time allowed are intended to be an accurate representation of the exam environment. The option to customize your quiz allows you to create custom exams from selected domains or chapters, and you can further customize the number of questions and time allowed.

To take a test, follow the instructions provided in the previous section to register and activate your Total Seminars Training Hub account. When you register, you will be taken to the Total Seminars Training Hub. From the Training Hub Home page, select your certification from the Study drop-down menu at the top of the page or from the list of Your Topics on the Home page, and then click on the Total Tester link to launch the Total Tester. You can then select the option to customize your quiz and begin testing yourself in Practice Mode or Exam Mode. All exams provide an overall grade and a grade broken down by domain.

Performance-Based Questions

In addition to multiple-choice questions, the Microsoft Azure Fundamentals (AZ-900) exam includes interactive performance-based questions (PBQs). You can access the PBQs included with this book by navigating to the Resources tab and selecting the quiz icon. You can also access them by navigating to and selecting **Microsoft Azure Fundamentals All-in-One (AZ-900) Resources** from the Study drop-down menu at the top of the page or from the list of Your Topics on the Home page. After you have selected the PBQs, an interactive quiz will launch in your browser.

Technical Support

For questions regarding the TotalTester or operation of the Training Hub, visit **www.totalsem.com** or e-mail **support@totalsem.com**.

For questions regarding book content, visit **www.mheducation.com/customerservice**.

agility   The ability to rapidly develop, test and launch capabilities that drive business growth at speed and scale.

AI (artificial intelligence)   Computer-oriented capabilities that emulate human intelligence. Combining math and logic, the system can emulate the logic that humans use to learn new information and make decisions.

AKS (Azure Kubernetes Service)   AKS, also known as Azure Kubernetes Service, is Azure's open source fully managed container orchestration service. The service is available on the Microsoft Azure public cloud. AKS allows for the deployment, scaling and management of Docker containers and container-based applications within a clustered environment.

alerts   Alerts notify a user when an issue is discovered with infrastructure or application using your monitoring data in Azure Monitor. The alerts help to mitigate issues before they become evident to the end user.

alternate region   A region that uses Azure's existing footprint within a data residency boundary. Under these conditions, the original recommended region may also exist. Alternate regions help reduce latency. They also supply a secondary region for disaster recovery needs, although they are not used to support Availability Zones.

Apache Spark   A parallel processing framework that supports in-memory processing that can boost performance of big-data analytic applications in Azure.

App Service   A fully managed platform that allows a user to build, deploy, and scale web apps in Azure.

append blob   Made up of blocks and is optimized for append operations. When you modify an append blob, blocks can be added to the end of the blob only, via the Append Block operation.

Application Insights   Application Insights is a feature within Azure Monitor that extends Application Performance Management (APM) services for developers and DevOps professionals. You can use Application Insights to check live applications, which automatically detects performance anomalies as well as allows for the diagnosis of issues.

Archive tier   Blob storage that is infrequently accessed and stored for at least 90 days.

ARM templates   A way to declare objects, types, names, and properties in a JSON file that can then become checked into source control and managed as a code file. ARM templates can be treated like infrastructure as code.

artifacts   Allows developers to easily discover, install, and publish NuGet, npm, and Maven packages using Azure DevOps.

authentication   The process of proving that you are who you say you are.

authorization   The act of granting or giving an authenticated permission the ability to act to do something.

autoscale   Enables a user to apply the right number of resources to handle the load of an application. A user can specify a minimum and maximum number of instances to run and add or remove VMs automatically based on a set of rules.

Availability Set   A collection of virtual machines managed together that can provide application redundancy and reliability. Availability sets ensure that at least one virtual machine environment stays available during a maintenance event, planned or unplanned.

Availability Zones   A high-availability location offering that protects your applications and data from data center failures. Considered a dedicated, unique location, Availability Zones are physical locations within an Azure region. Each zone consists of one or more data centers equipped with independent power, cooling, and networking.

Azure Active Directory   A cloud-based identity service in Azure that allows a user to authenticate and authorize users.

Azure Active Directory B2B   An Active Directory collaboration feature allowing external identities to connect to internal resources within a network. In other words, you can invite guest users to collaborate with your organization.

Azure Active Directory B2C   An Active Directory service that uses an identity store outside of your company. It is an authentication service for publicly facing applications.

Azure Active Directory Connect   An Active Directory solution that supports the integration of off-premises workloads with Azure identity resources.

Azure Advisor   Solution that analyzes various configurations within your Azure instances, including usage telemetry, and offers personalized, actionable recommendations. Metrics that Advisor helps optimize include reliability, security, operational excellence, performance, and cost.

Azure Blueprints   A solution package used to create standards and requirements for governing Azure services, security, and design in a reusable manner to ensure consistency and compliance.

Azure Boards   Tolls built into Azure to help teams manage cloud-based software projects.

Azure Bot Services   An integrated environment that allows users to build chatbots inside of Azure.

Azure Command-Line Interface (CLI)   A command-line interface that allows a user to manage Azure services from key operating systems such as Windows OS, macOS, and Linux.

Azure Cloud Shell   An interactive, authenticated, browser-accessible shell alternative built into Azure Portal for managing resources.

Azure Container Instance (ACI)   An Azure-based service allowing developers to deploy containers on the Azure without requiring any underlying infrastructure.

Azure Cosmos DB   Azure's own NoSQL database platform intended for modern enterprise application development.

Azure Cost Management   A free SaaS-based solution in Azure allowing users to monitor, allocate, and optimize cloud spend in one or more cloud environments.

Azure Database for MySQL   A fully managed relational database service in Azure powered by the MySQL community edition.

Azure Database for PostgreSQL   A fully managed-as-a-service relational database service based on the open source Postgres database engine that is known for handling enterprise-class mission-critical workloads with predictable performance, security, high availability, and dynamic scalability.

Azure Databricks   As a serverless, PaaS-based solution, Azure Databricks is used to for processing and transforming massive datasets as well as exploring the data through machine learning models.

Azure Dedicated Host   Provides physical servers that act as a host to one or more Azure virtual machines.

Azure Defender   A premium Microsoft security solution that offers alerts and advanced threat protection for virtual machines, SQL databases, containers, web applications, and endpoint protection for a network when enabled.

Azure DevOps   Offers a suite of developer services to plan work, to support code collaboration, and build and deploy applications.

Azure DevTest Labs   Allows a developer or members of a team to self-manage virtual machines images and PaaS resources without requiring approvals or built-in workflow requirements.

Azure Files   A service that allows a user to create a virtual file share in the cloud similar to a local share drive.

Azure Firewall   A managed, cloud-based network security service that offers protection to virtual network resources.

Azure Functions   A serverless solution allowing you to build task-based applications without having to support all the cloud infrastructure and resources.

Azure Machine Learning   Azure-based cloud service offering allowing users to build, test, and deploy predictive analytics solutions using their own datasets.

Azure Marketplace An online store operated Microsoft that offers products and services to assist those looking to deploy Microsoft Azure–related technologies.

Azure Mobile App An Azure Portal companion to handle many of the common tasks offered from its web-based companion, including monitoring resources, deploying virtual machines, diagnosing and fixing issues, and running commands to manage Azure resources.

Azure Monitor Allows a user to review the availability and performance of their applications and services in Azure.

Azure Pipelines Azure DevTest–based solution that automatically builds and tests code projects for rapid deployment, making applications available to others.

Azure Policy An Azure service allowing a user to create enforceable and controllable properties for resources.

Azure Portal A web-based, graphical-unified console alternative to the command-line tool to manage all Azure Cloud capabilities.

Azure PowerShell A command-line interface to manage Azure services from the desktop.

Azure Repos A set of version control tools within Azure DevTest that is used to manage code.

Azure Reservations Provides a significant discount for use of Microsoft-based products on Azure cloud by committing to one-year or three-year plans.

Azure Resource Manager A visual-based deployment and management service in Azure that enables you to create, update, and delete resources in an Azure account.

Azure Resource Manager templates JavaScript Object Notation (JSON)–based files that define the infrastructure and configuration for a Azure project.

Azure Security Center A unified infrastructure security management system that focuses on your data by offering advanced threat protection across your hybrid workloads in the cloud, either in Azure or on-premises.

Azure Sentinel A cloud-based security information event management (SIEM) and security orchestration automated response (SOAR) solution that helps investigate threats with artificial intelligence and hunt for suspicious activities.

Azure Service Health A personalized dashboard that provides notifications, guidance, and technical support guidance where there are known issues, updates, or planned maintenance issues that will impact Azure resources.

Azure sovereign regions Dedicated physical and logical network–isolated cloud infrastructure to ensure data protection. There are three sovereign regions besides public cloud: U.S. Government, Germany, and China.

Azure Sphere Combined with the Azure Micro-controller Unit (MCU), along with its operating system and application platform, this IoT solution enables the creation of secured, Internet-connected devices that support the updating, controlling, monitoring, and maintenance of devices remotely.

Azure SQL Database The cloud-computing based version of the popular Microsoft SQL Server. Azure SQL Database, is considered a Platform as a Service but can also be referred to as a Database as a Service. Azure SQL Database allows one to host and use a relational SQL database in the cloud without requiring any infrastructure.

Azure Synapse Analytics Considered the next-generation SQL Datawarehouse, Synapse is a Platform as a Service analytics service that offers data integration, enterprise data warehousing, and big data analytics either as a serverless-on-demand offering or as a provisioned resource at scale.

Azure Test Plans A DevOps solution within Azure, the solution offering provides all the necessary capabilities to successfully test applications. Developers can also create and run manual test plans, generate automated tests, and collect feedback from users with the solution set available.

billing zones A geographical grouping of Azure regions for the purposes of billing.

blob storage Type of Azure storage intended for massive amounts of unstructured data. Also referred to as container storage.

block blobs Composed of blocks and identified with a Block ID, a block blob is optimized for uploading large amount of data efficiently.

business analytics tools Tools that extract data from business systems. These tools then integrate into data repositories including data warehouses, where it can be analyzed. Analytics tools range from spreadsheets such as Microsoft Excel with statistical functions to sophisticated data mining and predictive features found in Power BI.

capital expense Up-front cost, which has a value that reduces over time, often having no recurring cost after an initial spend.

circuits A logical connection between your on-premises infrastructure and Microsoft Cloud Services that is configurable in ExpressRoute.

Cloud Adoption Framework for Azure A collection of documentation, implementation guidance, best practices, and tools created by Microsoft employees, business partners, and customers that are proven to accelerate your cloud adoption journey.

cloud bursting A configuration that is set up between a private cloud and a public cloud should the resource capacity exceed 100 percent capacity in the private cloud, overflow traffic is sent to the public cloud.

cloud computing A delivery model for computing resources where servers, applications, storage, databases, network connectivity, security, and other resources are made available as a service for consumption by a service provider over the Internet.

cluster   A group of connected computers, also referred to as nodes, that work together as a single system.

Cognitive Services   A compilation of machine learning solutions and algorithms that Microsoft has developed within the Azure platform to solve problems using artificial intelligence.

compliance documentation   Centrally located website to locate global compliance and regulatory controls Microsoft Azure complies with across all geographies.

composite service-level agreement   An aggregate service-level agreement support level since there is support across multiple services supporting applications, each with different availability terms.

Conditional Access   A tool integrated within Azure Active Directory that brings authentication and authorization signals together to make decisions and enforce organizational policies.

container storage   *See* blob storage.

Cool tier   Storage that is optimized for storing data not accessed for at least 30 days.

Cost Management   Also referred to as Azure Cost Management, this SaaS solution allows permitted users and organizations to monitor, allocate, and optimize cloud spend in their cloud environments.

Data Protection Addendum   A policy document provided by Microsoft that explores their obligations with respect to the processing and security of customer data and personal data in connection with the online services, notably Azure.

Database Transaction Unit (DTU)   Describes a performance unit metric for the Azure SQL Database that is a way to charge individuals for usage. DTU is a mixture of four metrics: CPU, Memory, Data I/O and Log I/O. There are three different service tiers; each one offers different scalability and features.

DDoS Protection Defense in Depth   Azure's approach to support security protection based on dedicated monitoring and machine learning. The suite of security solution utilize DDoS protection policies tuned to an organizations virtual network, which profiles its application's normal traffic patterns, intelligently detecting malicious traffic and mitigating attacks as soon as they are detected.

DevOps   The union of people, process, and technology to enable continuous delivery of value to customers. The practice of DevOps brings development and operations teams together to speed software delivery and make products more secure and reliable.

disaster recovery   The process whereby when an outage occurs at a primary location, assuming there is redundancy in place, a failover to secondary location takes effect and takes over operations. Once primary operations are restored, the load is distributed back to its normal state.

disk storage   The only type of block storage to support both Windows- and Linux-based clustered or high-availability applications using cloud-based shared-disk space.

Docker   A PaaS-based container engine that uses the Linux kernel to create containers on top of an operating system.

elastic computing   To dynamically provision and de-provision computer capacity, which includes processing, memory, and storage resources, in order to meet changing demands.

elastic pools   A way of managing Azure SQL Databases where one can apply a simple, cost-effective solution for managing and scaling multiple databases with unpredictable usage demands.

elasticity   Ability to automatically scale hosted resources as needed and on demand against configured parameters.

ExpressRoute   Allows an organization to extend its on-premises networks into the Microsoft cloud over a private connection using a connectivity provider.

fault domain   More than two virtual machines in an availability set that fail concurrently.

fault tolerance   Ability to continue operating in the event of an operational failure.

Foundational Region   A core service that is available across every Azure region deemed generally available.

General Availability (GA)   Features that have been evaluated and tested that are released to customers as part public availability for the Azure community to use, consumer, and potentially purchase.

geography   A defined boundary for data residency that containing two or more regions. The boundaries may be within or beyond national borders, which includes countries or even continents. Geographies are influenced by tax regulation. Every geography has a minimum of one region.

georeplication   Ability to automatically replicate content such as blobs, tables, and queues within a regional pair.

git   A free and open source distributed version control system.

GitHub   The world's largest web-based open source code hosting platform for version control and collaboration, letting users work and collaborate from anywhere.

GitHub Actions   A platform within Github to automate, customize, and execute software development workflows right inside a GitHub repository.

governance   A way to maintain control over your applications and resources.

General Data Protection Regulation (GDPR)   A regulatory framework that provides guidance on how any organization or individual who conducts business and handles personal information should protect data for those that live in the European Union (EU).

Hadoop   Also referred to as Apache Hadoop, a software library framework that supports the distributed processing of large datasets across clusters of computers using simple programming models.

HDInsight   A managed-data analytics service offered by Microsoft that allows a user to run Apache Hadoop–based services such as Apache Spark, Apache Hive, Apache Kafka, and Apache HBase in Azure Cloud.

high availability   Systems that are highly dependable, with the intent of not failing. Should failure occur, there is ample redundancy to ensure no loss of service.

horizontal scaling   Adding more capacity, which may include virtual machines to a pool of resources.

Hot tier   Blob storage optimized for data that is accessed frequently.

hybrid cloud   Cloud capability that combines public and private cloud, allowing data and applications to be shared between both.

hypervisor   The underlying software that allows for a host computer to support multiple guest virtual machines by virtually sharing its resources, such as memory and processing.

Infrastructure as a Service (IaaS)   A virtualized computer environment that delivers services over the Internet using a cloud service provider such as Microsoft. Infrastructure offerings include servers, network equipment, storage, security, and software.

identity   A user or object tied to a username and password that requires authentication through a secret key or certificate.

identity and access management (IAM)   Security approach to help defend against malicious attacks and protect credentials using a combination of risk-based access controls, identity protection tools, and strong authentication options.

images   *See* virtual machine.

Internet of Things (IoT)   The ability for interrelated, Internet-connected objects to collect and transfer data over a wireless network without requiring human intervention.

Internet of Things (IoT) Central   An IoT-based application developed by Microsoft that consists of a web UI letting users monitor device conditions, create rules, and manage millions of devices and along with their data throughout its lifecycle.

Internet of Things (IoT) Hub   An Azure-managed service that acts as a central message hub for bi-directional communication between an IoT application and the devices it manages.

key vault   Cloud-based service that allows one to securely store and access secrets, including API keys, passwords, certificates, and cryptographic keys.

Log Analytics   A tool in the Azure portal allowing one to run and edit log queries from data collected by Azure Monitor. Log data can be interactively analyzed across various applications.

Logic Apps   A serverless cloud service allowing one to automate and orchestrate tasks, business processes, and workflows. Logic apps unlike functions are intended to integrate apps, data, systems, and services across enterprises or organization.

Mainstream Service   A type of Azure service available in recommended regions. Such services are available within 90 days of regional general availability or alternate regions where demand is warranted.

machine learning   The process when mathematical models are used to predict outcomes versus relying on a set of instructions to produce outcomes. The outcomes bear resemblance to how humans learn and think over time, and with greater accuracy given the data patterns, predictive decisions, and analytical models used.

managed domains   A domain that is configured to perform a one-way synchronization between Azure Active Directory to provide centralized access to a set of users, groups, and credentials.

managed instance   Appropriate for customers looking to migrate many apps from an on-premises or self-managed IaaS infrastructure to a fully managed PaaS cloud environment.

Management Groups   Containers that help you organize and manage access, policy, and compliance across all Azure subscriptions.

meters   A way resources are tracked in Azure across a given time period.

Microsoft Azure   Microsoft's cloud platform that hosts all related service offerings pertaining to Platform as an Infrastructure (IaaS) and Platform as a Service (PaaS) capability.

Microsoft Privacy Statement   Explains all facets of how Microsoft handles personal and corporate data with its applications, including Azure cloud.

multifactor authentication (MFA)   Requires two or more security authentication options in order to grant a user access. One option will be a username and password. The second will be a one-time option like a code generated from a device or application that is not easily duplicated and is often time-bound.

network security   Process to take preventative measures to protect networking infrastructure from inappropriate usage under various secure conditions in order to create a secure platform for technologies and people to operate.

node   A virtual machine that is a single instance within a cluster is called a node.

node pool   When using Azure Kubernetes Service (AKS), nodes, which are representative of virtual machine environments, are configurations grouped together into node pools. A node pool, or a series of VM that are like-kind, will run together in a group.

nonregional services   Azure service where no dependency exists on a specific Azure region. Nonregional service deploys services to one region. If there is failure in one region, a secondary region picks up the workload for the failed region.

NoSQL   A class of nonrelational database technologies developed with unique capabilities to handle high volumes of unstructured and changing data.

Notebook   Microsoft Azure's implementation of the popular widely used open source Jupyter Notebook.

network security groups (NSG)   A way to activate a rule or access control list, which in turn allows or denies network traffic to a virtual machine image on a virtual network.

OAuth   An open standard for access delegation, used as a way for Internet users to grant websites or applications access to their information on other websites without having to give provide usernames and password credentials.

Online Service Terms   Location of all Azure terms of service.

on-premises   Located onsite or at an organization's facility. Commonly associated with a large internal data center.

operational expense   Also referred to as OpEx, these are ongoing cost of doing business that are billed under a pay-as-you go model in Azure.

page blobs   Collections of 512-byte pages, that offer the ability to read/write arbitrary ranges of bytes. Page blobs are used to store index-based data structures like OS and data disks for virtual machines.

pass-through Authentication   Allows one to sign into both on-premises and cloud-based applications by using the same passwords, whereby the password can be validated against the on-premises Active Directory if available.

password hash synchronization   The synchronization of passwords between on-premises and that of the password hash, which is located in Azure AD.

peering   When one Internet connection can directly connect to another network connection, enabling a faster throughput and exchange of information without incurring any additional charges.

Platform as a Service (PaaS)   Cloud-based service offering supported by cloud service providers that supports the complete infrastructure, versus having the customer manage their own infrastructure. The responsibility of the end user or organization is limited to developing an application within the environment.

Pricing calculator   A free cost estimation and management provided by Microsoft to help determine cloud costs for implementing deployments, or specific services available within Azure.

private cloud   Cloud services offered over the Internet to select users, not the public. Private internal networks may be included in private cloud.

Private Preview   Beta-tested product offered to a limited number of Azure customers that is intended for evaluation purposes exclusively.

public cloud   Cloud services offered over the public Internet and available to anyone, corporate or individual, who would like to acquire them.

Public Preview   Beta-tested service offerings in Azure available to all users that come without any service-level agreement terms.

recommended region   Region offering a broad range of service capabilities. Designed to support Availability Zones now, or in the future depending on geography.

region   Geographical-based parameter bound by national borders. Regions will contain one or more data center. Azure pricing varies based on available services and offer types at the region level. A region is typically paired with another region, forming a regional pair, which will be a data center several hundred miles away for the purposes of redundancy and data integrity.

regional pair   Consists of two regions within a given geography.

regional service   Targeted Azure services within a specific region. The customer can specify where services can be deployed in the targeted region.

resource   Any item that is part of your Azure solution. Azure services allow you to enable resources across different product categories including storage, networking, databases, security, and virtual machines.

Resource Groups   A virtual container in Resource Manager that holds related resources together. These resources can be associated with an application or project.

resource locks   A way an administrator can prevent users in an organization from accidentally deleting or modifying critical resources.

role   A way to control access and assign users, groups, and services to specific Azure resources.

role-based access control (RBAC)   A way to provide fine-grained access management to resources to segregate duties within an organization, so that you only grant the amount of access to users they require.

role-based application model   A method of restricting network access using fine-grained access control among users within an enterprise.

Software as a Service (SaaS)   Cloud-based complete software solution that can be purchased on a pay-as-you-go basis from a cloud service provider. All users can access these applications using their web browser.

scalability   The ability for a cloud compute environment to handle an increased load.

Scale Sets   The ability to create and manage a group of load-balanced VMs, which can increase or decrease in response to demand or a defined schedule to support high availability.

scope   A way of setting resources access to a role based on how you grant a security principal. There are four group ways to assign a scope: at the management group, subscription, resource group, and resource level.

serverless computing   A delivery model where an organization and its developers can build an application but are not responsible for the infrastructure to host that application. The onus is on the service provider to maintain the infrastructure.

service-level agreement (SLA)   The agreement that describes Microsoft's commitments for uptime and connectivity. Each Azure service has a specific set of terms.

service lifecycle   The stages a Microsoft Azure product goes through from development, known as Private Preview, to General Availability, which is when all users can consume the product or service. There are three distinct service lifecycle stages: Private Preview, Public Preview, and General Availability.

shared responsibility model   A cloud framework that explains how security requirements for a cloud computing service provider and its customers should be handled, to ensure proper accountability.

single sign-on   A way to automatically authenticate and authorize users to multiple accounts if they are on the same network so they do not have to type their username and password in repeatedly.

specialized service   Demand-driven Azure services that are available across regions based by custom-built hardware.

Spot Virtual Machines   A method of saving on your virtual machine infrastructure when there is unused capacity on Azure infrastructure for a particular region. if capacity is no longer available the virtual machine becomes unavailable. Pricing scales based on availability and region.

storage tiers   A way to store blob object data in the most cost-efficient manner possible. There are three tiers: Hot, Cool, and Archive.

subscriptions   A customer agreement set up with Microsoft enabling one to attain Azure services.

Tags   Can also be referred to as Resource Tags. An indexing method, or way to create user-focused metadata, that enables you to categorize resources according to user specific requirements. Typically used for managing resources or billing.

Total Cost of Ownership calculator   Allows a user or organization to estimate the cost savings that can be achieved by migrating compute capabilities to Azure.

Trust Center   A single location to find all the security, privacy, and compliance requirements and settings associated with Microsoft Azure.

update domains   Virtual machines in an Availability Set that are updated concurrently.

upgrade domains   Logical sets of availability instances that are updated as a group. There will never be more than one domain updated at a given time within Azure.

vertical scaling   Vertical scaling refers to adding more resources (CPU, RAM, Disk) to your server on demand based on application demand.

virtual core (vCore)   A virtual core (vCore) is how Azure recognizes logical CPU units available for your server, which is also made among distinctions between generations of hardware.

virtual machines   A computer file, commonly referred to as an image, that acts like a physical computer.

virtualization   Instead of creating a compute environment on physical hardware, the environment is replicated in an emulated environment to mimic a like-kind configuration including computer hardware, operating system, storage devices, and so forth.

virtual network (VNETs)   Network connectivity that is between all your own Azure resources. The connection is isolated from all other Azure-based tenants.

virtual network peering   Ability to connect two or more virtual networks within Azure.

VPN gateways   A method of setting up connections between virtual networks as well as between an on-premises network and one or more virtual networks. With a VPN gateway, you can control the IP address blocks, DNS settings, security policies, and route tables within a virtual network.

web apps   Azure supplies a platform to build an app in Azure without requiring one to deploy, configure, and maintain any virtual machines infrastructure.

web hooks   User-defined HTTP endpoints triggered by an event.

Windows Remote Desktop   A program accessible on the Windows operating system that allows a user to connect to a computer in another location. The software allows the user to access another desktop and interact with it as if it were local.

Windows Virtual Desktops   A virtualized app-based desktop that runs on the cloud.

zonal services   A resource that is assigned or pinned to a specific zone.

INDEX

A

ACI. *See* Azure Container Instances (ACI)
Active Directory, 210–213, 264
    Conditional Access, 213–214
    multi-factor authentication (MFA), 214–216
    single sign-on (SSO), 216–217
Advanced Research Projects Agency Network
    (ARPANET), 1
Advisor, 127–130, 264
agility, 21, 263
AI (artificial intelligence). *See* artificial intelligence
AKS. *See* Azure Kubernetes Service (AKS)
alerts, 186, 197, 263
    cost alerts, 244–245, *246*
Apache Hadoop, 152, 270
Apache HBase, 152
Apache Interactive Query, 152
Apache Kafka, 152
Apache Spark, 152, 263
Apache Spark for Azure Synapse, 151
Apache Storm, 152
App Service, 77, 263
    benefits of, 79–81
    creating a web app, 79, *80, 81*
    service plans, 77–79
append blob, 263
Application Insights, 263
Application Rules, 201
Arc, 185
architecture framework, 38–39
architecture model, *11*
Archive tier, 263
ARM. *See* Azure Resource Manager (ARM)
ARM template tool kit (arm-ttk), 131
ARM templates, 118, 131–132, 222–223, 263, 266
Artifacts, 170, 264
artificial intelligence, 155, 156, 263
artificial intelligence solutions, 155–162
authentication, 209–210, 264
authorization, 209–210, 264
autoscaling, 96, 239, 264
availability, 18
Availability Sets, 51, 76–77, 92, 264
Availability Zones, 49–51, 76–77, 92, 264
    and cost, 234
    See also management groups

Azure Active Directory, 210–213, 264
    Conditional Access, 213–214
    multi-factor authentication (MFA), 214–216
    single sign-on (SSO), 216–217
Azure Active Directory B2B, 211, 264
Azure Active Directory B2C, 264
Azure Active Directory Connect, 264
Azure Advisor, 127–130, 264
Azure App Service, 77–81, 263
Azure Arc, 185
Azure ARM templates, 118, 131–132, 222–223, 263
Azure Artifacts, 170, 264
Azure Blueprints, 222–223, 264
Azure Boards, 167–168, 264
Azure Bot Service, 161–162, 264
Azure China Cloud, 226, 227
Azure Cloud Advisor, 118
Azure Cloud Shell, 32, *33*, 118, 119, 124–126, 265
Azure Cognitive Services, 159–161
Azure Command-Line Interface (CLI), 118, 119,
    123–124, 264
Azure Container Instances (ACI), 81–82, 265
    creating, 82–86
Azure Cosmos DB, 95, 100–101, 265
Azure Cost Management, 244–246, 265
Azure Dashboard, *122*
Azure Database for MySQL, 95, 99, 265
Azure Database for PostgreSQL, 95, 99–100, 265
Azure Databricks, 153–155, 265
Azure DDoS Protection, 201–202
Azure Dedicated Hosts, 195–196, 265
Azure Defender Service, 182, 185, 197, 265
    security alerts, 186
Azure DevOps, 132, 265
    Azure Artifacts, 170
    Azure Boards, 167–168
    Azure Pipelines, 168–169
    Azure Repos, 168
    Azure Test Plans, 169
    overview, 165–166
Azure DevTest Labs, 172–174, 265
Azure ExpressRoute, 107
Azure ExpressRoute Direct, 107–108
Azure Files, 93, 265
Azure Firewall, 196, 198, 200–201, 265
Azure Functions, 163, 164, 233, 265
Azure German Cloud, 226–227